People Get Ready

CATHOLIC PRACTICE IN THE AMERICAS

People Get Ready

RITUAL, SOLIDARITY, AND LIVED
ECCLESIOLOGY IN CATHOLIC ROXBURY

Susan Bigelow Reynolds

FORDHAM UNIVERSITY PRESS
New York   2023

Fordham University Press has no responsibility for the persistence or accuracy of URLs for external or third-party Internet websites referred to in this publication and does not guarantee that any content on such websites is, or will remain, accurate or appropriate.

Fordham University Press also publishes its books in a variety of electronic formats. Some content that appears in print may not be available in electronic books.

Visit us online at www.fordhampress.com.

Library of Congress Cataloging-in-Publication Data available online at https://catalog.loc.gov.

Printed in the United States of America

25 24 23   5 4 3 2 1

First edition

For Nora, Lucy, and Julia,
and for the people of St. Mary of the Angels Catholic Parish/
Iglesia Santa María de los Ángeles in Egleston Square

Contents

The joys and hopes, the grief and anguish of the people of our time, especially of those who are poor or afflicted, are the joys and hopes, the grief and anguish of the disciples of Christ as well. Nothing that is genuinely human fails to find an echo in their hearts. For theirs is a community of people united in Christ and guided by the Holy Spirit in their pilgrimage towards the Father's kingdom, bearers of a message of salvation for all of humanity. That is why they cherish a feeling of deep solidarity with the human race and its history.

GAUDIUM ET SPES, *Pastoral Constitution on the Church in the Modern World (1965), Preface*

If you have come here to help me, you are wasting your time. But if you have come because your liberation is bound up with mine, then let us work together.

LILLA WATSON, *Aboriginal activist*

Introduction
Unstable Communities of the Faithful

The Communion hymn at the English Mass begins with a low hum.

Pew by pew, we knit ourselves into the center aisle and process forward in two steady lines to receive the Eucharist. Crisp October sunlight sifts through the garden-level stained-glass windows, bathing the small sanctuary in an ethereal glow. When Anita starts to sing, the air in the sanctuary shifts, suspending the dust and shadows that swirl in the windowlight.

> People get ready, there's a train a-comin.'
> You don't need no baggage, you just get on board . . . [1]

I recognize "People Get Ready" as an anthem of the civil rights movement. Here, the Curtis Mayfield freedom song doubles as a gospel hymn. Standing in the Communion line, I have a habit of looking at the floor—first, instinctively, out of reverence, and then because I become mesmerized by the movement of feet: scratched boots and new sneakers and those wide black Velcro shoes that keep elderly folks on their feet, the occasional cane, the staccato prance of a loose toddler, all of them shuffling together and not quite together in the same direction. Our footsteps settle into the song's slow swing, and we hum and sway our way to the altar.

Anita has a soulful, deliberate voice and the second-most extensive hat collection in the parish. Next to her is Victoria, who greets me every Sunday morning with a warm Jamaican accent and a broad hug. Greg, a sandy blond millennial who acts in community theater and bikes to Mass, is soft spoken and kind and sings an understated tenor. A brown-robed Capuchin brother from the friary a few miles away in Jamaica Plain plays the keyboard. The director of the choir is a folk guitarist named Jim. Originally from California, he's wryly funny and speaks in drawn-out West Coast syllables, his voice equal parts sincerity and wonder. He once reminisced, unprompted, that the years after Vatican II "were like Jesus and surfing were one." Behind the singers and musicians, Harry operates the enigmatic soundboard with a heavy hand. A large Irish American man with an affinity for obscure railroad history, Harry drinks hot tea from a lidless Styrofoam Dunkin' Donuts cup as he feverishly presses buttons and adjusts levers. The sound system is in a perpetual state of malfunction and rarely improves with these interventions. (When the Spanish Mass choir arrives to set up, they start by undoing Harry's sound engineering.)

We settle back into our pews as the hymn winds to a close. Now everyone in the church joins in, repeating the final line of the refrain:

You just thank the Lord . . .
Thank the Lord . . .
Thank the Lord . . .
Thank the Lord.

Saint Mary of the Angels is a basement with a roof. If not for the ivory-painted statue of the Virgin Mary gazing tranquilly toward the bus stop from behind a wrought-iron gate and an inauspicious sign on the corner, nothing about the stubby building would resemble a Catholic church. It was built at the turn of the twentieth century to serve working-class European immigrants in the Egleston Square neighborhood of Roxbury, then a streetcar suburb of Boston. Builders broke ground on the church's foundation the same year that Boston Elevated Railway trains first rumbled over the heads of residents. The new parish signaled Boston Archbishop John Joseph Williams's confidence that Roxbury would soon become a flourishing center of Catholic life. As would-be parishioners awaited the construction of their new church, they gathered for Mass down the block in the West End Street Railway Car Barn. Over the clatter of train cars overhead, Rev. Henry A. Barry entreated the assembly to pray for the church's swift completion. As it turned out, the archbishop's vision—and the building plans that accompanied it—had been more than mildly optimistic. Catholics remained a marginal presence in Egleston Square. Few Catholics meant little money to invest in finishing the church. Instead, a hasty roof was built over the basement chapel. On March 8, 1908, the first parishioners of St. Mary of the Angels processed down a narrow set of stairs and into their new, underground church.

More than a century later, St. Mary's remains an unfinished project. Inside, the basement sanctuary evinces generations of slow revisions. Ruddy carpet covers thick floorboards. In the corner behind the choir looms the skyline of a bricolage sound system, its stacked speakers connected by a labyrinth of cables. On the slim crucifix carried by an altar server during Mass, Jesus's left arm clings to the cross by a rubber band looped around his wrist like a scrunchie. Here, in the words of Curtis Mayfield, passengers from coast to coast don't need tickets or baggage to get on board—just faith.[2]

If the twentieth century was supposed to be a story of upward mobility for American Catholics, St. Mary's had apparently missed the memo. Midcentury Catholicism traded on an image of stability, proving its American bona fides by publicly binding together the Catholic faith with symbols of national stability: military service, the Hollywood silver screen, suburban life, the white nuclear family, the university, the presidency. In its own way, the American parish emblematized this stability, mapping notions of holiness and sacramentality onto territorial belonging. St. Mary's, however, was the antithesis of this facade, both predating and outlasting it. In many ways, the community it served represented the underside of that history, the untold story of urban Catholic life on Boston's social, economic, and ecclesial peripheries. If European Catholic immigrants spent the twentieth century "becoming white,"[3] as the narrative goes, the people of St. Mary's spent much of that same period negotiating their place within a church that the National Black Catholic Clergy Caucus in 1968 called "primarily a white racist institution."[4] By the time the Second Vatican Council summoned the church to solidarity with the world, St. Mary's had long since thrown in its lot with the people of Egleston Square, forging community and working for peace in the face of racism, poverty, violence, and institutional neglect. While their suburban counterparts were supposedly busy ingratiating themselves into the American middle class, St. Mary's was serving a Black, Caribbean, Latin American, Laotian, Irish, and Italian American community of immigrants, refugees, and workers. St. Mary's never enjoyed the sort of stability that Catholics supposedly achieved during the twentieth century. The stability that St. Mary's offered its people was wrought neither by suburban proximity to wealth and security nor by the comfort of an insular cultural haven. Rather, it was won through decades of enduring presence. When the 2004 tidal wave of Boston parish closures tried to come for St. Mary's, the *Boston Globe* declared the tiny church the "lifeblood of the neighborhood."[5] By the time I moved to Roxbury, St. Mary's had spent more than a century operating on a shoestring budget in a basement church in the heart of Egleston Square.

How did the people of St. Mary's manage to defy the racial and cultural fragmentation that has so long defined U.S. parish life in general and Boston Catholicism in particular? This is the sort of question ordinarily pursued by sociologists and historians of religion. In this book, I ask it as a theologian. Specifically, this book examines the Catholic world of Egleston Square—its rituals, its histories, and its people and their stories— through the lens of ecclesiology, the theological study of the church. Since Vatican II, few questions have so occupied the attention of church scholars as that of the relationship between ecclesial unity and cultural diversity. Yet despite the need for more critical ways of thinking theologically about race, culture, and community, Catholic ecclesiologies have largely neglected the concrete experiences of diverse communities on the ground, consigning the study of parish life to historians and sociologists on one hand or those concerned primarily with pastoral guidance on the other. In turn, the church has struggled to perceive racism, ethnocentrism, economic inequality, and other structures of injustice not only as ethical problems but as ecclesiological ones. St. Mary's, it seemed to me, was not merely an interesting counterexample to historical dynamics or liturgical trends, a quirky parish in an iconic Catholic city that has beaten every conceivable odds. The things that made St. Mary's unique were visible signs of the constructive, communal theological work that had been unfolding there over the course of decades. What I encountered in Roxbury was a community that had stayed alive by making solidarity with its neighborhood and among parishioners central to its way of being. Taking seriously the theological agency of the people of Roxbury meant reading parish practices, past and present, as living ecclesiological sources—loci of revelation about the meaning and nature of the church in the world.

I arrived at St. Mary's in the fall of 2011 after stumbling on an ad seeking a graduate student willing to work for the church in exchange for a room in the parish house. St. Mary's shared a pastor with two other parishes and had long operated without a priest in residence. The community relied on lay volunteers to maintain a sense of presence at the parish—to keep the lights on and shovel the walk and wake up in the middle of the night when the church security alarm went off, as it often did. One young woman lived there already, a bilingual social work graduate student and former Jesuit Volunteer named Catherine. But the work was a lot for one person, and—I later learned—community members had begun to worry about the safety of a woman living alone in the house. Sight unseen, I responded to the ad and moved into the parish house, la casa parroquial, a solid, three-story Victorian-era estate house that towered over the basement church next door. The house had peeling paint and webs of cracks in the ceiling plaster and a broad, inviting front porch. Parishioners never called it a rectory. No matter who happened to be living there, the house belonged to everyone. In our case, we were Catholic women in our twenties living in a space designated for clergy within a tradition that reserves ordination for unmarried men. But to parishioners, our presence was far from subversive. St. Mary's had a long tradition of opening the parish house to lay residents—volunteers, missionaries, students. Dr. Paul Farmer, cofounder of the global health nonprofit Partners in Health, had lived on the third floor while he was in medical school at Harvard in the late 1980s.[6] In exchange for our rooms above the kitchen, we did a host of odd jobs and pastoral work. On Saturday mornings, we helped to clean the church with a weekly rotation of volunteers from the Spanish and English Mass communities. I taught fifth grade catechesis classes and compiled the Sunday bulletin. Catherine gave Spanish lessons to some of the English-speaking older women and led Communion services in the chapel on mornings when there was no priest to say weekday Mass. After the two Sunday Masses, it was our job to set out the mammoth vat of coffee and a few dozen Dunkin' Donuts, dutifully cutting the pastries into quarters in an attempt to feed as many people as the minuscule budget would allow.

It was a raw time for Catholics in Boston. When I moved to the city, it had been nine years since the *Boston Globe*'s 2002 "Spotlight" reports exposed decades of clergy sexual abuse and cover-ups. The revelations had blown through the archdiocese like a wildfire whose flames were still smoldering almost a decade later. The crisis devastated Boston Catholics' trust in the church hierarchy and ignited calls for greater lay leadership.

With its open, inclusive ethos and storied tradition of lay participation, St. Mary's was the kind of parish that people otherwise disillusioned with the church and its leaders described as the only place "keeping them Catholic." Two years after the abuse revelations came to light, Archbishop Seán O'Malley announced the impending closure of more than eighty of Boston's smallest and most financially unstable parishes. The wave of closures forced nearly thirty thousand Catholics to find new parish homes,[7] further upending communities already suffering from institutional betrayal. St. Mary's parishioners were stunned to find their church—despite its thriving social justice ministries and vibrant intercultural community—on the closure list. Neighbors and parishioners launched a solidarity campaign aimed at convincing the archdiocese that St. Mary's was too vital to the stability of the neighborhood to close. The campaign became one of few success stories in the wave of resistance that erupted across the archdiocese in the wake of the shutdowns. That St. Mary's continues to exist at all makes it an anomaly in Boston.

Moving into the parish house was like opening a new book to page 200 and beginning to read. I found myself in the middle of a story for which I had little context, filled with characters who, to everyone else, needed no introduction. Many parishioners were relatively recent migrants, but others had been parishioners for decades, some for much of their lives. They banded together with community activists in 1969 to halt an expansion of Interstate 95 that would have cut the neighborhood in half. They revered the memory of Fr. Jack Roussin, the late St. Mary's priest known for brokering peace among youth in rival gangs during the 1980s and '90s. Some had joined Voice of the Faithful in the wake of the abuse revelations and spent a night in the pews to protest the church's closure. Together, they had put their bodies and souls on the line for their community. The margins of my fieldnotes from those early months are filled with lists of names and events and other things St. Mary's parishioners regularly talked about that I didn't understand (*Who is Sixto? "Hands Around St. Mary's"? What is a CORI?*[8]).

In addition to a room of my own and all the potluck leftovers I could eat, my year in the parish house afforded me the rarest of opportunities: the chance to experience the life of a parish from the inside out. There is a reason why, until recently, most intimate portraits of Catholic parishes have been written by men, and usually priests.[9] Within the hierarchy of the church, clerical status affords a researcher both a more direct path to parish insiderhood and, in the eyes of parishioners, the presumption of credibility. Women may be the heartbeat of parish ministry, but our authority and access stops at the rectory door. My year in the parish house was an exhilarating immersion in the ordinary: the too-long meetings and fiery debates over how best to extend the life of the office printer cartridge (remove, shake, reinstall), the ambient echo of ambulance sirens through city streets at night, and the riotous laughter of the church matriarchs who lingered in the parish house after weekday Mass to drink coffee and watch *The Price is Right*. These moments were their own kind of revelation, a glimpse of the deep and abiding continuity between church and neighborhood, ritual and the rhythm of everyday life.

I had moved to Boston from the border city of Brownsville, Texas, where I had worked as a social studies teacher and children's church choir director in a small parochial school. Both daily life and parish life in Brownsville were shaped by the rich cultural porosity, political complexity, and tensive disjunctures of the U.S.-Mexico borderlands. Two thousand miles north of the Rio Grande Valley, I was surprised to encounter at St. Mary's another kind of borderland. In many ways, the unusual Roxbury parish was as much a place of cultural convergence, spatial negotiation, ritual hybridity, contested identities, half-visible divisions, unexpected alliances, and creative solidarity as the border city I had once called home. "Borderlands are physically present," wrote the late Chicana poet, author, and theorist Gloria Anzaldúa, "wherever two or more cultures edge each other, where people of different races occupy the same territory, where lower, middle, and upper classes touch, where the space between two individuals shrinks with intimacy."[10] St. Mary's was a place defined by cultural, linguistic, racial, bodily, economic, theological, and generational differences. As I came to see, it was also a place where distance shrank with intimacy, where the borders were always more porous than they appeared.

As I gradually learned, the community's history supported this impression. More than a century of local, national, and international migrations had shaped and reshaped the cultural landscape of Egleston Square, transforming cross streets into religious and ethnic borderlines and St. Mary's into a way station in the midst of them. By the 1920s, the parish boundaries encompassed the contentious borderline between

Catholic- and Jewish-occupied blocks of upper Roxbury. In the 1940s and 1950s, African Americans moving northward during the Great Migration settled in the neighborhood, eventually catalyzing urban white flight and transforming St. Mary's into a home for Black Catholics. Successive migrations from Puerto Rico and the Dominican Republic prompted the addition of a Spanish Mass in 1971. By 1979, St. Mary's had also become a religious and social hub for Catholic Laotian Kmhmu refugees in the city, while a Haitian community prompted the ad hoc addition of French and Creole ministries. By the 1980s, the tiny church was sustaining a community of some forty nationalities.

The parish was also a borderland in less obvious ways. In a church and city where class segregation runs nearly as deeply as racial and cultural divides, St. Mary's welcomed housing-insecure neighbors and city councillors, hotel housekeepers and architects, doctors and professors and community organizers. And as Roxbury became an epicenter of gang violence in Boston during the latter part of the twentieth century, St. Mary's served as a vital meeting ground for youth and their families across charged neighborhood and gang lines. When I lived there, a host of community organizations still held their meetings around the long rectangular table in the parish house.

Studies of congregational life have been unequivocal in demonstrating that most Americans worship with people who are racially, ethnically, and economically similar to themselves. While Catholic parishes are growing increasingly diverse, most "multicultural" parishes are in fact home to cultural subgroups that operate largely in parallel, sharing space but little else.[11] Against the inertia of segregation and cultural siloing that characterizes many faith communities, St. Mary's remains an outlier. These days, the community that gathers for nine o'clock Sunday morning Mass in English is composed primarily of middle-aged and older African American, Jamaican, Trinidadian, Haitian, Cape Verdean, and white parishioners. There are a smaller number of Spanish-speaking attendees from South America and the Caribbean and a handful of teenagers, young professionals, and families with children. The Spanish Mass community that gathers two hours later is much larger and younger. Most members are Dominican or Puerto Rican, while others trace their roots to Cuba, Ecuador, Mexico, Spain, and elsewhere in Latin America and the Caribbean. Both communities serve primarily working-class and middle-class parishioners who live in the vicinity of the church. Both have been welcoming of gay and lesbian Catholics. Both rely on unusually high levels of lay participation and leadership.

What makes St. Mary's unique, however, is not merely the coexistence of these two distinct, internally diverse Mass communities. This kind of multicultural space-sharing has become typical in parishes throughout the United States.[12] More striking is the community that emerges between and beyond the two Masses. During the hour-long crosscurrent between the closing hymn of the English Mass and the opening announcements in Spanish, parishioners of different races, languages, ethnicities, and generations linger with each other in the church's in-between spaces: the entryway and sanctuary aisles, the sacristy and parish house kitchen, on the parish lawn and at the top of the stairs and around the small, cracked parking lot. In one language or another or a combination of two, they ask about each other's families and exchange news. They laugh and whisper and high-five each other's kids, trading meeting reports and hugs and kisses on the cheek. These conversations do not seem forced, the product of labored intentionality or superficial politeness. Rather, these glimpses of intimacy hint at the presence of something far more elusive: deep and hard-won bonds of affection.

Solidarity as an Ecclesial Virtue

This book is a winding attempt to understand the mystery of love in a community of difference. The questions that first fueled my research were simple and open ended: *What is going on here? What stories does this community tell about itself? What draws these people together? When does it go wrong? What am I not seeing?* Gradually, my questions grew more refined: *How do people here ritualize togetherness? In a community on and of borders, what role does a parish play?* Larger theoretical and methodological questions also shaped the work's development: *What would it mean to take the ritual of a meeting as seriously as the ritual of the liturgy? How might we theorize streets, intersections, church aisles, subway stations, bus stops, and other corridors and crossings as sites of relationship? How do we read the material culture of an urban parish and neighborhood as a collection of theological sources? Nearly sixty years after Vatican II, how can ethnography sharpen and concretize reflection on the church in the modern world?* The result is a constructive theological account of solidarity, ritual, and the local church, told through ethnographic accounts that marry description, storytelling, and image with historical and ecclesiological inquiry.

The curiosity driving these questions was propelled from two directions that slowly collided. First and foremost, they arose from my year in the parish house and the five years that followed, during which I remained a parishioner and researcher at St. Mary's. When I moved in, I wasn't seeking a case study. I was looking for a place to live and a faith community to ground my ecclesial existence beyond the world of academia. The questions found me there. The complex ecology of rituals that made up the lifeworld of St. Mary's soon impressed itself upon my attention as a site of intricate border crossings. It seemed to me that, in their doing, the people of Egleston Square were saying something that had not yet been said.

Simultaneously, this work was driven by theoretical questions that emerged from analysis of post–Vatican II ecclesiological discourse on unity and diversity, emblematized in the idea of the church as communion. Communion ecclesiology lauds the neither-Jew-nor-Greek, communitarian spirit of the early Christian church and heralds a future of oneness in Christ, making it an oft-invoked ecclesiological framework for reflection on diversity in the Catholic church. But between the early church and the eschaton, the concrete task of Christian communities is less clear. Engaging communion ecclesiology from the site of a parish like St. Mary's revealed, among other things, the undertheorized status of power, race, ethnicity, class, and other forms of social difference in much of contemporary Catholic ecclesiology. As a theological foundation for diversity, communion struck me as quixotic and perplexingly overreliant on the insinuation that the sacraments of baptism and the Eucharist functionally ameliorate social division. I was far from the first person to grow impatient with communion ecclesiology's idealism,[13] but even the most salient critiques missed what seemed to be its most glaring problem. When applied to the church in history, communion is often used to glorify a postracial vision of Christian community in which difference itself is dissolved. It provides for the nominal celebration of diversity without concomitantly calling into question the structures of sin and circuits of power that divide communities in history. The result is a pervasive naiveté regarding historical and structural dimensions of division in ecclesial communities. Despite communion ecclesiology's Trinitarian insistence on the inherent goodness of difference (isn't God three in one, after all?), it became clear to me that the inability of most ordinary church communities to deal well with difference was reflected in theologies of church that similarly did not know how to conceive of human difference as anything other than a challenge. If ecclesiology had anything meaningful to contribute to the work of justice in the local church, it needed to stop insisting on its own colorblindness.

As I participated in St. Mary's ritual life, delved into its radical history, and listened to parishioners recount stories of their church, neighborhoods, friendships, and lives, I came to see that what the people of Egleston Square had spent decades working out was a lived ecclesiology of solidarity. Taking as my guide the lived practice and complex history of a parish that managed to hold together a diverse community not by transcending ethnicity but by ritually affirming difference, this book challenges prevailing ecclesiological understandings of unity in diversity. Moving beyond preoccupation with communion ecclesiology's beguiling but in some way forgivable idealism, I attend to the specific hazards it poses as a paradigm for racial justice and cultural pluralism in the local church. I argue instead for a retrieval of Vatican II's notion of ecclesial solidarity as a basis for conceiving of the mission of the local church today. While the reception of the council has largely focused on its call for solidarity *ad extra*—between church and world—the theological notion of solidarity has just as much to say about what it means to negotiate difference *ad intra*, across the intimate, immediate borderlines within ecclesial communities. Solidarity centers human difference as a good; lifts up the agency, authority, and practices of grassroots communities; reaches toward a vision of the common good; makes demands of those with power; and, with eyes open to the pain of reality, maintains, against all odds, a fierce determination in the power and possibility of love. It requires, in the words of Gustavo Gutierrez, a conversion to the neighbor.[14] In each of these ways, solidarity eschews the tendency toward ecclesial colorblindness and political apathy that prevailing ecclesiological approaches to unity in diversity wittingly or unwittingly sanction. If communion describes the eschatological character of the church, then solidarity proposes the shape of its task in history.

This book argues for an understanding of solidarity as an ecclesial virtue cultivated through embodied practice. Through stories gleaned from archives, letters, newspapers, and the long memories of parishioners and neighbors, I trace how the people of St. Mary's constructed rituals of solidarity as a practical foundation for building community, interrupting violence, sustaining both parish and neighborhood, and negotiating the borders in their midst. Looking beyond liturgy and sacrament alone, I examine solidaristic practices threaded throughout the parish's entire ritual ecology: from announcements at the end of Mass to the reflection at the beginning of Parish Pastoral Council meetings, from the Good Friday Way of the Cross through the streets of Egleston Square and Holy Week processions around the block to the protest rituals staged in and around the church in the wake of the 2004 closure announcement. Such practices, I argue, disclose a recognition that salvation in both the immanent and spiritual sense is a communal reality—that the future of one is bound up with the futures of all. For the people of Egleston Square, such rituals are the language of community. In the absence of a common spoken language, culture, or history, ritual becomes a kind of body language—a choreographed dance, an embodied script, a shared itinerary. Through this ritual language, communities practice joining together across difference. At St. Mary's, ritual's capacity to build bridges allowed it to encompass ambiguity without demanding uniformity. Creative, processional, embodied practices cultivated space for the renegotiation of power and the reformation of relational imaginations, making possible the kind of conversion to the other that the work of solidarity demands.

City and Parish as *Locus Ecclesiologicus*

This book is a work of lived ecclesiology, situated methodologically at the juncture between sustained ethnographic fieldwork in a church and constructive theological work about the church. I understand ethnography as the methodological corollary to Vatican II's summons to read the signs of the times in light of the Gospel (*Gaudium et Spes* 4)—to anchor theological reflection, especially reflection on the church, in the intricate, fragile complexities of the human condition and particular human communities. In turn, I view the parish as a *locus ecclesiologicus*, a source of theological insight about the nature and mission of the church in the world.[15] It is worth bearing in mind that the term "parish" refers not only to a church building or its membership but to the entire territorial space encompassed by a parish's boundary lines. If we think of the parish as the totality of this space, then to speak of the parish as a *locus ecclesiologicus* is also, necessarily, to regard the city as a space of ecclesiological revelation. To tell the story of an urban neighborhood is to tell a story about the church. This remains true even in an age in which enclaves of ethnic-Catholic urban life are mostly the stuff of great-grandparents' memories. Urban neighborhoods like Egleston Square are borderlands, making them important sites of reflection on the reality of the church today. Natalia Imperatori-Lee, drawing on the work of late mujerista theologian and ethnographer Ada María Isasi-Díaz, observes that "the church in the United States . . . is a displaced church, made up in large part of people Isasi-Díaz calls 'multi-sites persons' who live in the interstices of cultures."[16] As city parishes are transformed by migration, displacement, transnational belonging, gentrification, and other forms of social change, they remain rich sources of insight on the possibilities and limits of community in an in-between church.

Within the study of urban religion, public rituals are often described as sanctifying streets or making profane space sacred. Yet such descriptions seem, often, to be burdened by an exaggerated distinction between sacred and profane. According to a religious imagination formed along this Durkheimian binary, ritual sanctions the flow of holiness in one direction: from clergy to laity, church to world, religious symbol and story to brick and asphalt and billboard advertisements for pay-by-the-minute cell phones. As Robert Orsi writes, within this imagination of the sacred, "The very idea of 'city religion' [strikes] many as an oxymoron." White, middle-class Americans are "more likely to identify mountaintops and oceans and beaches as places evocative of religious feelings than street corners and the basements of housing projects."[17] The operative religious sensibility that governs the ritual life of St. Mary's, by contrast, has much more in common with Latinx theological reverence for lo cotidiano, the sacred everyday.[18] Sidestepping Western religious anxieties about the distinction between religion and not-religion, these rituals rely on a fundamental conviction in the holiness of the neighborhood and its people. It would have surprised me, for example, to hear participants in the Good Friday Way of the Cross through Egleston Square describe the ritual as somehow imparting holiness to the streets. (No one did). Though many gestured at the procession's transformative, prophetic character, no one seemed to view the ritual as producing sacred space. Instead, I got the sense that when walkers took to the streets, they perceived themselves to be moving through space already charged with divine presence.

If we regard the city as a site of ecclesiological revelation, then the faith practices people undertake in these streets are also ecclesiologically meaningful. The stories of the people of God are part of the story of the church. Lived theology relies on a conviction that faith communities themselves are "bearers of theology."[19] What these individuals and communities do—the rituals they practice and stories they tell, the questions they ask and the conflicts they negotiate, the joys they inhabit and anguish they bear—are real-time theological acts. As Imperatori-Lee rightly contends, Catholic ecclesiologists have long relied upon church doctrines and magisterial pronouncements as their primary, and sometimes only, sources of reflection. The result has been a misrepresentation of the story of the church as a "single story." As living expressions of the *sensus fidelium* (the "sense of the faithful"), ritual practice, art, drama, music, literature, and other lay embodiments of faith add to these typical sources a fuller sense of the church's living tradition.[20] The rituals the people of St. Mary's perform in the streets around their parish disclose the community's own memories and hopes, their struggles and yearnings for new life. This is polyvocal ecclesiology—the story of the church told in the vernacular of many lives.

I hesitate to call this book an "ecclesiology from below," a category that I find draws too fine a distinction between institutional and popular dimensions of ecclesial identity and practice, flattening the mutually constitutive, often mixed-up relationship between the creeds, doctrines, and liturgies of the institutional church and the devotional faith of the people. "Ecclesiology from below" also seems to exculpate those working "from above" from taking its insights seriously. Instead, like all theologies of church, it is an ecclesiology from a place. I have simply sought to clarify what that place is and who I am as an interpreter of that place.

Ethnography and the Parish

Though speaking of diversity in congregational life often conjures associations with emerging realities and recent trends, parishes have been sites of cultural, ethnic, and linguistic negotiation for centuries. The outsized legacies of national and ethnic parishes in American Catholic historiography, combined with the passage of restrictive immigration laws in the 1920s and the Americanizing impulse of white Catholics in the post-World War II period, can offer the impression that until recently, most parishes were relatively culturally homogenous. Such impressions are misleading, however. Until the mid-nineteenth-century spike in immigration from predominantly Catholic European countries and the U.S. conquest of nearly half of Mexican territory in the 1840s and 1850s, Catholics were an extreme minority throughout much of the United States.[21] Where parishes were few and far between, Catholics of different nationalities and ethnicities often worshipped together by default. In these cases, everyday social interaction among neighbors of different cultures helped to foster an "ethos of cooperation" within the context of worship and parish governance.[22] Even in archdioceses like Boston, where the establishment of national parishes was a common solution to the pastoral and liturgical exigencies posed by waves of European immigration, territorial parishes remained the norm. At the height of the national parish era in New England between 1880 and 1930, only about 30 percent of new parishes were designated to serve a particular cultural group.[23] The rest, like St. Mary of the Angels, were territorial, theoretically tasked with serving every Catholic residing within their boundaries, regardless of race, ethnicity, or language. Because immigrants often settled in enclaves, territorial parishes in cities like Boston often functioned as de facto national (often Irish) parishes. And because of the pervasive racial discrimination Black Catholics suffered in their local parishes, the establishment of African American ethnic parishes was both an opportunity for Black Catholics to practice their faith unfettered by white racism and an institutionally sanctioned excuse for whites to continue excluding Black coreligionists from "their" parishes.[24] In telling the story of St. Mary's in this book, I have drawn on significant historical data from the parish in part to demonstrate that "diversity in the church" is not a contemporary phenomenon, nor are diverse parishes outliers. In many ways, U.S. parishes have always been sites of boundaries, borders, and bridges.

Despite the role that parishes continue to play as sites of racial and cultural negotiation, however, we know remarkably little about the inner lives of such communities. Indeed, as Brett Hoover notes, theologians have been curiously hesitant to assign theological significance to the parish.[25]

This is ironic, given that parishes remain many Catholics' primary, and sometimes only, connection to the universal church and to the sacraments, rituals, stories, songs, communities, and creeds that encompass the practice of their faith. As Karl Rahner suggested more than sixty years ago, the parish is overdue for theological consideration.[26] A large body of literature examines multiethnic Protestant congregations, but comparable ethnographic studies of diverse Catholic parishes are sparse.[27] This is surprising for two reasons. First, Catholic parishes are, on average, more racially and ethnically diverse than Protestant congregations.[28] Second, broadly speaking, Catholic approaches to theology and ministry tend to be more affirming of cultural particularity than Protestant ones. Comparing Catholic and evangelical Protestant approaches to diversifying their churches, sociologist Kathleen Garces-Foley observes that whereas evangelical congregations tend to locate unity in the notion that Christian identity supersedes culture and ethnicity, Catholic theological understandings of inculturation and hospitality, particularly since Vatican II, more explicitly affirm the persistence of cultural, ethnic, and linguistic particularity.[29] In other words, whereas evangelicals might proclaim that believers are one in Christ despite their differences, Catholics might respond that believers are one in Christ by virtue of their differences.

Yet despite Catholicism's ostensibly affirming attitude toward cultural particularity, the lack of ethnographic accounts of diverse parishes bespeaks larger difficulties these complex communities pose to scholars. First, studying parishes presents a different set of epistemological, methodological, and theological concerns than does studying Protestant congregations. These consequential distinctions mean that the theoretical categories and analytical frameworks of congregational studies do not seamlessly apply to parish contexts. The most obvious distinction between the two is the territorial basis of the parish system. Even though many Catholics no longer feel particularly compelled to adhere to their parish boundaries, parish belonging is still more geographically determined than Protestant congregational membership. Because parochial belonging is less the result of voluntarism, and new parishes are established and staffed by the diocese based largely on population needs, intentional efforts among Catholics to cultivate a unique sense of intercultural mission and identity in their churches can be less overt and, in turn, more difficult to characterize.

Second, data on Catholic parish diversity reveal little about actual levels of interaction among parishioners of different races, ethnicities, or cultures within parishes. Because cultural subcommunities often participate in distinct Masses and ministries within the same parish, pinpointing the locus, extent, and significance of actual intercultural interaction within these "communities of communities" can be difficult.

Third, while the coexistence of multiple cultural groups within the same parish is not new, the emergence of what Hoover terms the "shared parish" as an institutionally recognized model of parish life is a relatively recent phenomenon. While shared parishes are not temporary arrangements, the cultural coexistence that happens there feels to many within them like an ad hoc solution, something that works for the time being but also bears a sense of impermanence. The task of offering a cohesive account of an arrangement that many feel to be provisional and awkward seems daunting if not impossible. Such communities can seem far from both the idealized images of church described in the pages of systematic ecclesiologies and from highly mission-driven, self-consciously multiethnic Protestant congregations that make up much of the relevant congregational studies literature.

In order to describe this complexity while avoiding the temptation to idealize it, I have taken methodological cues from the field of lived religion and from its more emergent, confessionally oriented cousin, lived theology.[30] In this work, I have been most influenced by Robert Orsi, whose commitment to reading the devotional lives of Catholic city dwellers on their own terms is unparalleled.[31] More recently, Alyssa Maldonado-Estrada's study of Catholic men's devotional lives in Williamsburg, Brooklyn, upends prevailing understandings of gender and the body in the devotional culture of a parish.[32] Neither Orsi nor Maldonado-Estrada is a theologian, but in many ways that makes them more, not less, willing to affirm traces of divine presence where it lies—in streets and basements, invented rituals and gift shop statues, clothing and tattoos, and above all, in the relationships that comprise the networks of everyday holiness.

Unlike lived religion, lived theology is complicated by the fact that it is necessarily both descriptive and normative. The relationship between these two aims is the subject of continued debate among scholars and poses myriad challenges for writing a book like this one.[33] I have found that centering analysis on a community's rituals, as I have done throughout this book, is a helpful way of parsing the relationship between the two aims. Ritual is communal action located at the juncture between the descriptive reality of what is and the moral force of what could and should be. In Christian terms, ritual contains an implicit admission of sin and human failure, a recognition of the distance between history and eschatology. A community's rituals reveal something about who that community is, but they reveal even more about who those in the community wish they were and believe themselves to be. At St. Mary's, ritual was a template, an embodied script through which participants practiced being the kind of community or neighborhood or church they wished they could be all the time.

Methods

In her book *Lifeblood of the Parish*, Maldonado-Estrada draws on sociologist Erving Goffman's distinction between a performance's "front region" and "backstage" to examine the hidden places where the work of parish maintenance happens and the unexpected agents of this devotional labor.[34] At Brooklyn's Our Lady of Mount Carmel, Maldonado-Estrada spends most of her time in the church basement among the tattooed Italian American men who count money and paint statues in preparation for the church's annual feast. My research for this book involved similarly protracted sojourns into the basement. In the case of St. Mary's, however, the basement was also the sanctuary. For five years, I attended English, Spanish, and multilingual liturgies, devotions, weddings, baptisms, and funerals in the underground church. Beyond the basement, I marched in public processions, prayed at "nights of reflection" during Advent and Lent, ate and danced at parties, hauled aluminum casserole pans to potlucks, and perused parishioners' donated housewares at parish bazaars in the parking lot. Once I bought a microwave whose former owner chided me for the ten dollars I spent on it. "Why you didn't tell me you need a microwave?" she asked. "I would have given it to you for free!" In very different ways, these were the public-facing "front stage" events of parish life and ministry at St. Mary's. Yet even more of my participation at St. Mary's took place within the intimate, day-to-day work of parish maintenance and preparation that unfolded backstage: meeting, planning, practicing, counting, translating, setting up, decorating, cleaning, mouse-trapping, evaluating, advocating, making-do, visiting, record-keeping, printing, calling, e-mailing, listening, negotiating, storytelling, worrying, imagining, and praying. The general lack of space at St. Mary's, coupled with the fact that virtually everybody at the parish was given some responsibility for planning or leading or cooking or donating, meant that front-stage devotion and backstage preparation were often unfolding simultaneously, depending on where one happened to look.

In chapters 4 and 5, I focus on Holy Week, the liturgical period between Palm Sunday and the Easter Vigil, and in a particular way on Good Friday. Here, I follow Latinx theologians and scholars of religion including Karen Mary Davalos, Alyshia Gálvez, Roberto Goizueta, Virgilio Elizondo, and Christopher Tirres in affirming the significance of public Holy Week devotions for communities on the margins.[35] Indeed, this was the point in the liturgical year at which lay participation and intercultural collaboration at St. Mary's reached their peak. The bilingual liturgies and rituals of Holy Week were multilingual and lay coordinated, each one relying on the participation of dozens of parishioners from all walks of life. The time and effort demanded by this ritual work drew parishioners together and gave the week a frenzied energy. "There's an intensity in the planning of it and the frenetic-ness of making it happen and the satisfaction of it coming together," an English Mass parishioner named Amelia explained to me. "We're helping to create a space for people to experience the Passion, you know, and that's pretty profound, I think."[36]

To understand the complex migration and transportation histories of Egleston Square, I combed through parish records, photographs, and clergy personnel files in the archives of the Roman Catholic Archdiocese of Boston (RCAB) and of the *Boston Pilot*, the archdiocesan newspaper. Most intriguing was the nearly eight decades of available correspondence between the chancery, St. Mary's priests, and parishioners. (Files from the mid-1980s forward were still sealed). As I narrate in chapter 3, these letters were mostly a litany of laments. In the early decades, priests wrote to the cardinal to complain about the lack of Catholics in the neighborhood, the lack of funds, the scandal of parishioners marrying outside the Catholic church, the perennially decrepit state of the parish house and basement church, and one another. Parishioners wrote to the chancery to decry their pastor's controlling personality and rambling, outrageous homilies. In the years following Vatican II, however, the tone of these letters changed dramatically. Complaints about facilities and budget shortfalls were accompanied by distressing accounts of the violence overwhelming the neighborhood and the inhuman living conditions suffered by parishioners. They contained pleas for greater pastoral commitment to Roxbury and other "inner-city" neighborhoods. The chancery, for its part, had its own complaints—particularly about the headstrong, lay-led Parish Pastoral Council that formed at St. Mary's in the years following Vatican II. These archived correspondences told the story of a parish trying desperately to read and respond to the signs of the times, not merely as an exercise in liturgical experimentation but as an act of survival. Careful record-keeping by longtime parishioners offered even greater insight into the years for which RCAB archives were unavailable. Files containing meeting minutes, handwritten notes, printed e-mails, letter drafts, newspaper articles, liturgy programs, and ritual scripts detailing the protests that the community staged against St. Mary's closure in 2004 provided the source material for the final chapter. I remain grateful to parish leaders for entrusting me with these artifacts.

In addition to everyday conversations with parishioners, I also conducted several rounds of formal interviews in Spanish and English. These I recorded, transcribed, translated when necessary, and coded.[37] My conversations with longtime parishioners often lasted for ninety minutes or more, resulting in rich oral histories of St. Mary's and Egleston Square. If there was one thing St. Mary's people were good at, it was talking about St. Mary's. They were well practiced at it—telling their story in word and ritual to a variety of publics helped to save the parish from closure—and most people were eager to add their voices to the record. The challenge came in corroborating stories, matching fading memories with elusive historical records, and learning to ask the kinds of questions that would later help me sift through nostalgia.

In recorded interviews, I found that parishioners from the Spanish Mass community had less to say than I had anticipated about the challenges of working with the English-speaking community (sound system–related grievances excepted). There are several potential explanations for this. It is possible that participants were telling me what they believed I wanted to hear, fearing that they would offend me, a white, English-speaking parishioner. Perhaps my university affiliation lent me the illusion of institutional power and gave our conversations an inhibiting ethos of formality. In any case, recent émigrés generally expressed gratitude for the welcome they felt they had received from Spanish and English speakers alike. Longtime leaders had more to say about the everyday tensions that arose between Spanish- and English-speaking parishioners over the years, but even these long-timers tended to emphasize the positive. For example, the famously blunt lay leader Claudia gushed about her decades of collaboration with the English Mass community. "I could *write a book* about how beautiful it was to work with the Anglos," she once declared to me. Even the Dominican women with whom I had become close friends— women who had no problem speaking candidly with me about the good, the bad, and the ugly of their experiences at St. Mary's—had few critical words about their cross-cultural interactions. When they did describe tensions, they often did so in familial terms. "We fight. We make up," choir member Marisol said with a shrug. "It's like a family."[38]

More than likely, Spanish Mass parishioners had simply spent less time than their English-speaking counterparts mulling over the intricacies of St. Mary's multicultural mission. To the English Mass community's largely progressive, social justice–oriented crowd, diversity was part of what made St. Mary's an attractive parish. The Spanish Mass community was also deeply committed to the parish's intercultural identity, as illustrated in chapter 6 by their offense at the archbishop's suggestion that they simply attend the Spanish liturgy at another nearby parish should St. Mary's close. But for many, it was the internal diversity of the Spanish Mass community, which encompassed parishioners from across the Caribbean, Latin America, and occasionally Spain, that posed more immediate challenges. Disagreements over musical styles in the liturgy, negotiations about how to celebrate everyone's preferred Marian feast days, conflicts between traditional and progressive members about the role of the priest in the community, and the perennial challenge of serving their third-culture youth were all more pressing than macrolevel questions about their relationships with the English speakers. Ultimately, for Latinas/os in the Northeast, belonging to a parish that offers Mass in Spanish almost invariably means attending a "shared" parish. Diversity is less a progressive virtue and more a fact of ecclesial existence.

My year in the parish house came to an end when I got married and moved across town to Brighton. But I remained an active parishioner and participant-researcher there until we moved out of state in 2016. During my five years at St. Mary's, I sat for a time on the Parish Pastoral Council and agreed to briefly join the leadership team of the Liturgical Committee, a role that confirmed that my gifts lay elsewhere. I lectored and read the announcements at the end of Mass and sang an occasional psalm. My oldest daughter was baptized at six weeks old at the Easter Vigil Mass one chilly April night. I attended Red Sox games and birthday parties and ate around more kitchen tables than I can count. I got my haircuts and gossip from a parishioner who owned a salon and furnished our first apartment with hand-me-downs from several others. After we left Boston, I returned to St. Mary's several times to conduct follow-up interviews and fieldwork and visit with friends from the parish. On my first trip back, no sooner had I stepped through the sanctuary doors than I was recruited to read the English half of the Solemn Intercessions at that evening's bilingual Good Friday liturgy. It was nearly impossible for anyone to attend Mass at St. Mary's and not be drafted into involvement, and I was no exception.

During my time in Egleston Square, I inhabited many subjectivities simultaneously: that of a Catholic woman, white person, English speaker, parish resident, researcher, and theologian. Gradually, I added others: spouse, then mother; later, professor. Marriage and motherhood turned out to be credentials that mattered in ways I hadn't anticipated. My husband—a social worker and former high school Spanish teacher, outgoing and earnest and happy to volunteer for every conceivable thankless church task (for two years, he found himself the "temporary" director of the eclectic English Mass choir)—immediately endeared himself to the entire parish, procuring for me a nearly boundless supply of goodwill from parishioners in both Mass communities. To many, especially older women and Spanish Mass families, the fact that I had a family of my own granted me a subtle air of legitimacy, as though these things made me a real adult rather than "just" a student. They made me—and, in turn, the research I was doing—legible to those who might have otherwise been skeptical of or confused by my presence. They also occasioned empathy. Women from both Mass communities mourned with me after I suffered one, then two, then three miscarriages. They told me their own stories of loss and cried their tears in front of me. Relationships were not ancillary to the work. In many ways, they were the work. St. Mary's was a community that had staked its survival on bonds of mutuality, friendship, and love. In my research, I strove not for some illusory objectivity. Rather, what I hope this book demonstrates is that it is through deep embeddedness in the local church and in the lives of people that theologians can begin to uncover exactly what is at stake in ecclesiological debates. I maintain that taking seriously the parish as a *locus ecclesiologicus* entails a fundamental shift in commitment and scholarly accountability. The lived experiences of communities on the margins are not raw data to be extracted and carried away to academic conferences and peer-reviewed journals. Instead, doing theology from the site of a parish beckons theologians to sustained dwelling in and with a community—to solidarity with the local church.

It is probably clear by now that my position at St. Mary's was not without complications. Living in the parish house meant that I became, upon arrival, a literal gatekeeper. Alongside my housemate, I held the keys to the church and parish house. I answered the door and the phone and set the security alarm at night. As a resident-researcher, I was examining the parish's practices of inclusion while I was partially responsible for managing its porous boundary between insider and outsider. I myself was part insider, part outsider. My positionality conditioned my own implicit prejudices, bodily habituations, interpretive biases, and the power relationships that developed between myself, other parishioners, and the various diocesan and Jesuit clergy who served the parish. My first day at St. Mary's, I realized later with incredulity, marked the first time in my life I had worshipped among a community of Black Catholics. And though I spoke Spanish, I often struggled to understand the Dominican accents of many parishioners. Never having lived anywhere near the Northeast, even Boston initially felt like another world. It took months to move beyond the self-consciousness I felt as a newcomer in a church of long-timers and as a white person in a racially diverse parish. As I became part of the community, I came to recognize that the initial awkwardness I felt was in fact fear, a by-product of my lifelong racial habituation as a white Catholic in mostly racially homogenous ecclesial contexts. I did not know how to be different, and even my best intentions could not tell me what to do with difference once I encountered it. Ten years later, this book is an attempt at an answer.

Names, Terms, Languages, and Identifiers

Whenever possible, I let parishioners speak for themselves, citing interviews in order to weave together a tapestry of voices. To allow parishioners to speak freely, I use pseudonyms for most individuals, with some
exceptions. I occasionally cite quotations from parish members originally
printed in the *Boston Globe* and other media. Since these are part of the
public record and parishioners offered interviews with the explicit intention of making their voices heard, I attribute them using real names. I identify by name William and Hector Morales, the St. Mary's brothers whose
story I recount in chapter 4. Will Morales became a well-known community leader in Boston, and the story of his brother Hector's death in 1990
occupied news headlines for weeks and was the subject of a highly publi-
cized investigation into police conduct. I similarly retain the real names
of deceased parishioners and priests, except for parishioners who have
died since I initially interviewed them. I use the real name of Fr. John
"Jack" Roussin, the legendary city priest who led St. Mary's during the
turbulent years from 1976 to 1992. Others who are still alive but whose
leadership of St. Mary's has been widely documented, such as Fr. David
Gill, S.J., are also identified by name, as are all public figures, local politicians, bishops, cardinals, activists, and community leaders.

Both the terms researchers use to describe race and ethnicity and the
identifiers individuals at St. Mary's used for themselves are fluid and often imprecise. The term "Latinx" had not yet come into popular use during my early years at St. Mary's; in this book, my occasional use of the
contested descriptor to identify persons and communities of Latin American descent reflects scholarly convention, if not consensus. I employ the
similarly contested term "Hispanic" to describe Spanish-speaking communities, especially when referencing church contexts in which the term is
more common (e.g., "Hispanic ministry"). In general, however, I defer to
contextual norms to determine these markers of identity. The St. Mary's
community primarily employed monolithic terms like these—"Asian"
rather than Kmhmu, "Latino" in place of Dominican, Puerto Rican, and
so on—when offering a snapshot of parish demographics to the archdiocese or public. Blanket descriptors like "Black" and "Latina" sometimes
obscure more than they reveal, particularly in a community that, at various points, has included people who are African-born, descendants of

enslaved Africans, Caribbean and African Caribbean, Mexican, Latin American, and Spanish. Whenever possible, I opt for specificity, identifying people as they identified themselves—often by their country or culture of origin—except where identifying one's home country would make one's identity obvious. I use the terms "white" and "Euro-American" interchangeably, except where the latter refers to a specific community of European origin. I capitalize "Black" except when part of a title or quotation.[39] Finally, I occasionally refer to older members of the parish as "elders." Many English speakers in the parish used this term as one of endearment and respect for the community's most senior members. By way of disambiguation, however, note that "elder" does not indicate a formal congregational leadership position, like "deacon" or "priest," as it does in some Protestant denominations.

I primarily identify the groups of regular attendees at each of the parish's two Sunday masses as the "English Mass community" and the "Spanish Mass community." In emic terms, English speakers usually referred to these two communities simply as the "Spanish community" and the "English community" or, even more colloquially, as the "Nines" and the "Elevens," a reference to the times on Sunday morning at which each Mass began. Some Spanish-speaking parishioners referred to the two communities as "los hispanos" and "los ingles," "los americanos," or "Anglos." But these terms, too, were imprecise, and not only because a good half of the English-speakers were not white or born in the United States. There were English speakers who attended the Spanish Mass and Spanish speakers who attended the English Mass and some who attended either and sometimes both, depending on the week; many parishioners were multilingual and still others spoke languages other than English and Spanish. Such descriptors should not suggest that language and Mass affiliation were the only consequential identity signifiers at St. Mary's. Parishioners conceived of difference and belonging along many different lines, language and Mass attendance being two of the most salient.

Readers will notice that though I recount the presence of a small but active Laotian Kmhmu community at St. Mary's throughout the late 1970s, '80s, and '90s, no interviews from members of this community appear in the book. By the time I arrived at St. Mary's in 2011, this community was no longer an active part of the parish. The first Easter Vigil Mass I attended in 2012 was celebrated trilingually in English, Spanish, and Lao. A Kmhmu family who had since moved out of Boston returned to read these parts of the liturgy. According to longtime parishioners, this family—one clearly known to and beloved by many—was one of several who periodically returned to Egleston Square, often during Holy Week, to celebrate with the parish. Beyond that interaction, however, I had few encounters with the Kmhmu community.

In the parish mission statement, St. Mary's defined itself as "multicultural and multilingual," language I occasionally echo throughout the book. When I do so, I am employing parishioners' self-definition as "multicultural" in the colloquial sense, not in the now-outmoded political one. Alma, a longtime parishioner who helped to lead the mission statement writing process in the early 2000s, recalled that even at the time, "multicultural" seemed an imperfect descriptor, but it was the term that parishioners felt most adequately captured what they were about. Because St. Mary's is a multilingual parish, I have chosen not to italicize words and phrases in languages other than English, with the exception of song lyrics and theological terms.

Itinerary

This book begins by deconstructing prevailing ecclesiological approaches to unity in diversity, and then uses ethnographic storytelling and analysis to construct a vision of ecclesial solidarity. Chapter 1 examines how Vatican II (1962–65) changed the way that the church conceived of its relationship with "others." In ways both seismic and subtle, the council reenvisioned the church's once-fortified internal and external borders as porous. This reorientation was manifested at the most local level, the parish. Once the center of the parallel societies Catholics constructed for themselves in cities like Boston, the parish became the site at which ordinary Catholics translated and transacted the council's developments. There, improvising on Vatican II's themes, structures, and practices, parishioners experimented with new approaches to inclusion, authority, and public witness. I argue that Vatican II laid the groundwork for an understanding of the parish as a school of solidarity. Yet as magisterial attention shifted to emphasize communion ecclesiology as the predominant interpretation of Vatican II's ecclesiology, the ecclesiological implications of the council's vision of solidarity have gone largely overlooked. A critical examination reveals the inadequacy of communion ecclesiology as a theological basis for racially and culturally diverse communities. By the end of the chapter, the shape of the dilemma emerges. Prevailing interpretations of the council's ecclesiology leave us with a vision of unity in diversity that takes insufficient account of the borderlines within local ecclesial communities. By ignoring the stark asymmetries of power that definitively shape the liturgical, sacramental, and social life of a parish, the communion paradigm ultimately underwrites ecclesial colorblindness and renders unclear the mission of the local church with respect to racial justice.

Chapter 2 begins a constructive response to the question of ecclesial community in difference by turning to St. Mary of the Angels. Attending to welcome rituals during Mass announcements and parishioners' accounts of their arrivals at St. Mary's, I trace the evolution of parish and neighborhood through the century of local, national, and international migrations that shaped them both, situating these movements within the larger story of twentieth-century Catholicism in the urban Northeast. I propose an understanding of the parish as a way station in an urban borderland, a community whose practices were shaped by the confluence of cultures, migrations, and histories.

In chapter 3, through the lens of a present-day Parish Pastoral Council meeting, I contrast two attempts at solidarity propelled by Vatican II. The first was a 1965 attempt by Boston's Richard Cardinal Cushing to provide pastoral intervention to "inner-city" parishes through a missionary program called the Roxbury Apostolate. The initiative, examined here for the first time, sought to reimagine parish structures and clergy roles in light of the council's reforms. Yet despite the archdiocese's attempt to revive the Roxbury parishes it had long neglected, the program was undone by its own idealism and undermined by the capricious nature of institutionally led solidarity "from above." The second was the establishment of the St. Mary's Parish Pastoral Council around 1969. Drawing on archival data and oral histories, I analyze how parishioners' reception of the liturgical and ecclesial reforms of the Second Vatican Council radically reframed their relationship with the local community. Seizing the postconciliar ethos of openness to the modern world, laity leaned hard into their newfound power in order to make structural decisions that placed their struggling parish into a relationship of costly solidarity with the increasingly

marginalized community it served. The creative public practices that en-
sued solidified St. Mary's status as a borderland in the otherwise highly
segregated social and ecclesial ethos of twentieth-century Boston.

Chapter 4 weaves together text, photography, and song in a phenomenological analysis of how public devotional practice functions as a site
of border negotiation and source of solidarity in communities of faith. I
focus on the annual Good Friday Neighborhood Way of the Cross, which
emerged as an ecumenical, popular-liturgical response to gang violence
in Roxbury. Winding through the streets of Egleston Square, the Stations
of the Cross are places—street corners, storefronts, apartment stoops—
marking the neighborhood's own passion. Participants' memories of
migration—international, transnational, parochial, spiritual—converge in
the streets, woven together in the present through the shared body language of footsteps and the Christian aesthetic vernacular of suffering,
death, and resurrection. By crossing neighborhood lines, parish boundaries, and gang territories, parishioners reconfigured local space and
actively defied structures of segregation, violence, and displacement.

Chapter 5 considers the relationship between ritual practice and solidarity in contexts of difference. Prevailing studies of multiethnic congregations emphasize the role of ritual in transcending racial and ethnic
differences. Refuting such claims, I suggest that at St. Mary's, effective
ritual does not erase difference but instead affirms it, inviting participants
to join with others in their otherness. Interpreting solidarity rituals at
St. Mary's against the backdrop of social reality in Roxbury, I contend that
in contexts of profound difference, ritual can itself become the language
of community. Distinguishing solidarity from a Turnerian notion of *communitas*, I ask how the people of St. Mary's use parish ritual to work out
in practice the vision of community they seek. Drawing on the work of
Catherine Bell, I propose an expansive vision of ritual in parish studies,
one that looks beyond liturgy alone in order to take seriously the ecclesial
work that happens in meetings and marches. I argue that all parish rituals should be understood within their broader ecologies of practice. Engaging the idea of lay-led ritual as "dialogue on the ground" developed
by the late Indian Catholic ethnographer Selva J. Raj, I suggest that it is
through the body language of ritual that parishioners form and perform
themselves into a community.

Chapter 6 concludes by drawing on parishioner records to tell the story of the solidarity campaign mounted by the community to protest the closure of St. Mary's in 2004. Rather than emphasizing sentimental connections to their church, drilling down on unwieldy grievances with the Catholic hierarchy in the wake of the abuse crisis, or becoming mired in expensive litigation or improbable Vatican appeals, as other churches had done, they mounted a case aimed at convincing the archdiocese that St. Mary's was too vital to the delicate urban ecology of Egleston Square to close. Incensed by the archbishop's proposal that members be divided up among nearby parishes along linguistic and racial lines, parishioners' rejection of the closure decision was, I argue, ultimately the refusal of a certain kind of ecclesiology, one unable to imagine a community like theirs. That the campaign was ultimately successful when most others were not testifies to the notion that for the people of St. Mary's and Egleston Square, solidarity was and remains an act of salvation.

The 1983 Code of Canon Law defines the parish as a stable community of the faithful. Yet as mass migration, shifts in religious practice and commitment, struggles for racial justice, nationalist violence, and demands for institutional change in the wake of continuing abuse revelations reshape the American Catholic landscape, it is instability that most characterizes twenty-first-century parish life. The grief and disorientation of the COVID-19 pandemic have accelerated these changes, magnifying inequities and suffusing even the most durable institutions with an aura of fragility. Within this milieu of profound change and destabilized identities, ecclesial communities survive by becoming way stations for a church on the move. By reenvisioning the local church through the lens of solidarity, it is possible to glimpse new futures for the Catholic church that respond for a new age to the challenge that catholicity continually poses: how we remain together.

1   Beyond Unity in Diversity

Dios nos ha juntado. Pero uno tiene que trabajar para la unidad.
(God has united us. But you have to work for unity.)

Marisol, St. Mary of the Angels Spanish Mass choir member

On August 27, 1963, thirty-two busses carrying 1,299 passengers departed from Carter Playground in Lower Roxbury bound for the March on Washington. Among the Bostonians who donned "Mass. Freedom Rider" armbands and boarded the caravan that morning were seven Catholic priests. Six more arrived in Washington, DC, by air. Of the thirteen Boston clergy who attended the March on Washington, three served parishes in Roxbury: St. Joseph, St. Francis de Sales, and St. Mary of the Angels.[1]

Four weeks later, marchers came to them. On Sunday, September 22, 1963, between six thousand and ten thousand people processed through the streets of Roxbury to demand an end to de facto segregation in Boston public schools. Organized by the Boston chapter of the NAACP, the March on Roxbury took place two days before the city's school board primary election, one week after the deadly KKK bombing of 16th Street Baptist Church in Birmingham, Alabama, and on the heels of a summer of failed negotiations with the Boston School Committee led by anti-integrationist chairperson Louise Day Hicks. Marchers arrived from two directions. In Lower Roxbury, they departed once again from Carter Playground. In Upper Roxbury, they streamed past St. Mary of the Angels on their way to Washington Park. Processing through the streets singing "We Shall Overcome," demonstrators converged in front of Roxbury's Sherwin School, which served an almost entirely Black student body. The ninety-three-year-old brick structure looked, in the words of Birmingham civil rights attorney Orzell Billingsley, Jr., a 16th Street Baptist Church member who had traveled to Boston for the march, like "a dilapidated ware-house" unfit for children of any race.[2] "Now, you know that we went on the March on Washington . . . and now we are marching here in Roxbury," march coordinator Archie Epps declared to the crowd, gesturing to the school. "You know what it's all about. You can see it right behind me! You see the school here built in 1870, and then you see the Prudential Center rising above that in the back. This is what we're talking about—*the difference!*"[3]

The same week that Black and white Bostonians marched through the streets of Roxbury to protest the separate and unequal state of Boston schools, Boston's Richard Cardinal Cushing boarded a TWA flight bound for Rome to begin the second session of the Second Vatican Council.[4] The council represented another kind of confrontation with the spiritual, social, political, and economic demands of human freedom. Cushing was no stranger to Boston's racial disparities. The de facto segregation that defined its schools also defined its parishes, and for many of the same reasons. On a flyer advertising the March on Roxbury, a hand-drawn sketch titled "The Problem" portrayed two men side by side. The man on the left, captioned "Sweet Home/Suburbia," stood in the doorway of a neat, modern house in a suit and tie, a pipe in his mouth. The man on the right, captioned "High Rent/Roxbury," leaned against a dirty, crumbling wall, his tattered clothing and thin face betraying his poverty.[5] The illustration was meant to capture disparities in wealth and housing, but it could just as well have described the racial and economic realities of parish life in the Archdiocese of Boston. Middle- and upper-class white Catholics who had left the city increasingly belonged to newer, wealthier suburban parishes, while poor, Black, and Hispanic Catholics were disproportionately concentrated in urban centers and worshipped in underresourced churches like St. Mary of the Angels. Cushing encouraged Christian mobilization in support of civil rights and regularly seized opportunities to denounce the racial chasm dividing the church and nation. The week before the March on Washington, Cushing had sent a statement condemning Catholic apathy in the struggle for racial equality to priests at all 407 parishes in the archdiocese to be used, he directed, as the basis for every sermon that Sunday, August 25.[6] But on the question of integration, white Catholic opinion in Boston sided overwhelmingly with Louise Hicks, not with the priests who marched on Washington and Roxbury.[7]

In his opening address to the second session of Vatican II, Pope Paul VI declared his desire that the council become a "spring awakening of the immense spiritual and moral energy latent within the heart of the church." The time had come, the pope counseled the thousands gathered in St. Peter's Basilica, for the church to offer "a more thoughtful definition of herself." In "faithful adherence to the words and thoughts of Christ," the task before them was to "clarify the conscience of the church."[8] For Catholics in the United States, the church's examination of conscience could hardly have come at a more consequential time. As was clear in Roxbury, the civil rights movement had brought questions of freedom, justice, human dignity, and institutional authority squarely into the center of the public sphere. Now these themes would be taken up ecclesially.[9] By the time the council concluded its final session in December 1965, the concern for social justice, embrace of local cultures and vernaculars, support for ecumenical and interreligious dialogue, and the clarion call to read the signs of the times marked a formal end to the magisterium's adversarial stance toward the modern world. Shifts propelled by the council softened the perceived borderlines around and within the church: between God and believers, church and secular world, Europe and the global church, clergy and laity, Catholics and those of other faiths, and among the faithful themselves. This profound reconfiguration of ecclesial borders recast relationships within and beyond the church as infused with the potential for dialogue rather than defense. At the conclusion of the council, Paul VI likened its spiritual and pastoral sensibility to the parable of the good Samaritan (Lk 10:25–37): "A feeling of boundless sympathy has permeated the whole of it. The attention of our council has been absorbed by the discovery of human needs."[10] Like the Samaritan in the parable, the council had assumed a stance of mercy—a willingness to see and unite itself to the wounds of humanity.

At the highest level, these shifts catalyzed a new era in the church's self-understanding. But they were also manifested, perhaps more acutely, in the way that the council was received locally. In racially stratified Boston, Cushing viewed Vatican II in part as a referendum on the future of pastoral commitment to the inner city, a perception intensified by the council's conjuncture with both the struggle for civil rights and the beginning of the War on Poverty. As we will see in chapter 3, through the Roxbury Apostolate and other urban missionary endeavors, Cushing and other church leaders attempted to respond to the council's call to solidarity with the poor by reenvisioning traditional parish structures and clergy roles. For laypeople, Vatican II both affirmed and catalyzed a fundamental shift in imagination already nascent in parish life and religious practice.[11] In addition to the sweeping liturgical reforms brought about by *Sacrosanctum Concilium* aimed at "full, conscious, and active participation" (SC 14), Vatican II also commenced a new era of lay leadership in ministry. Propelled by a renewed understanding of the baptismal priesthood of all believers, the captivating image of the church as the people of God, the invitation to work across boundaries of religion and culture for the common good, and a more expansive sense of the church's mission, Vatican II offered Catholic laity new structures and language for the work of solidarity. As the primary locus of participation in the church, the parish was where the outcomes of the council were transacted most vividly.[12]

Given the social and historical contexts within which Vatican II unfolded and the transformations in parish life that followed, one would expect to discover that the council's compelling vision of a church in solidarity had ignited widespread efforts to build community across differences of race, culture, and class in local parishes. One might further expect to find that the notion of solidarity had become the foundation for decades of robust theological reflection on the relationship between the church's mission and the concrete task of racial justice. Neither assumption would be correct. Within the United States, the council's call to solidarity beckoned Catholics to concern for the poor and oppressed around the world, but with notable exceptions, it did not seem to have much of an effect on the way white Catholics in cities like Boston viewed the racial and ethnic borderlines in their own backyards. Theologically, solidarity assumed a starring role in Catholic social thought, but it did not enter the postconciliar ecclesiological lexicon with the same force. This chapter investigates the source of these divergences.

Why begin here? In the chapters that follow this one, I turn to an ethnographic account of an urban Catholic community in Roxbury to trace a different reception of the council—one that, I suggest, offers vital insight for a church once again on the cusp of radical change. But in order to appreciate the theological and historical significance of the solidarity work inventively ritualized in Egleston Square, we must begin by assessing the ways that Vatican II transformed—and failed to transform—understandings of the church in general and the parish in particular. The first part of this chapter examines the implications of Vatican II's vision of solidarity for the mission of the local church. I frame this discussion using the heuristic distinction between the church's mission *ad intra* (with respect to its own internal relationships) and *ad extra* (outward to the world). These categories, proposed during preparations for the council by Belgian Cardinal Léon Joseph Suenens in order to clarify the scope of its work, were ultimately reflected in *Lumen Gentium*, the Dogmatic Constitution on the Church (*ad intra*) and *Gaudium et Spes*, the Pastoral Constitution on the Church in the Modern World (*ad extra*). The council's theology of mission proceeds outward, from the church to the world. Here I take the opposite approach, beginning by analyzing the council's most expansive reimagining of borders—those between the church and the world—and culminating with the most granular—those of race, culture, language, and class within the local community. This approach requires that we read *Lumen Gentium* (LG) and *Gaudium et Spes* (GS) together, mapping GS's expansive moral vision of solidarity onto the notion of the church as the people of God in LG.[13]

I contend that Vatican II's vision of solidarity laid potential but unrealized groundwork for a transformation in the ways that Catholics negotiate difference at the local level. Rather than appealing to the call to solidarity to frame the task of ecclesial community-in-difference, leading voices instead approached cultural diversity in the church through the notion of the church as communion. But critical analysis of the communion paradigm reveals its weaknesses in this respect. Unlike solidarity, communion ecclesiology largely shies away from critical engagement with difference and power, while its overly efficacious view of sacramental participation renders the eschatological gift of ecclesial unity largely indistinguishable from the demanding historical task of justice. While privileging the ideal of local belonging, communion ecclesiology ignores the impact of structural and residential racism on constructions of the local. Prevailing interpretations of conciliar ecclesiology thus offer a vision of unity in diversity that takes insufficient account of the borderlines within concrete communities. By ignoring the power asymmetries that shape ecclesial practice, the communion paradigm continues to underwrite a colorblind approach that renders unclear the mission of the local church with respect to racial justice.

Solidarity with the World

Ecclesiological debates are often portrayed as pendular: from the rigid ul-tramontanism of Vatican I to the expansive and inviting image of the church as the people of God at Vatican II, then back to rigidity when lib-erationist embrace of the council's reforms threatened the guardians of orthodoxy. What such framing fails to capture are the diverse trajectories of conciliar reception that unfolded locally. As examinations of parish-based activism have demonstrated, the theological and structural out-comes of the council gave oxygen to the fire of lay social commitment at the local level.[14] For communities like St. Mary of the Angels, the coun-cil's most important legacy was its espousal of solidarity as an ecclesial virtue, an orienting moral force for the renewal of relationships, practices, and structures.[15]

Among the final documents promulgated at Vatican II, *Gaudium et Spes* can be interpreted as a summation of the council, its "last word." In it, the council fundamentally reconceived the moral status of the world and in so doing reimagined the relationship between the world and the Cath-olic church. Underwriting this relationship is both an understanding of mission as "ecclesial presence in the world"[16] and a vision of solidarity in which laity are primary agents. The striking preface of *Gaudium et Spes* became agenda-setting language for the church after the council. In pro-fessing the church's desire to draw near to the "joys and hopes, the grief and anguish" of humanity, *Gaudium et Spes* called the church to "deep soli-darity with the human race and its history" (GS 1).[17]

The council's vision of solidarity was the culmination of a notion that had been evolving in papal writing and ecclesial practice for seven de-cades. Pope Leo XIII's *Rerum Novarum* (1891) introduced the idea of soli-darity into the social doctrine of the church. Though the term itself does not appear, its roots are present conceptually in the encyclical's support for the rights and dignity of workers and the promotion of the common good.[18] Forty years later, Pope Pius XI's encyclical *Quadragesimo Anno* re-iterated and expanded the notion of the common good and the call for cooperative membership in the human family. During this period, Euro-pean schools of thought including German solidarism and personalism in-fluenced papal commitment to solidarity as a moral, social, and economic obligation.[19] A robust sense of social solidarity—both between social classes and between lay and ordained—also undergirded the praxis of many of the Catholic movements that emerged during the early twentieth century, from the worker priests of France to the social projects of Jesuit Alberto Hurtado in Chile, from Belgian Cardinal Joseph Cardijn's Young Christian Workers to the Catholic Worker movement of Dorothy Day and Peter Maurin in the United States. As the work of the council unfolded, solidarity was simultaneously becoming an explicit centerpiece of papal writings. A succession of social encyclicals—John XXIII's *Mater et Magistra* (1961) and *Pacem in Terris* (1963) and Pope Paul VI's *Populorum Progressio* (1967)—developed and refined the moral demands of solidarity in the realms of human rights, war and peace, international relations, human development, and economic justice.[20]

In the years immediately following the council's conclusion, it became clear that this vision of ecclesial solidarity was among its most consequential outcomes for the world church. The 1968 CELAM (Latin American Episcopal Conference) gathering in Medellín, Colombia, convened in order to interpret the meaning of Vatican II for Latin America, introduced the preferential option for the poor into magisterial thought. The 1971 Synod of Bishops, whose theme was "Justice in the World," concluded that work on behalf of social justice and the transformation of the world was "a constitutive dimension of the preaching of the Gospel" and of "the Church's mission for the redemption of the human race and its liberation from every oppressive situation."[21] The theme of solidarity would come to define, albeit in different ways, the papacies of both John Paul II and Francis.

If solidarity describes the council's relational vision, then dialogue was its praxic corollary.[22] In council documents, dialogue has two senses. First, it denotes the concrete practice of intentional communication among two different parties aimed at deeper understanding. In a more capacious sense, however, the council uses the notion of dialogue to signify a disposition of openness to the gift of the other—a spirit of warmth, mutual exchange, and friendship. In the words of French Dominican theologian Marie-Dominique Chenu, a *peritus* (invited theological advisor) at the council, dialogue carried with it a

> whole wealth of meaning: recognition of the other as other, loving others as they are and not as people to be won over, accepting that they

are different from me, without trying to encroach on their consciences and on their searching, without asserting my reservations before I give my trust.[23]

Conciliar documents explicitly call for dialogue when describing the interaction of the Catholic church with the world beyond itself: with other Christians and faith traditions, with the social and natural sciences, and with the modern world in general.[24] Yet a spirit of dialogue in the second, more expansive sense is the through-line in virtually every meaningful relationship the council takes up—even the foundational relationship between God and humanity. *Dei Verbum* portrays revelation as God's ongoing dialogue (*colloquium*) with the church: "God, who spoke in the past, continues to converse [*colloquitur*] with the spouse of his beloved Son" (DV 8). Reading this passage with Chenu's understanding of dialogue in mind renders its use of familial language for Christ and the church striking. God speaks to the church with the same intimacy one feels when talking with a daughter around the kitchen table. Seen in this light, tradition becomes the church's family story, the Holy Spirit its guardian. The divine-human conversation called revelation is the basis for other dialogical relationships within the church: for collegiality among bishops (LG 23), collaboration among lay and ordained (*Apostolicam Actuositatem* 10, 20), and "mutual esteem, reverence, and harmony" among all believers in their diversity (GS 92).

To center dialogue as a metaphor for the church's internal and external relationships, then, was to abandon in a gentle yet definitive way the defensiveness that had long characterized the church's stance toward the world. In the centuries prior to the council, the institutional church's relationship with the world around it had become, in the words of Sandra Schneiders, "one of nearly total mutual estrangement."[25] The Reformation, Enlightenment, and eventual loss of the Papal States (1870) decentered the Catholic church's once-sweeping influence in the religious, political, economic, and intellectual spheres. In turn, the four hundred years between the Council of Trent (1545–63) and Vatican II saw the church grow increasingly insular. The church came to define its relationship to the world primarily "as a non-participant . . . except as a moral checkmate to secular developments."[26] In the United States, Catholics constructed an entire social ecology parallel to the secular one comprising Catholic schools,

hospitals, sodalities, social welfare organizations, fraternal benefit societies, publications, recreational sports leagues, and of course, parishes.
Some of these institutions, like schools and hospitals, served Catholics
and non-Catholics alike, but the purpose of this Catholic infrastructure
was clear: to cultivate a world otherwise than the world, a nonworldly
world, insulated from the heresies of modernism and the dangers of anti-
Catholicism. In response to the church's diminished position on the world
stage, the short-lived First Vatican Council (1869–70) was motivated by a
desire to "preserve the independence of the church by securing its voice
in a world that seemed, in many ways, increasingly opposed to its very
existence."[27] Consequently, Vatican I was pervaded by what Ulrich
Horst calls a "security-mentality" (in German, *Sicherheitsdenken*), an
anxiety-laced desire for control in the face of instability that resulted in a
stark consolidation of papal authority.[28] A succession of antimodernist
papal decrees—among them Pius IX's "Syllabus of Errors" (1864), Pius
X's encyclical *Pascendi Dominici Gregis* (1907) and Apostolic Constitution
Lamentabili Sane (1907), and the "Oath Against Modernism" (1910–67)—
further codified this adversarial stance.

Vatican II refashioned the relationship between the church and world
by first redefining the meaning of "the world." The preface of *Gaudium et
Spes* describes it as follows:

> The world which the council has in mind is *the world of [people]*, the
> *entire human family* seen in its total environment. It is the world as the
> theatre of human history, bearing the marks of its travail, its triumphs
> and failures. It is the world which Christians believe has been *created
> and is sustained by the love of its maker*, has fallen into the slavery of sin
> but has been freed by Christ, who was crucified and rose again in or-
> der to break the stranglehold of the evil one, so that it might be fash-
> ioned anew according to God's design and brought to its fulfillment.
> (GS 2; emphasis mine)

Prior to the council, a sense of mutual exclusivity governed the church-
world relationship. It was as though the world ended at the church's door-
step. The council abandoned the once-normative language of the church
as *societas perfecta*, a term that connoted self-sufficiency and the idea that
the church did not need anything from the secular world in order to fulfill its mission.[29] In a clear contrast to previous understandings, *Gaudium*

et Spes begins by recognizing that the church is not only *in* the world but also *with, for,* and even to some extent *of* the world in its own humanity and historicity.[30] The church is people—the same people who dwell in the world of everyday life, rife with its disappointments and injustices, its beauty and potential for transformation.

As many have observed, Vatican II was different from councils that preceded it in that it explicitly embraced historical consciousness, a sense of its own situatedness in history, and an acknowledgment of the evolutionary nature of institutions, traditions, texts, and doctrines.[31] For the council, historical consciousness was not limited to a more robust sense of tradition and the past, captured by its method of *ressourcement* (returning to the sources), nor even to its recognition of the need to respond to the unique exigencies of the present, as in the guiding idea of *aggiornamento* (updating). Historicity also disclosed a sense of the future—both the eschatological future and the ordinary and more immediate earthly future, infused with the possibility of liberation. The hope and imagination that followed from Vatican II were in many ways reflections of its historical consciousness—the idea that the church could change, because it already had.

Following from this newly articulated historical consciousness, the council evinced on behalf of the church a self-conscious awareness of its own capacity to listen, evolve, and be moved by the recognition of human needs. In exhorting the church to "read the signs of the times" (GS 4), the council effectively bound together history and the Gospel, pastoral sensibility and doctrine.[32] The call to read the signs of the times is not about gaining content knowledge of current events to add a veneer of relevance to preaching or ministry. Nor does it point to the mere application of preexisting doctrines to new circumstances. Rather, as Ormond Rush points out, it constitutes a deep theological principle, one bound up with the council's expansive notion of revelation: "The God who has spoken within history *in the past* speaks in a new way *in the present,* because the historical conditions of the present are different from the conditions of the past. Through these historical dimensions of human existence, God is teaching the church new things about the meaning of the Gospel *for this time and place.* To discern what God is saying, the church needs to understand 'the world of today.'"[33] The church's dialogue with the world is inseparable from its dialogue with God. Outside the world, there is no revelation:

The church's very mission depends on willingness to see the Spirit at work in the world.

In *Gaudium et Spes*, the council describes several such signs of the times: the specter of nuclear war, the growing global chasm between rich and poor, rapid scientific and technological advancement, the decline of traditional institutions and familial models, and movements for social equality—all of them shaped in some way by the influence of evolutionary theory on understandings of human development and progress (GS 5–9). The understanding of the human condition laid out in *Gaudium et Spes* is defined by deep-seated anxiety prompted by the inherent contradictions of the age: the ambiguity of the notion of history-as-progress in a world where many are abandoned to suffer, and the persistence of fundamental questions about human life and its meaning even in the face of unprecedented scientific advancement. The council attended to this anxiety not by anathematizing its causes but by extending the church's solidarity. It is impossible to overstate the magnitude of the shift this sympathetic gaze represents. Equally groundbreaking was the idea that the times themselves had anything to say to the church, much less anything that informed its interpretation of revelation. The Council of Trent spoke of the times as "calamitous."[34] Vatican I declared anathema anyone who would suggest that the unfolding of time could alter the interpretation of dogma.[35] By contrast, *Gaudium et Spes* declares that the council "can find no more eloquent expression of [the church's] solidarity, respect and love for the whole human family, of which it forms part, than to enter into dialogue with it" about the challenges and fundamental questions of modern life (GS 3).[36] Dialogue with the world is an act of love for that world. Rather than condemnation, the church offered friendship.[37]

In reconceiving the boundary between church and world as porous and dialogical, Vatican II also transformed the position of the parish. No longer enclaves of spiritual refuge in a hostile world, parishes were now relativized within the fabric of their local civic, social, and religious ecologies. This shift in self-understanding created the conditions for new local practices, structures, and relationships. As neighbors, Catholics and non-Catholics could be coagents in common projects for justice and peace. It also altered the landscape of parish-based public ritual. Scholars have interpreted the public practices that dotted the landscape of urban Catholic devotional life in the century before Vatican II as one way Catholics asserted the presence of the messy antimodern within the rationalism of the American cities they called home.[38] In their aesthetic force and extensive materiality, public rituals blurred the vertical boundary between sacred and profane. Vatican II's emphasis on the liturgy (SC 10), and particularly the Eucharist (LG 11), as source and summit of the Christian life and thus as the primary locus of the divine-human encounter had the unintended (and, some would argue, lamentable) consequence of sparking a decline in extraliturgical devotional practice.[39] But public ritual did not fade away. Instead, some communities used ritual to negotiate the newly porous boundary between church and world, parish and neighbor. As the rest of this book demonstrates, ritual became a site and means of the local reception of the council—a space where communities worked out the meaning of church-world solidarity in the context of their own neighborhoods. It is to the parish that we now turn.

Solidarity *Ad Intra* and the Question of Community

No single outcome of Vatican II reoriented the Catholic popular imagination as deeply and broadly as *Lumen Gentium's* characterization of the church as the people of God. The image staked the church's place in the world and its history, at once relativizing its place in that world and binding it to the world in an integral way. In foregrounding the church's collective human identity, the motif served as a corrective to what had been an outsized emphasis on the church as an institution[40]—one whose hierarchical structure was also perceived to indicate an ascending order of holiness. Within this order, clergy and bishops occupied the highest echelons of spiritual perfection while laity assumed a sort of second-class ecclesial citizenship, their immersion in the ordinary world sentencing them to a life of B-grade holiness. The church's revaluation of the world also entailed a profound reconsideration of the role of laity as agents of the church's mission. The council planted the seeds for a vision of "integral salvation,"[41] one that saw God at work in the transformation of human society toward the realization of a "genuinely human life" for all (GS 26). If the church—the people of God—is the sacrament of integral salvation, then the entire faithful, lay and ordained alike, partake in its mission. *Lumen Gentium* foregrounded the significance of baptism, through which all members of the Body of Christ come to share in an equal way in the gift of God's grace. As baptism is one, so too is holiness: "In the various types and duties of life, one and the same holiness is cultivated by all who are moved by the Spirit of God." (LG 41). Responding to this universal call to holiness (LG 39–42) is the right and duty of every Christian, lay and ordained alike.

While solidarity is a hallmark of *Gaudium et Spes*, more rarely is it considered in its relationship to the local church. Yet considering *Gaudium et Spes* and *Lumen Gentium* in tandem discloses deep resonances between the language of solidarity in the former and the notion of peoplehood in the latter. The motif of peoplehood permeates conciliar documents. In *Gaudium et Spes*, a relational theological anthropology and communitarian vision of society undergird its vision of mission (e.g., GS 23–25). *Lumen Gentium*, too, portrays salvation relationally, as God's desire to "make women and men holy and to save them, not as individuals without any bond between them, but rather to make them into a people who might acknowledge him and serve him in holiness" (LG 9). For the council, holiness has a fundamentally communal character. Accordingly, the incarnation is described as an act of solidarity, as Jesus "[taking] his place in human society" (GS 32). Jesus did not merely become an individual; he became a member of a community, a person who, like all people, was woven into the fabric of a particular family in a particular place and time. In so doing, Jesus sanctified the ties that bind ordinary human life. The image of the church as the people of God, then, accents the fundamentally communal characters of holiness and salvation.

At the local level, a key dimension of the reception of the council's ecclesiology was an emphasis on the idea of the parish as a community. Of course, prior to Vatican II, parishes functioned as communities, in many ways more effectively than they do today. The difference was that community in the sociological sense—a group of people united by common beliefs, goals, identities, or practices into a shared sense of connectedness and reciprocity—came to be seen as a principle for ecclesial renewal.[42] The idea of parish-as-community expressed the conviction that the church, in its essence, is about relationships (*Gemeinschaft*) more than it is a hierarchically structured society (*Gesellschaft*).[43] The renewed emphasis on community retrieved much of its theological energy from the organic, communitarian description of the early church in the Acts of the Apostles and found expression in the Greek New Testament term *koinonia*, loving communion and fellowship (Acts 2:42ff). Reflecting the council's move away from a juridical and rigidly structured conception of the church, the community model tended to subordinate the church's institutional and hierarchical dimensions to the "really real" of the church: graced communion among believers and with God. As Avery Dulles notes, the emphasis on church as community spoke directly to the signs of the times. People searching for meaning and connection in life find that they encounter these things not in institutional structures but "in terms of the informal, the personal, the communal."[44]

For most believers, it was in the parish that the council's softening of borderlines had the most immediate effect. Popular reception of the people-of-God ecclesiology disclosed a desire for the transformation of power relationships and ministerial roles within parishes. Rather than a static arbiter of salvation, dispenser of sacramental grace, and insular refuge from the threats of the modern world, the parish was now seen as a historically and contextually situated community of pilgrims on a shared journey. Though the council's use of the image of the people of God was not intended to suggest a democratization of parish governance or ecclesiastical leadership, many interpreted it this way, mapping on to the metaphor their hopes for a more participatory church. The council's reaffirmation of the common priesthood of the faithful (LG 10) and thoroughgoing spirit of dialogue recast church life as a participatory endeavor. As Bradford Hinze argues, "This formulation amounted to an invitation to all the faithful to reclaim their baptismal inheritance by cultivating their own authority and agency based on their discernment of the faith of the church."[45] The idea of collaborative ministry, a centerpiece of the Decree on the Apostolate of the Laity (AA 10, 20, 24), supplanted an emphasis on the hierarchy as it gave rise to new models of lay leadership and pastoral ministry.[46] Chief among these was the advent of diocesan and parish pastoral councils (see chapter 3). For their part, priests were now considered responsible not only for the care of souls but for the cultivation of a community, one that was "turned outward to the diocese and the whole world."[47]

Studies that assessed the council's reception in the decades following its conclusion affirmed this burgeoning vision of the parish as a participatory community. The landmark Notre Dame Study of Parish Life conducted throughout the 1980s found that beyond the pastor, 83 percent of leaders (and 94 percent of unpaid leaders) within U.S. parishes were lay-people.[48] During the same decade, a comparative study of post–Vatican II parishes in the United States, Australia, Europe, and the Philippines found that the council had effectively catalyzed a transition in the self-perception of laity from deferential, passive "helpmates" of clergy to active, agentic participants in the life of the church.[49]

The conciliar vision of the parish as a community was also reflected in the 1983 revision of the Code of Canon Law, which defined the parish as "a certain community of the Christian faithful stably constituted in a particular church [diocese]" (Canon 515 §1). Describing the church as a community was an intentional choice on the part of the commission charged with drafting the code. An early version described the parish with the Latin word *portio*—as in portion of a diocese—to describe the parish. Such terminology suggests a view of the parish as essentially a logistical division meant to facilitate the task of ministry within the geographical expanse of a diocese. A later draft of the Code of Canon Law replaced *portio* with *communitas*—community—because, the commission later explained, it better indicated the sense of "dynamic interaction" and unity among parishioners.[50]

Despite the enthusiasm, a question remained: *What is community?* The biblical notion of *koinonia*, though rich and evocative, is also highly ambiguous, as Dulles and others note. Are intimate social bonds always correlated with a mystical relationship with God? What is the relationship between the human community and institutional structures? Between human communities and God? What is the community for? As Dulles contends, the image of church as community "fails to give Christians a very clear sense of their identity or mission."[51] Moreover, how is this community to be constructed and maintained? Since the Council of Trent, territorial parishes have existed, on a basic level, because they are established by the bishop in order to serve whoever happens to reside within the parish borders. Communities, on the other hand, are not a given; they have to be cultivated. A community is more about space than place; its very existence is tied to the quality of relationships therein, the "sense of community." Communities can decline and die—and then what? Most critically, the borderlines that define and divide life beyond the parish—lines of race, culture, and class, of segregation and social privilege—do not simply cease to exist at the parish doors. They have to be interpreted and negotiated within the parish, too. Vatican II unwittingly made parish life into a project without a clear template for accomplishing it or even a sense of what, exactly, was to be accomplished.

Vatican II's thoroughgoing revaluation of culture further complicated the question of community. Karl Rahner famously characterized the council as commencing a third epoch in church history, the church's self-realization as a "world Church."[52] This meant, paradoxically, a discovery of its own cultural particularity. Rahner compared the church's activity in and to the world beyond Europe prior to the council to that of "an export firm which exported a European religion as a commodity it did not really want to change but sent throughout the world together with the rest of the culture and civilization it considered superior."[53] To discover itself as a world church, then, required that it first come to terms with itself as a European church, recognizing that the theological paradigms and aesthetics that it long held as universal were in fact quite particular. The council marked the beginning of a retreat from universalism, from the notion of a church whose truths were unchanging and ahistorical, whose point of view was from nowhere and everywhere, whose culture was static and whose borders were absolute. The introduction of the vernacular into the liturgy was only the visible tip of this larger iceberg of recognition. (As Rahner put it, "Latin could not become the liturgical language of a world Church, since it was the language of a small and particular cultural region."[54]) This embrace of cultural particularity laid the groundwork for the postconciliar emergence of the notion of inculturation—the conviction that the Gospel could take root and find expression in any culture, in a form that was meaningful and familiar to its people.[55] The council began to chip away at the church's Eurocentrism, laying the groundwork for a more diffuse and egalitarian notion of unity in diversity.[56]

Vatican II's renewed understanding of cultural difference marked, in Rahner's words, a "qualitative leap."[57] Yet the dawning of the new "world church" era raised deeper and more critical questions, ones that in many ways the church was unprepared to answer. In calling for full, active, and conscious participation in the liturgy, the council made cultural and linguistic inclusion in parish life and access to the Mass a matter of justice. What did this demand of parishes like St. Mary of the Angels, where a variety of languages were spoken? In what did "legitimate diversity" (GS 92) consist, and who was the arbiter of this legitimacy? How could the church hear the joys, hopes, fear, and anguish of people whose languages it did not understand, whose histories it could not comprehend, whose epistemologies and cultural norms it had long rejected, and, in some cases, in whose conquest and enslavement it had been historically complicit? In short, what did the council's vision of solidarity and dialogue mean for the church *ad intra*? In the United States, Vatican II and its immediate aftereffects coincided with the civil rights and Chicano movements and, in the Catholic sphere, with the continued decline of the culturally siloed national parish as a pastoral strategy for ministering to new immigrants. Thus, the question put to the parish after Vatican II was not simply "What does it mean to be a community?" but "What does it mean to be a community of difference?"

Communion Ecclesiology and Unity in Diversity

The council's emphasis on community, coupled with its cultural approbation and world-church orientation, lent new urgency to ecclesiological studies of the relationship between unity and diversity in the church. In the postconciliar era, no understanding of church has been more influential in this respect than *koinonia*, more commonly identified by its Latin counterpart, *communio*, or communion. Beginning in the mid-1980s, communion ecclesiology emerged as the predominant interpretation of Vatican II's ecclesiological outcomes. This was primarily the result of its promotion by the 1985 Extraordinary Synod of Bishops, which was convened by John Paul II two decades after the conclusion of Vatican II in order to address certain "deficiencies and difficulties" in the ongoing reception of the council.[58] In its final report, the Synod concluded that an excessive focus on the renewal of church structures after Vatican II, coupled with insufficient attention to God and Christ, indicated on the part of the faithful a failure to distinguish between "openness of the council to the world" and "acceptance of a secularized world's mentality."[59] In other words, it seemed to some in power that the church's boundaries had become too porous. Without saying so explicitly, the report's focus on communion appeared to push back against what many prelates saw as an overly enthusiastic embrace of the idea of the church as people of God. The Synod concluded that *koinonia/communio* was the "central and fundamental idea of the council's documents," and the "foundation for order in the Church, and especially for a correct relationship between unity and pluriformity in the Church."[60] German Cardinal Walter Kasper, the special secretary of the Synod, later argued for communion ecclesiology's even more fundamental status, writing that communion "lies behind all . . . biblical images for the description of the nature of the church."[61] And Joseph Ratzinger once insisted, "Ultimately there is only one basic ecclesiology," communion ecclesiology.[62] Given its magisterial stamp of approval, Clare Watkins critically observed that "the language of koinonia [emerged] at the start of the twenty-first century as an established orthodoxy."[63]

Embraced by Roman Catholic, Orthodox, and Protestant theologians, the literature in communion ecclesiology is vast.[64] Here, I will simply outline its contours. Communion ecclesiology offers a vision of ecclesial unity grounded in sacramental participation and dialogue. The concept of communio expresses both the vertical dimension of the Christian life (communion with God) and the horizontal dimension (communion among believers).[65] Theologian Dennis Doyle identifies four basic emphases that communion ecclesiologies share: the experience of the early church, spiritual fellowship among believers and with God, shared participation in the Eucharist as a sign and sacrament of unity here and now, and attentiveness to the dynamic between unity and diversity.[66] Because of its expansiveness, it has often served as the theological basis for systematic ecclesiological reflection and has proven fruitful for ecumenical dialogue in describing the positive relationship among the separated Christian churches. Its dual emphases on the fundamental unity of the church and on the goodness of diversity have also made communion ecclesiology a popular hermeneutical framework for interpreting cultural pluralism within the church in general and parishes in particular. Though the lens of communion, the parish is the place where believers of different races, languages, and backgrounds are united as one in Christ through the waters of baptism and the sacrifice of the Eucharist.

Communion ecclesiology is grounded in a comprehensive Trinitarian understanding of ecclesial identity, theological anthropology, and social reality. The triune God is the "highest exemplar and source" of unity (Unitatis Redintegratio 2), the font of and template for ecclesial communion. Human beings, created in the image of a God who is a community of persons, are themselves inherently oriented toward relationship. This innate intersubjective desire for community is fulfilled most fully in the church, which is the sacramental and social locus of communion in the midst of a fragmented world. At the baptismal font, one undergoes an ontological transformation from a mere individual into a member of the ecclesial community.[67] Reflecting Vatican II's centrifugal understanding of mission, the love that exists within the communion of the church—a sharing in the self-giving love of the triune God—overflows outward into mission to the world. The church, then, is at once the sacrament of communion and icon of the Trinity. The bonds of unity among believers make visible God's love for the world.[68]

Another prominent feature of communion ecclesiology is its thoroughgoing liturgical and sacramental orientation. In the celebration of the Eucharist, writes Walter Kasper, "the Church understood as *communio* becomes concrete reality."[69] The Eucharistic liturgy is both an active, historical inbreaking of communion with God and others and a foretaste of the fullness of communion in the life to come. Ecclesiologies of communion frequently appeal to the experience of the early Christian community to illustrate this dynamic. Orthodox theologian John Zizioulas describes the early church as shaped by what he terms a "eucharistic consciousness," a sense that the act of gathering as one body and sharing in a common meal effectively suspended, even dissolved, the social, ethnic, and biological divisions that existed among the Christian faithful.[70] Zizioulas contends that in and of itself, the act of "coming together in brotherly love" was not what made early Christian communities unique. Rather, it was the inclusive composition and equal standing of all those so gathered, bonded as they were through a common baptism: Jew and Greek, male and female, adult and child, rich and poor, master and slave (Gal 3:28).[71] On this point, he notes the absence of "specialty" liturgies in the practice of the early church—that is, those celebrated for a particular generational, linguistic, ethnic, or social cohort, as is common practice in some churches today (a youth Mass or Spanish Mass, for example).[72] Instead, the communion of the local church was embodied in that every liturgy included all Christians within the geographical area. Liturgical gathering fostered unity through "the transcendence of all divisions in Christ."[73] Taking as paradigmatic this interpretation of the early church, Zizioulas contends that today, in gathering across difference, Christians continue to become a living sign of the incarnation, reaching toward the eschatological fulfillment of the prayer of Jesus on the eve of his death that "all may be one" (Jn 17:21).[74]

Communion, Diversity, and the Parish

Given both its emphasis on relationship and the magisterial context of its rise to prominence, communion has become an agenda-setting paradigm for theological and pastoral approaches to cultural diversity. Understood as unity in diversity, communion grounds a vision of mutual recognition, dialogue, and harmonious coexistence among people of different cultures, races, and backgrounds. From bishops' documents to parish studies to theologies of community, its normative status is evident.

U.S. Bishops' Documents

Since the 1985 Synod, communion ecclesiology has served as the central organizing principle in bishops' documents on immigration, diversity, and intercultural ministry.[75] The capaciousness of *communio* is evident in the multitude of ways it is employed in bishops' writings and its apparent resonance with a wide variety of cultural paradigms and pastoral exigencies. Late twentieth- and early twenty-first-century documents of the United States Conference of Catholic Bishops (USCCB) on Hispanic ministry, for example, use communion as the governing metaphor for the church's mission and identity. Here, the language of communion resonates with Hispanic ministry's emphasis on *pastoral de conjunto*, the collaborative, relational model of ministry at the heart of Latinx pastoral practice. In both the *National Pastoral Plan for Hispanic Ministry* (1987) and *Encuentro and Mission* (2002), *pastoral de conjunto* is defined as "communion in mission"—language that would later become central in the bishops' 2013 and 2014 publications on intercultural ministry in shared parishes.[76] Communion is also a focus in bishops' documents on intercultural ministry, as in *Best Practices for Shared Parishes: So That They May All Be One* (2013) and *Building Intercultural Competence for Ministers* (2014). In *Encountering Christ in Harmony* (2018), a pastoral response to ministry with Asian and Pacific Island Catholics, the bishops transpose the concept of harmony, central in many Asian cultures, into the language of communion. Both harmony and communion, they write, are oriented toward the fundamental unity of the human community: "The importance of harmony in Asian and Pacific Island communities offers a fruitful cultural analog to help us deepen our insight into the revealed mystery of the communion of the Church."[77]

Communion ecclesiology similarly frames the vision of ecclesial community in U.S. bishops' writings on immigration. In their 2000 pastoral letter on immigration, *Welcoming the Stranger Among Us: Unity in Diversity*, the bishops invoke John Paul II's call to "conversion, communion, and solidarity" among all people, defining communion as unity in diversity.[78] In an echo of Zizioulas, the bishops argue that it is only in overcoming ignorance and mistrust of the "stranger in our midst"—that is, in trading fear for hospitality and openness—that genuine communion is possible. Privileging the liturgy as the primary locus of this encounter, they center the Eucharist as the ultimate embrace of the other.[79]

The USCCB's most recent pastoral letter on racism, *Open Wide Our Hearts* (2018), shows a similar influence.[80] Yet a subtle but critical distinction is evident, one that perhaps forecasts a shift in magisterial use of the term. In *Open Wide Our Hearts*, the language of communion is employed only in the eschatological tense. The letter describes "communion of all peoples and nations" as the heavenly *telos* of the Christian life and thus the orienting vision of restored relationship toward which humans are called to strive.[81] But communion is not used as a metaphor for church life here and now. The absence of church-as-communion in *Open Wide Our Hearts*—language employed with such abandon in the pastoral documents on cultural issues that preceded it—could be interpreted as an implicit recognition, in the document's words, of "the ways that racism has permeated the life of the Church."[82]

Parish Studies

In an ethnographic study of a Latinx and Euro-American shared parish in the Midwest, Brett Hoover proposes communion as a new "folk paradigm" for cultural diversity in U.S. parish life.[83] He argues that the two prevailing paradigms, assimilation and multiculturalism, have long shaped both the narratives American Catholics construct to make sense of cultural diversity and the church's strategies for dealing with immigration. Assimilation and multiculturalism each offer particular and quite different sets of assumptions about the nature of cultural diversity. Yet, as Hoover rightly observes, neither paradigm has proven very effective at challenging the problem of cultural encapsulation in parish life, which he defines as "an isolation of perspectives, where members of socially disconnected groups judge all things by their own cultural perspective and have trouble identifying or understanding the perspective of members of other groups."[84] Hoover proposes communion ecclesiology as a way forward, a new folk paradigm for diversity in the church: "[Communion] provides a vision of church unity that does not require cultural uniformity, but it also demands more of Christians than simply a vague and distant tolerance."[85]

Theologies of Community and Place

Theologians have similarly appealed to communion ecclesiology as a basis for the virtue of local belonging. *Communio*'s emphasis on the local church and its resonance with the notion of catholicity make it a fitting theoretical framework for theological reflection on community, diversity, and place. Making a case for recommitment to the territorial parish, theologian Vincent J. Miller draws on communion ecclesiology's motivating concern for the spiritual toll of individualism on the church. Miller describes how the spiritual ungroundedness and social homophily of a postmodern, globalized age have rendered the virtues of the territorial parish less clear. This disjuncture is manifested most clearly in the prevalence of "parish shopping." Instead of gathering with the proverbial here-comes-everybody of the neighborhood church, people increasingly seek out parishes that suit individual preferences: better music, more competent homilies, greater emphasis on social justice, more traditional liturgical styling, better generational fit. As believers sacrifice local diversity for the comfort of like-minded enclaves, Miller argues, they "lose the habits of cohabiting with people who are different from them," in some way undermining the very catholicity of the church.[86] As an antidote, he urges Catholics to resist the temptation to parish shop and instead embrace "communion in place," grounding ecclesial belonging in their local communities, however imperfect they may be. In an age of extreme polarization, Miller's work suggests, resisting the consumerist urge to self-sort can be countercultural.

The broad influence of communion ecclesiology in the work of bishops and scholars alike suggests, using Hoover's framework, that communion's vision of unity in diversity has already become a folk paradigm for diversity in the church. Yet the same elasticity that lends communion its broad applicability simultaneously prevents it from critically addressing issues of power and inequality within the local church.

Critiquing Communion, Challenging Ecclesial Colorblindness

Both despite and because of its capaciousness, some have found communion ecclesiology suspect. Scholarly critiques of communion primarily largely fall along three lines: that its idealized image of the church is at odds with reality, that it blunts the urgency of mission, and that any theological benefits it might offer are offset by the conservative, reactionary context of its 1985 promotion. Nicholas M. Healy's well-known critique of *communio* as the paradigmatic "blueprint ecclesiology" epitomizes the first trajectory of criticism. Healy takes issue with the obvious disjuncture between idealized ecclesiological models and the realities of sin and division in the church. Abstract metaphors, he argues, "frequently display a curious inability to acknowledge the complexities of ecclesial life in its pilgrim state."[87] Clare Watkins sharpens this critique, arguing that communion rhetoric "[seduces] us into the un-evangelical belief that the Church is a tame and humanly comfortable reality, whose main purpose is the general feeling of well being and inclusion for its members."[88] Accentuating internal harmony among its members, Watkins maintains, communion ecclesiology promotes complacency while diverting attention from critical questions about the nature and exercise of authority in the church. Far from being an asset, the capaciousness of *communio* is actually a sign of its inability to do any real ecclesiological work. At best, Watkins observes wryly, "*Koinonia* is eminently marketable!"[89]

Neil Ormerod offers an even more expansive critique of communion ecclesiology's idealism, connecting it to the deeper conflict he perceives between communion, church history, and mission. *Communio*-centric models, he argues, "describe a Church that we would all want to belong to. But when we look at the Church as an historical concrete reality we may wonder about the discrepancy between the idealized form and the historical facts."[90] Working deductively (from an abstract theological vision of the church) rather than inductively (beginning with historical data about the church) means that the gap between the ideal and the real remains unaccounted for and thus becomes a threat to the model's theoretical coherence. Change, too, becomes both threatening and unnecessary, since it would unseat the already-achieved perfection of the present.[91] Communion ecclesiology is at its most compelling when it is deliberately cast as a contrast against the atomistic individualism of postmodernity. Yet this should also give us a hint of its highly context-bound (which is to say, nonuniversal) character. After all, in societies where communal forces are more stifling than they are consoling, the idea of the church as an all-encompassing community loses its utopic appeal.[92] Like Healy, Ormerod also finds the model's reliance on a social analogy of the Trinity to be suspect. Divine triunity cannot be a template for human unity; on the contrary, "The divine unity is where God is *most different* from God's creatures, even the creation that we call Church."[93] Ultimately, Ormerod argues, mission, not communion, should be understood as the central organizing principle of the church because it captures the church's historical, teleological orientation toward the kingdom of God.[94]

The third area of critique—that conservative magisterial machinations in 1985 placed communion ecclesiology at odds with the council's vision of the church as the people of God—has been articulated most thoroughly by Belgian-born Latin American liberation theologian José Comblin. Comblin argues that communion ecclesiology has undermined popular reception of Vatican II's original ecclesiological vision, promoting a rigidly hierarchical, "disincarnate church"[95] over one that is localized, concrete, and lay oriented. The promotion of communion by the 1985 Synod and subsequently by the Congregation for the Doctrine of the Faith intentionally neutralized the possibility of liberation in the church, Comblin argues. Not merely inadequate, *communio* denies the dignity and agency of the poor and the militates against the council's transformative vision.

In different ways, each of these critiques concludes that ecclesiological idealism matches neither the experience of the church in history nor the need for transformation in the present. Yet there remains more to say. The wounds with which the church and its members contend today are not abstract concepts—division, imperfection, and so on—but life-or-death situations, refractions of the legacy of colonial domination in many dehumanizing forms: white supremacy, forced migration, searing economic inequality, and institutional complicity in abuse, to name just a few. If post–Vatican II ecclesiology is to reckon with the signs of the times, then the grief and anguish occasioned by these social wounds are worthy of careful consideration. In light of this present, what appears most consequentially underdeveloped in communion ecclesiology is its capacity to reckon with power—to address the sources of domination and division in ecclesial communities and to offer, in turn, a serious and open-eyed vision of solidarity within the local church. Three tensions illuminate the limits of the communion paradigm in this respect: its ambiguous operative understanding of difference, its view of sacramental participation as an effective social equalizer, and its inattentiveness to colonialism broadly and structural and residential racism particularly in its conception of the local. Despite good intentions, the communion paradigm ultimately underwrites ecclesial colorblindness, a vision of church unity predicated upon an impossible unseeing of difference. These issues point to its inadequacy both as a theological paradigm for parish life and as a fulfillment of Vatican II's vision-in-germ of solidarity *ad intra*.

Diversity or Difference?

First, communion ecclesiology centers the conviction that equal sharing in the discipleship of Jesus Christ through a common baptism renders irrelevant social, economic, ethnic, or biological distinctions. Galatians 3:27–28 is frequently cited as a thesis statement on ecclesial unity: "As many of you as were baptized into Christ have clothed yourselves with Christ. There is no longer Jew or Greek, there is no longer slave or free, there is no longer male and female; for all of you are one in Christ Jesus." This radical vision of a discipleship of equals modeled on the inclusivity of the early church has guided contemporary reflection on the church of communion. Canadian theologian Jean-Marie R. Tillard's analysis of Eucharistic unity sums up the point: "The sacrament shows that communion with Christ renders null and void any distinction of race, dignity, or social status. In Christ, all are equal."[96]

Yet there remains a tension in communion's vision of equality. In one sense, difference is regarded as a source of strength for the church, a gift, and a fundamental reflection of a God who is three in one. At the same time, Christians are encouraged to look both backward to the experience of the early church and forward in eschatological hope, two points at which these same differences, now interpreted as obstacles to unity, were and will be rendered "null and void." The sacraments of baptism and Eucharist are regarded as privileged sites of the foretaste and momentary inbreaking of true communion—that is, of unity unburdened by human distinctions. In this light, Tillard's inclusion of the category of race alongside those of dignity and social status is a telling detail, as it betrays an implicit sense of racial difference as inherently negative in the same way that differences in dignity and social status are inherently negative. It is possible to imagine a utopic future in which all people enjoy the same dignity and social status. But attempting to imagine a world in which all share the same race becomes more troubling. Is this a world in which everyone becomes white? One in which people "don't see color"? Perhaps a variation on José Vasconcelos's notion of "la raza cósmica," the "cosmic race" born of mestizaje?[97]

Lest this critique appear overly literal, evidence of my drilling down too hard on a single point, it is important to note that the equation of unity with the transcendence of race is a pervasive feature of the genre. Communion's framings of early Christian liturgical communities evince a similar emphasis, as exemplified in Zizioulas's work. Early Christians, he writes, "soon came to believe that they constituted a *third race*, but this was only to show that in fact it was a 'non-racial race.'" They were a people who "declared . . . that they did not care about the difference between a Greek and a Jew once these were members of the Christian Church."[98] Yet as critical scholarship on early Christian communities has pointed out, early Christians did in fact care about the difference, even as they sought to do something new. Tensions of race, ethnicity, class, religious belonging, gender, and citizenship marked the emerging self-understanding of the early church in ways that should counteract the tendency to idealize its communitarianism.[99] Zizioulas's quixotic analysis of the early church illustrates the subtle but critical contradiction at the heart of the church-as-communion framework: Because it reflects a certain Trinitarian theological anthropology, it affirms difference as vital for unity. Yet because actual human relationships across difference rarely approach anything bordering on perichoresis, ultimately difference must be overcome for the sake of unity. Racial and ethnic differences, in particular, are consistently portrayed as features of human existence that Christian belonging does not merely transcend but elides. The implication is that racial difference is inherently lamentable and an obstacle to unity in Christ.

Distinguishing between rhetorics of *diversity* and *difference* aids in understanding this ambivalence. Within social, political, and ecclesial discourse, diversity is typically framed in a positive light. Postcolonial theorist Homi Bhabha argues that in both scholarly and everyday speech, invocations of diversity implicitly partake of and perpetuate misconceptions about the nature of culture. For Bhabha, rhetorics of diversity posit culture as an ahistorical category, a static marker of identity untouched by colonialism, hybridity, or generational change.[100] Within the church, cultural diversity is most associated with "traditional," aesthetic cultural expressions such as food, music, language, dress, Marian apparitions, saints, feasts, popular devotions, and other broadly legible customs. Critically, as anthropologist Thomas Hylland Ericksen notes, diversity discourse relies on a superficial misreading of these cultural features as morally and politically neutral.[101] What we call cultural diversity, then, trades on the idea of "the separation of totalized cultures that live unsullied by the intertextuality of their historical locations, safe in the Utopianism of a mythic memory of a unique collective identity."[102]

Difference, conversely, is often associated with practices, epistemologies, narratives, authorities, and bodies that are disruptive of the status quo. As Ericksen concludes, in Western contexts, "there is considerable support for diversity in the public sphere, while difference is increasingly seen as a main cause of social problems associated with immigrants and their descendants."[103] Within the church, M. Shawn Copeland observes that "difference connotes suspicion, if not disdain. Difference communicates that which is and those who are to be avoided." What results, then, is "the temptation to dissolve difference—to ignore it or to meet it with sly or shame-faced side-long glances."[104] Copeland cites anthropologist Johnnetta B. Cole, who warns, "To address our commonalities without dealing with our differences is to misunderstand and distort that which separates as well as that which binds us."[105] Ecclesial rhetorics of unity in diversity are complicit in this pattern, celebrating cultural diversity while eschewing difference.

The dissonance between appreciation of abstract diversity and suspicion of concrete difference is a pattern reflected in contemporary parish life. In a 2015 survey of Catholics who belonged to culturally diverse parishes by Georgetown's Center for Applied Research in the Apostolate (CARA), white respondents were more likely than their Hispanic, Asian, Black, and Native American counterparts to describe their parishes as "multicultural." This difference echoes research suggesting that white people tend to perceive exaggerated levels of diversity in situations in which any people of color are present.[106] In the survey, whites were also less likely than nonwhite parishioners to perceive tensions between different cultural groups in their parishes, and predictably, they were least likely to report feeling like outsiders at their parishes because of nationality, race, ethnicity, language, or culture. Yet despite their seemingly rosy views of the status of diversity in their parishes, only about one in five strongly believed that "celebrating cultural diversity" or "understanding the different cultures that exist within the parish community" should be parish priorities. These same white respondents showed abysmal levels of support for the prospect of greater diversity in their parishes. Support for welcoming immigrants, non–English speakers, and specific communities of color into their churches was markedly lower among whites than it was among Hispanic, Asian, Black, Native American, and multiracial respondents. But white parishioners were not altogether against welcoming outsiders. Their support increased significantly for opening the parish doors to people who were not explicitly nonwhite, such as persons with disabilities, young adults, inactive Catholics, divorced parishioners, and non-Catholic spouses.[107] In other words, according to these data, white Catholics seemed to feel more instinctive kinship with non-Catholic whites than with fellow Catholics of color. The CARA survey suggests that white Catholics who belong to culturally diverse parishes largely view their communities through rose-colored lenses, perceiving harmony where it does not exist, promoting complacency where action is called for, and paying lip service to multiculturalism while continuing to act as racial and ethnic gatekeepers.

Communion ecclesiology's imprecision about the status of difference is not incidental or merely semantic. Rather, it points to larger Christian philosophical and theological difficulties with difference. As ecclesiologist Elochukwu Uzukwu observes, Christian theology and practice have been shaped by Platonic thought, adopting its preoccupation with unity. The result has been the inherent association of unity with perfection and difference with imperfection.[108] As Bryan Massingale has argued, within the Christian imagination, notions of perfection and unity—even "unity in diversity"—are bound up tightly with white, Euro-American cultural symbols and norms.[109] Indeed, in Hoover's study, white parishioners tended to express comfort with diversity only "when accompanied by some momentum toward uniformity." For them, "unity 'feels right' when framed as uniform belief and practice."[110] Particularly when manifested in liturgical expressions that fall outside of accepted Euro-American norms, racial and cultural difference can provoke among white churchgoers not only general feelings of discomfort but also a sense that difference itself is inherently un-Christian, a violation of orthopraxy or right worship.[111] Thus, in deference to an aspirational notion of liturgical harmony, the communion paradigm conceals inequalities even as it flattens perceptions of what and who count as "truly Catholic."

Baptism, Eucharist, and Social Equality

Identifying the tendency to value abstract diversity over actual difference raises a second and related critique, one already partially articulated above. As in the work of Tillard and Zizioulas, communion ecclesiology relies heavily on the sacraments of baptism and the Eucharist to function as efficacious social equalizers, effecting a concrete change in the relationships and social hierarchies that govern everyday life. Tillard, referencing Chrysostom, sums up this position: "At the baptismal font and at the Eucharistic table, there no longer exists any hierarchy, any preferential treatment."[112] While this utopian vision expresses Christianity's deepest eschatological hopes, it is far from the case here and now. Discrimination and preferential treatment have long shaped ecclesial practice in reality. Indeed, throughout history, sacramental practices have often been used to reinscribe the very racial and social hierarchies they claim to subvert.[113] Such inequalities persist in ways both obvious and insidious. Accounts by Catholics of color detail patterns of liturgical discrimination—being denied the sign of peace by white Massgoers seated around them, questioned like outsiders by ushers in their own churches, and refused the Eucharist by priests who assume they are not Catholic.[114] Liturgy can reinscribe power asymmetries, as when Spanish-speaking communities are offered the church basement rather than the sanctuary for their Masses and only at inconvenient times of the day. It is simply incorrect to contend that the sacraments can do the sort of real-time relational work with which communion ecclesiology tasks them. Falling into what Katie Grimes calls "sacramental optimism" suggests that the problem of racial inequality in the church can be solved by better catechesis—the notion that if people understood and practiced the sacraments more rightly, ecclesial unity would follow.[115] Such a perspective equates racism with individual feelings and intentions, neglecting its power as a social force operative both structurally and at the level of unconscious habituation. Without clearly accounting for the relationship between structural sin and ecclesial life, communion ecclesiology proposes a church immune from accountability for its failings.

Local Belonging and Residential Racism

The third weakness of communion ecclesiology as a theological framework for diversity in the church is the dissonance between its romanticized view of the local and the racialized systems and habits that configure local dwelling. The firm persistence of residential segregation in the United States complicates the assumption that a locally rooted ecclesial community will also be one characterized by racial, cultural, and economic difference, much less harmony. In the United States, residential dwelling is not the result of random chance or personal agency. Discriminatory housing policies, restrictive zoning laws, disparities in economic mobility and intergenerational wealth, income inequality, and the persistence of racial discrimination have contributed to the extreme residential segregation of African Americans and the moderate segregation of Latinas/os and Asian Americans in U.S. cities.[116] As we will see in the chapters to come, redlining had a catastrophic impact on Egleston Square and other Roxbury neighborhoods, setting in motion the cycles of poverty and violence that would later be used as evidence of the inner city's moral depravity.

The Catholic church's complicity in reinforcing these racial boundaries is well documented. As historian John McGreevy has demonstrated, white Euro-American parochial belonging structured residential communities and prevented integration from taking root in neighborhoods throughout the twentieth-century urban North, particularly in cities like Boston.[117] Parish boundaries were complex in their effects. On one hand, for new immigrants, parishes provided social solidarity and cultural refuge and promoted civic empowerment. On the other, as McGreevy demonstrates, these same parish enclaves often became "rallying points for bigotry" as Catholics "proved unable to separate 'community' from racial mythology."[118] McGreevy notes that historical records report startlingly high

rates of homeownership among working-class immigrant Catholics, rates
that exceeded even those of their more highly educated and economically
successful American-born, Jewish, and Protestant counterparts.[119] Homeownership slowed Catholics' participation in urban white flight, thus
serving at once as a stabilizing force for parishes and as a bulwark in maintaining the religio-racial purity of predominantly white Catholic neighborhoods. Virulent Catholic opposition to residential and school integration
efforts in cities like Boston meant that northern cities remained even more
segregated than southern ones.[120]

Given both the persistence of residential segregation and the legacy of
urban Catholic parishes in upholding it, simply belonging to one's neighborhood parish does little to guarantee that believers ecclesially "[cohabit]
with people who are different from them," as Miller writes.[121] Indeed, as
long as parish belonging is determined territorially, residential segregation is indelibly mapped onto parochial segregation. Thus, while consumer
choice often leads to the like-minded communities created in niche or
"boutique" parishes, as Miller argues, territorial parish membership is
also determined by choices—those of homeowners, real estate agents,
banks, lenders, policymakers, and business owners. In a society in which
the construction of place is shaped by structural racism and profound
economic inequality, "communion in place" risks sanctifying residential segregation.[122]

Ecclesial Colorblindness

Communion ecclesiology's appeals to the early Christian church as a "non-
racial" or postracial community, coupled with its inattention to social
and historical realities that problematize a number of its fundamental
claims, orient the communion paradigm toward what I call *ecclesial colorblindness*. Theorists define colorblindness as a strategy commonly employed by white Americans to deflect accusations of racism by insisting
that they "don't see race."[123] Underlying the logic of colorblindness is the
idea that such unseeing is possible, that the category of race only applies
to people of color (and hence that white people are racially neutral or race-
less), and that (nonwhite) racial identity obscures a person's dignity and
humanity. Ecclesial colorblindness, then, posits the suspension of racial
difference as a precondition for Christian unity. Ecclesial colorblindness

views Christian identity as an alternative to racial and ethnic identity, dismissing the possibility of discrimination in the church with an insistence that all are one in Christ. In this way, it functions as a strategy of conflict suppression, suggesting that the recognition (much less the reversal) of power asymmetries is, for the Christian, beside the point. As such, it both relies on and promotes a pervasive naiveté regarding historical and structural dimensions of division in the church: The Christian is one who is inoculated to perceptions of difference. The effects of colorblindness in the church are similar to those of colorblind ideology within broader society: the formation of a church in which a rhetorical insistence on welcome is coupled with a refusal to acknowledge the impact of structural racism, and thus the norming of white practices, experiences, histories, and bodies.

Conclusion: Retrieving Solidarity's Unfulfilled Promise for Parish Life

In the year 2000, fifteen years after the conclusion of the 1985 Synod and a year after John Paul II's *Ecclesia in America* accented the themes of conversion, communion, and solidarity, Black Catholic theologian Jamie Phelps, O.P., published an analysis of communion ecclesiology in *Theological Studies* in which she lauded its resonance with the goals of Black and Womanist liberation theologies and African traditional religions. Given these resonances, she argued that the then-burgeoning emphasis on communion offered a promising opening for the institutional church to definitively affirm the life and dignity of its Black members and others whose full humanity it had historically denied: "The Church in the U.S. must speak the truth of its sinful past, ask and give forgiveness, and commit itself to creating a visible worldwide ecclesial and human communion of reconciling love and solidarity."[124] Two decades later, communion has been well integrated into the church's ecclesiological and pastoral imagination. But the promise Phelps identified appears largely unfulfilled, evidence that communion's benign treatment of difference and avoidance of questions of power and authority have militated against the flourishing of its own vision.

Given the popular turn to the idea of the parish as community in the decades following Vatican II, one would expect that the council unleashed a cascade of critical theological reflection on the roles of race, culture, and power within the life of the parish. Yet little such emphasis emerged. For a church that, as Rahner argued, was only beginning to come to grips with culture, postconciliar ecclesiological frameworks were ill equipped to offer analyses of cultural pluralism within the church that did not explicitly or implicitly privilege uniformity and Euro-formity. Indeed, what we do not see in the wake of the council is a systematic theological application of the council's vision of solidarity to the life of the church *ad intra*. *Gaudium et Spes* condemned "every type of discrimination, whether social or cultural, whether based on sex, race, color, social condition, language or religion" as "contrary to God's intent" (GS 29)—that is, as sinful. But its powerful solidaristic vision was applied primarily beyond the church to "the world," not within the church to the parish, reinscribing the very boundary between church and world that the council sought to overcome. Today, progressive disillusionment over the unfulfilled legacy of Vatican II tends to coalesce around the stubborn persistence of the clerical/lay divide in Roman Catholic life. But a more critical and prophetic approach to racial and social justice within parish life is a perhaps even more unfulfilled promise of the council.

The chapters that follow trace a different story of postconciliar ecclesiology, one for which the theological notion of solidarity became the lynchpin for a radical reimagining of the role of a parish in turbulent times. The people of Roxbury's St. Mary's perceived in the council's call to solidarity a basis for the comprehensive reimagining of parish practices and power structures. Interpreting solidarity as a mandate for the transformation of the church *ad intra*, parishioners decided that it was not only the wall between the institutional church and the modern world that needed to come down, but also the walls that divided parish from neighborhood and parishioners of different races and classes from one another. They recognized in the council's elevation of the liturgy both the possibility for creative solidarity and the danger of further centering clergy as the lone arbiters of divine presence. Underlying the story of St. Mary's, I will suggest, is a case for the retrieval of solidarity as an animating vision for the urban Catholic parish in divided times.

Urban Borderlands

There's reasons why you live in a neighborhood and get comfortable in a community, and even when a community has changed some, there's a resistance to leave this community that felt so much a part of *you*. So it's like, which is easier? To move, or to adapt *a little*?

Michelle, longtime African American lay leader[1]

YAMARIS: Sunday is the day I look forward to the most because, well, I'm going to have a certain encounter with the Lord. It's an encounter that I have every day, but this is the day that I share it with the community.
ME: Ah, right.
I feel really good about this community.
How is it similar or different from your parish in Santo Domingo?
Well, it's similar because [at St. Mary's] they give you a big welcome when you come for the first time, or if you visit the parish for the first time. We share food after Mass, and back in [Santo Domingo] we shared like that, too. And I also helped with lectoring there, so that was similar. I felt that it was similar because there are also many people from Santo Domingo at the church, like half [of the parishioners]. So I feel at home.

Yamaris, Spanish Mass parishioner from the Dominican Republic[2]

At St. Mary's, the announcements at the end of Mass are their own ritual. Unlike the rest of the liturgy, laypeople—almost always women—preside over the announcements. This morning, it's Olivia's turn to read. Olivia looks about my age—a white woman in her late twenties sporting an adorable vintage-looking dress. She and her spouse would eventually become two of my most treasured friends in Boston. But at Mass this morning, I'm not sure that I remember her name, even though we have been introduced, probably more than once. I'm still new here. Over the course of the hour-long English-language liturgy, it becomes clear to me that nearly everyone here knows everyone else by name. During the sign of peace—which I am surprised to find falls in the middle of Mass rather than in its usual place after the Lord's Prayer—parishioners spill out of their pews to embrace one another as the choir breaks into "This Little Light of Mine." Around me, exchanges of "Peace be with you" are accompanied by "How are the kids?" or "Will you be at the meeting tomorrow?" In the small community, no newcomer arrives unnoticed. People ask me my name, where I'm from, what I study. I'm used to parishes where exchanges of peace reach their emotional climax in timid handshakes and polite smiles. Here, I'm being hugged by strangers. Olivia kisses me on the cheek.

Now, at the end of Mass, Olivia smiles broadly from the ambo, slowly directing her gaze around the small sanctuary. "We want to begin by welcoming those who are here for the first time, or those who have been away for a while and returned," she proclaims with the measured vigor of a prayer. "We invite you to stand."

I have been in many parishes where visitors and newcomers are welcomed. But I'm intrigued by the second part of Olivia's invitation: "those who have been away for a while." How many people are leaving and coming back that they merit their own category? A lifelong Catholic, I'm accustomed to homilies that invoke a dubious medley of causal claims to explain why people are leaving the church. But I've never been to a parish that welcomes them back.

I glance around and slowly rise, smiling nervously, a little self-conscious. I'm relieved when I realize that I am not the only one standing. Behind me, a middle-aged man is also on his feet. Parishioners seem delighted to see him, suggesting to me that he falls in the "been away for a while" category. Everyone applauds. Michelle weaves around the pews handing out bilingual parish registration cards to those of us who stood up. She leans in and smiles like she's telling me a secret. "Even if you don't wanna fill it out," she winks, "you can keep it as a souvenir to remember your visit to St. Mary's."

Two hours later, at the Spanish Mass, announcements begin with a similar invitation. This time, we who rise are met with an ebullient sung refrain punctuated with rhythmic clapping:

¡Bienvenidos, bienvenidos
A los que vienen en el nombre del Señor![3]

St. Mary of the Angels is a parish on and of margins. For more than a century, its small boundaries have encompassed some of Boston's most consequential religious and racial borderlines. Like nearly four in ten U.S. parishes, St. Mary's serves a culturally diverse community. Unlike most, however, it is not a "shared parish," an arrangement Brett Hoover defines as involving "two or more cultural groups, each with distinct masses and ministries, but who share the same parish facilities."[4] While cultural groups in shared parishes might come together periodically for bilingual liturgies or parishwide celebrations, most path-crossing happens informally, unintentionally, and rarely. Unlike such parishes, where chasms of language, culture, class, ethnicity, and life experience clearly delineate the church's subgroups, St. Mary's is more like a borderland, a place formed by the confluence of peoples and cultures. Through decades of practice and reimagined parish structures, the community sustained both language-specific Masses and a distinctive sense of shared belonging.

As I would learn, the welcome ritual at the end of Sunday Mass was as much about introducing St. Mary's to newcomers as it was about introducing newcomers to St. Mary's. The unconventional greeting—to the recently arrived, to the departed and returned—contained the parish's history in brief. In an otherwise highly segregated city and church, St. Mary's had become a hybrid parish formed over time by successive migrations. While most parishioners primarily identified as either English or Spanish Massgoers, their commitments to the "multicultural and multilingual" parish mission statement revealed a robust sense of interstitial belonging. Most Spanish Mass community members were first-generation immigrants. Some lived transnationally, commuting between Boston and the Dominican Republic or other homelands for work or family. Meanwhile, some older African American parishioners traced their families' arrivals in Boston to the Great Migration and spent summers visiting relatives along the Eastern Seaboard and in the South. Some parishioners were lifelong Bostonians, but others had moved to the city for school and knew their time at St. Mary's would be temporary. Clergy at the parish followed a similar migratory pattern. St. Mary's was served by a combination of archdiocesan and Jesuit priests, all of whom lived different sorts of transitory lives. The former were subject to regular transfer by the arch-bishop, though staffing tended toward extremes—there were years when no one was assigned to St. Mary's at all, and there were long stretches, sometimes a decade or more, with the same pastor. As the clergy short-age worsened, the archdiocese welcomed the assistance of priests from other shores. For most of my time at St. Mary's, the pastor was a Neocat-echumenal Way–affiliated priest from Spain. A rotation of Jesuits would also come to say Sunday Masses, further ameliorating the shortage. The "fan favorites," beloved for their good homilies, had been coming for years. Other Jesuit priests and transitional deacons from Latin America were stu-dents at Boston College. They would serve the parish for two or three years, devoting much of their effort to pastoral work in the Spanish Mass community. Invariably, by the end of their tenures they would be adored like sons, and everyone would hug them and take pictures and cry at their despedidas (going-away parties). The best friend I made during my first year at St. Mary's was a Chilean Jesuit deacon named Juan Pablo, at whose despedida I cried. Every Sunday, it seemed, someone was moving away or moving back or visiting, and in parishioners' long memories, they were all part of the story.

This chapter begins a constructive response to the questions of com-munity and solidarity raised in chapter 1 by attending to parishioners' ar-rival narratives, charting the migrations that made and remade Egleston Square and St. Mary's. Tracing the history of Egleston Square reveals its unique status as a religious, racial, and ethnic borderland in the heart of the city. Rather than attempting to secure a distinctive sense of cultural identity, St. Mary's adapted to its borderland reality by becoming a way station, a place of sojourn for journeying people.

Egleston Square as Urban Borderland

Egleston Square began to urbanize in the mid-1800s as Bostonians seek-ing a reprieve from the densely populated city moved to the nearby coun-tryside. In their 1893 petition for a national parish in Roxbury, a committee of German immigrants described settling in the area because their people "love the beauties and comforts of a garden."[5] Roxbury would eventually be incorporated into Boston's city limits and, by the mid–twentieth century, would become synonymous with its "inner city." Prior to the turn of the century, however, it was a serene escape from downtown, accessible by newly built electric streetcar lines. The transformation of Egleston from bucolic suburb to urban center was catalyzed by the construction of the Boston Elevated Railway. Elevated tracks were built above busy Washington Street, and a station was built in Egleston Square in 1906. The area quickly became a bustling transportation hub. An influx of Catholic settlement accompanied the railway expansion. By the early twentieth century, Egleston Square had become home to a growing number of working-class Irish, German, and Italian immigrants. They lived in newly popular multifamily, triple-decker housing and labored in the area's tanneries, print shops, factories, and breweries, and as domestic servants in the homes of wealthy merchants and brewers.[6]

That May, optimistic at the prospect of a flourishing Catholic community among Roxbury's working-class Catholic immigrants, Archbishop John Joseph Williams established a spate of parishes, each one within a few miles of another. The smallest was St. Mary of the Angels. The church was built on what was once a sprawling estate whose owner had deeded it to the archdiocese for one dollar. The large estate house would serve as the rectory.[7] Alongside it, plans were drawn up for a granite-block, Gothic-style church with a square tower overlooking verdant Franklin Park.[8] German and Polish Catholics had both recently established national parishes in the area. St. Mary's, by contrast, would be a territorial parish, built to serve all Catholics living within its archdiocesan-drawn boundaries. Glancing at a map of area parishes at the time shows how little territory St. Mary's contained by comparison. Its boundaries looked more like a large intersection than a substantive subdivision of the archdiocese. In 1907, a year after its establishment, St. Mary's served only 209 families. With the exception of a nearby mission, "No other Catholic church in all of Dorchester and upper Roxbury was supported by so few people."[9] Even accounting for the area's immigration-driven Catholic population boom, it is not at all clear why anyone thought that establishing the parish was a good idea in the first place. It was immediately evident that filling its pews and collection baskets was going to be a challenge.[10]

While the church was under construction, parishioners gathered for Mass in a makeshift sanctuary in the streetcar barn down the block. In a letter circulated to would-be parishioners, pastor Henry A. Barry likened their humble beginning to the nativity story:

> The birth of our parish life will be humble—like the beginning of Christianity; for we must not forget that Our Lord was born in a stable and was laid in a manger. . . . We will not disdain to adore Our Lord in humble quarters—it will refresh Bethlehem's story in our minds and fasten its incomparable fragrance on our hearts. We will join our minds and hearts in the noble effort to build Jesus a dwelling place.[11]

Though Barry undoubtedly believed that the parish's "humble quarters" would be temporary, he had forecasted its future more accurately than he realized. By the spring of 1908, builders had completed as much of the church as they could with the funds available. They placed a roof over the basement, and the archdiocese promised to oversee construction of the rest of the building as membership increased and money came in.[12]

St. Mary of the Angels was a borderland from the beginning. Its parish boundaries were among the smallest in the archdiocese, but they encompassed some of the city's most consequential dividing lines. While Archbishop Williams had predicted a vibrant Catholic future for upper Roxbury, Catholics soon became a minority in what had rapidly become Boston's first Jewish suburb.[13] In 1908, the Great Chelsea Fire displaced large numbers of Jewish residents, some of whom resettled in Egleston Square.[14] In the years that followed, a large Jewish community coalesced in the blocks surrounding St. Mary's. In 1913, Jewish congregation Beth Hamidrash Hagadol purchased land for a synagogue a few blocks north, further catalyzing Jewish settlement in the neighborhood. Egleston Square changed so rapidly that in 1919, St. Mary's pastor, Rev. Charles A. Finnegan, wrote to William Cardinal O'Connell to recommend that the archdiocese scale back resources from his own parish: "Having less than a thousand adults in this parish, three priests are hardly needed here. So many [Catholics] have moved away during the past year—their houses are now occupied by Jews—that three priests here are more than necessary for the work to be done."[15] In the fall of 1922, Congregation Mishkan Tefila, another significant Boston Jewish community, broke ground on a large temple less than a mile up the road from St. Mary's.[16] Six years later, Finnegan wrote that Walnut Avenue had become the stark dividing line between Jewish and Catholic blocks within his parish boundaries. East of Walnut Avenue, he noted, the parish boundaries encompassed 740 homes—only 12 of which were occupied by Catholic families.[17]

Roxbury's religious boundary line may have been invisible, but it was decisive. In his exhaustive study of Jewish and Catholic urban dynamics in Boston, Gerald Gamm cites the memoir of Theodore H. White, who grew up as a Jewish child in the enclave bordered by St. Mary's. White recalls the impact of the Catholic-Jewish divide on his childhood: "Within the boundaries of our community we were entirely safe and sheltered. But the boundaries were real. We were an enclave surrounded by Irish. Across Franklin Park to the west lay the lands of the lace-curtain Irish, who lived in Jamaica Plain and Roslindale; they were, if not friendly, at least not pugnacious." However, to the east, across the railroad tracks near Blue Hill Avenue, "lived very tough Irish—working class Irish." Venture beyond this boundary, White recalled, and bloody fights were sure to follow.[18]

The division persisted for decades. Census data from 1940 attest to the sharp divide between Jewish and non-Jewish blocks of upper Roxbury, with Walnut Avenue and St. Mary of the Angels marking the northwestern boundary of Jewish settlement in Roxbury and Dorchester. To the east of the church, at least 85 percent of white residents were Jewish; across the street, only between 10 and 35 percent were.[19] Because the boundary bisected the parish's already diminutive territory, parish membership remained small. By midcentury, St. Mary's was one of only four parishes in the Roxbury-Dorchester area without an elementary school.[20] Funds to complete the church remained small, too. Prohibition forced local breweries out of business, resulting in a loss of employment for many in the area. The Great Depression had a similar effect on other local industries and businesses. In the end, none of the hoped-for things—the Catholics, the money, the grand Gothic church—would arrive in Egleston Square. By 1935, plans to finish the building were abandoned for good.[21] St. Mary of the Angels would remain a basement church.

African American settlement also shaped residential dynamics and patterns of belonging at St. Mary's. Two Black Protestant congregations, St. Mark Congregational Church and Charles Street African Methodist Episcopal (A.M.E.) Church, arrived in upper Roxbury in 1926 and 1939, respectively. On a map, St. Mary's and the two churches formed a neat triangle, each one about a ten-minute walk from the others. These churches,

Gamm writes, "defined the first generation of African-American settlement in upper Roxbury, coordinating the formation of the area's black districts by effectively concentrating black demand for homes."[22] Clusters of African American families began to settle in the blocks around the two Protestant churches, attracted in part by the renowned St. Mark Social Center run by St. Mark Congregational Church.[23] Just as the new synagogues had done for Roxbury's Jewish residents, the Black churches acted as "nodes" for the formation of the city's nascent Black community.[24] By midcentury, the area's Jewish communities were rapidly leaving the city, relocating their synagogues to the suburbs.[25] As a territorially based institution, however, St. Mary's remained. By 1960, most nonwhite residents of Boston were concentrated in Roxbury.[26] St. Mary's small parish boundaries, once the site of Roxbury's religious dividing line, now encompassed the border between the few blocks that remained predominantly white and those home to Black families.[27]

Throughout the 1960s, Puerto Ricans began to settle in Egleston Square, followed by migrants from the Dominican Republic, Cuba, Haiti, Jamaica, Cape Verde, and elsewhere. Many of the new migrants who settled in the neighborhoods around Egleston Square were Catholic and made St. Mary's their parish home. To better serve its Spanish-speaking members, St. Mary's established a regular Spanish Mass in 1971. When Laotian Kmhmu refugees arrived in the late 1970s, St. Mary's became the headquarters for the Kmhmu-Lao Family Association of Massachusetts. St. Mary's pews reflected the cultural, racial, and linguistic diversity of the surrounding neighborhoods. In a 1986 report to the archdiocese, Fr. Jack Roussin estimated that St. Mary's was serving five hundred to six hundred people representing forty-three different countries of origin. The parish was offering liturgies and pastoral services in English, Spanish, Lao, French, Haitian Creole, and Portuguese.[28]

As Gamm convincingly demonstrates, the boundaries of many Roxbury Catholic parishes effectively functioned as racial barriers during the latter half of the twentieth century.[29] White urban-dwelling Catholics' well-documented recalcitrance toward racial and ethnic others did not automatically lead to white flight. In cities like Boston, it sometimes had the opposite effect. Attachment to their local parishes effectively bound Catholics to their neighborhoods, at least initially. As Gamm argues, "Parishes are the institutional fortresses of 'defended neighborhoods.'"[30] Par-

FIGURE 1. Neighborhood children create paper bag hand puppets at St. Mary of the Angels summer camp, July 18, 1978. Sister Rita Murray, *The Pilot*.

ish boundaries often functioned like border walls, restricting the possibilities for Black movement and settlement.

Why, then, did the parish boundaries of St. Mary's not hold? Why, in other words, did St. Mary's become a bridge rather than a wall? Several factors likely contributed. The boundaries of most nearby parishes coincided with major streets, railroad tracks, or other features of the urban landscape that also came to signify racial dividing lines. St. Mary's boundaries, on the other hand, were carved somewhat haphazardly from those of nearby St. Joseph Parish; they encompassed both sides of Washington Street and Columbus Avenue, two busy thoroughfares that would later mark racial borders. Additionally, St. Mary's was situated not only near the somewhat nebulous border between Roxbury and Dorchester, two sections of Boston with similar racial and economic profiles, but also on the border with Jamaica Plain, an area that remained relatively whiter. Finally, St. Mary's small size and economic precarity, coupled with the high degree of archdiocesan neglect suffered by inner-city parishes during this period, may have prevented it from becoming what Gamm terms a "strong parish" with "strong attachments."[31] Given the prevalence of shared family housing in Egleston Square and the working-class status of Catholics there, many parishioners did not own their homes, making them more vulnerable to population shifts.

For these reasons, St. Mary's became a community of difference, a place composed of borders—some porous, others less so. Successive migrations continually altered the demographics of the blocks in and around Egleston Square, but at the parish, the arrival of newcomers did not force the wholesale exodus of those who already worshipped there. Instead, many remained. Others who had moved away continued to attend Mass at St. Mary's, sometimes for decades and from a great distance. In the archdiocesan archive, I came across a 1977 *Boston Globe* feature on St. Mary's, a three-part investigation into the challenges faced by Catholic churches in the inner city.[32] I had to laugh when I realized that three of the women interviewed for the piece—two Black, one Italian American—were parishioners I had come to know well almost forty years later, all of them still active and involved in the parish.

Crossing Borders, Making Homes

Historian Thomas Tweed suggests that religious practice is about "making homes" and "crossing boundaries."[33] At St. Mary's, parishioners seemed to be doing both of these things at once. I usually began interviews by asking parishioners how they first happened to come to St. Mary's. As I listened to them narrate their arrivals, I began to see St. Mary's as a place where migrations of many kinds converged. The sense of cultural fluidity that shaped the church's past continued to define the community in the present. Many recent immigrants recalled coming to St. Mary's because of proximity or personal invitation. Yet I was surprised to find that nonimmigrant parishioners also drew on the lexicon of migration to narrate their journeys to the parish. Some described themselves as spiritual refugees, driven from former parish homes by poor leadership, ideological disagreements, or parish closures. For others, joining meant crossing denominational boundaries. These parishioners came to St. Mary's from other Christian traditions, compelled not by a desire to convert to Catholicism but instead by an invitation from a friend or family member to join this particular community. In almost every case, St. Mary's was the latest stop on a winding journey.

Crossing National Boundaries

Many new immigrants first came to St. Mary's by word of mouth. Yamaris, a woman in her midthirties who had recently moved to Boston from the Dominican Republic, had been attending Mass at a parish closer to her home when a friend invited her to St. Mary's. Her first Sunday there, she recalled, "I felt like I was at home because [other parishioners] treated me very well and I felt as if I were at my parish in Santo Domingo." Gradually, she said, "I started getting more involved . . . doing the readings [at Mass], helping with whatever activity was going on at church, with the collections . . . I always—whenever I have time—I always want to help out." She took public transportation across town or carpooled with other parishioners every Sunday morning for a year before buying a car. Now, she said, "it's easier because I can go to more activities and more things, like on days other than Sundays."³⁴

Ximena, a mother of two from Colombia who attended both English and Spanish Masses, also belonged to a different parish when a neighbor recommended she give St. Mary's a try. She didn't realize that the odd, half-underground building nearby was a church: "When I moved here, I didn't know any Catholic church around here. My neighbor who lives on the second floor just say one day, 'Why you go so far? There's a Catholic church around the corner.'" Unlike Yamaris, for whom the Dominican-accented liturgy evoked feelings of home, Ximena found it disorienting:

I thought, *This doesn't sound Catholic, because of the music.* The music at St. Mary's is more Caribbean. . . . It's very different. In [my home country] I used to go to a church [that was more traditional], the music was different. So [when I came to St. Mary's], I thought, *That's not Catholic. I used to look at the sign and say, That says 'Catholic,' but it's kind of funny.*³⁵

Ximena's instinctive association of the Spanish liturgy's merengue-style music with something foreign offers a sense of the internal diversity of the Spanish-speaking community at St. Mary's. On a broader level, it illustrates the inadequacy of monolithic perceptions of Latinx Catholics.³⁶ As she learned English, Ximena and her family began attending the English Mass, where the more muted ethos better matched her own experience of liturgy.

Dynamics of translocal and transnational belonging also shaped the seasons of parish life. Spring was for despedidas for the Jesuit deacons and recently ordained priests. New Jesuits were assigned in their place, and relationships would begin anew. In the summer, most parish group meetings were put on hold as parishioners left for vacations or family visits in the Dominican Republic or Puerto Rico or Atlanta. Most of them returned to Boston by the fall, but some returned months or years later. Others returned only to visit, and still others did not return at all, maintaining their connection to the community through updates from friends and family members who were still at the parish, social media, messaging platforms like Facebook Messenger and WhatsApp, and continued inclusion on the unwieldy parish e-mail list.

Crossing Parish Boundaries

Parishioners who were not themselves recent immigrants also spoke of their journeys to St. Mary's as migrations. Married couple Amelia and Tom started coming because they felt pushed out of their former parish by a newly arrived pastor who was difficult and myopically focused on abortion. "Our friends [from our former parish] had migrated over to St. Mary of the Angels," Amelia explained. "It was hard to leave, because we were very loyal to the people there. But we had this Jesuit friend who said, 'You need to go where there's life.'"[37] Crossing parish boundaries, they followed their friends to St. Mary's on a quest for spiritual survival. Indeed, many in the English Mass community echoed their experience of finding St. Mary's during a period of spiritual lifelessness or parochial homelessness. Some recounted feeling alienated from the institutional church after the sexual abuse crisis. Their arrivals at St. Mary's were prompted by a mixture of disgust with the institutional church, dissatisfaction with other nearby parishes, and a serendipitous personal invitation from someone else—a friend, coworker, fellow neighborhood activist, or priest.

For some white Massgoers, St. Mary's was a refuge from the racial homogeneity of other Catholic parishes. Eugene, a professor in his seventies, joined St. Mary's after becoming disillusioned with what he described as the whiteness and insularity of his former church. Gayle, a retired educator and longtime parish leader, arrived after her old parish—a small, struggling community not unlike St. Mary's—shut its doors. She and her husband were seeking a church that was progressive and diverse just as their old one had been. They tried joining the Paulist Center, a non-parochial community on Beacon Hill popular with progressive, highly educated Catholics, but they felt troubled that despite the community's emphasis on inclusivity, its membership was predominantly white. "It's not diverse enough in the ways that diversity is important to me," Gayle recalled thinking. The Jesuit pastor of St. Mary's invited them to visit one Sunday, and they never left.[38] Gayle admitted that what she viewed as the more conservative theological perspectives and practices of the Spanish Mass community were not always her cup of tea. But, she explained, she valued St. Mary's because it helped her to realize

> the range of who we are as Catholics, based partially on our language, on our culture, on our education, our life situation. I think it's something that when I've gone to churches that are very progressive and have beautiful liturgies but that are much more homogeneous, I don't have that experience. I have struggles with some of the experiences of St. Mary's, because we have to work hard at figuring out how we hear one another's voices.

For Gayle, belonging to St. Mary's meant choosing occasional disagreement and intentional compromise over the comfort of racial and ideological homogeneity.

For some, St. Mary's functioned as a node of residential settlement, in Gamm's terms. It kept some tied to the neighborhood when they would have otherwise moved away and compelled others who had initially commuted to Mass from well beyond Egleston Square to move into the neighborhood. Olivia, the woman who read the announcements at the English Mass during one of my first Sundays at St. Mary's, recalled how difficult it was for her to find a parish home after moving to nearby Somerville after graduate school. "I tried literally every single Catholic church in the greater Porter Square–Harvard Square area. And I wasn't feeling any of them," she lamented. "I was church-hopping and I was like, *I might as well not be going to church. This is terrible.* I have two requirements for a church," she continued. "One, that celebrating Mass is a *celebration*, and two, that there's a community. There's an *actual* community." Finally, a friend invited her to St. Mary's. "I just loved it. And I never left." She and her partner even moved closer to St. Mary's—a move that took her farther away from her workplace and into a neighborhood where they were the only white people on the block—so they could walk to Mass and become more involved in the life of the community.

The tendency to "parish hop" was not limited to progressive, diversity-seeking white Catholics. Victoria, the older Jamaican woman who sang in the English Mass choir, had been a parishioner since the 1980s. She proudly attested to driving right past "two parishes in my backyard" in order to get to St. Mary's.[39] And Michelle, who had been coming to St. Mary's since the mid-1990s, chose the parish for a combination of reasons. "I came here intentionally," she recalled. She hadn't been to church in two decades when members from her choir persuaded her to participate in a day of reflection in preparation for the National Black Catholic Congress, which many of them were planning to attend. At the event, she met a man who challenged her on her lack of church attendance:

> The man said, "If you don't go to church, you don't believe in God." And I challenged that bigtime. It's like, I believe in God, I'm just angry with the church, so I'm not going. And he continued to talk, and basically said, "Well one of the reasons for going to church is community." So, I liked that idea, and I talked to a couple of people who were at this day of reflection and said, "What is your church like, and what time are the masses, and does your church have music?"

She decided that if she were going to go back to church, it would have to be at a Black Catholic parish with good music. As it turned out, the St. Mary's gospel Mass had the latest start time and sometimes lasted only forty-five minutes, which struck Michelle as a much more sustainable commitment than the hours-long gospel Mass at the parish down the street. Michelle decided to give St. Mary's a try. As English-speaking attendance declined and the clergy shortage intensified, the noon gospel Mass was eventually combined with the other English Mass to create the 9:00 a.m. folk-gospel hybrid that existed by the time I arrived. Though not a fan of the earlier start time, by then, Michelle was in deep. When we spoke, she had been at St. Mary's for twenty years.[40]

Crossing Denominational Boundaries

For some African American parishioners, coming to St. Mary's began as an act of ecumenism. Florence, one of the most senior parish members, was Episcopalian when she first came to St. Mary's. "I used to live in that brick building right on the corner down there," she told me, gesturing out the chapel window and down the street. One day, the parish priest knocked on her door and invited her to Mass. "That was back in 1960 or '61," she recalled. "And I've been here ever since. All my kids were baptized here." Florence started volunteering, cooking lunches for the neighborhood summer camp that St. Mary's used to run. Eventually she joined the Parish Council, then the Finance Council, and then she became the parish secretary. "You can't tell me nothin's wrong with this church." She shook her head. "I love this church. I ain't goin' nowhere else."[41]

Martin, a longtime lay leader and English Mass attendee, also came to St. Mary's as a non-Catholic. Martin and his wife Alma moved to Egleston Square in 1976. Alma was Catholic, but Martin belonged to the A.M.E. church. His memories of moving into the neighborhood capture what was at stake in the residential transitions of this period:

> We bought a house less than a two-minute walk from St. Mary. The seller was a woman who was an Irish immigrant. I could tell she wanted to sell us the house, but I thought I needed to do something to solidify that potential sale, so I asked her where was the closest Catholic church? And she said, "Oh it's right there down the street. . . . Are you Catholic?"
>
> I said, "No, but I'm thinking about converting." Which was kind of a lie at the time, but that sealed the deal. (He laughed.)
>
> "I want you to have my house," [she said]. So we bought the house, and we still live in it.[42]

The Irish homeowner's desire to sell her house to a Catholic—even a Black would-be Catholic—illustrates the complex racial and religious push and pull that influenced white residential patterns in mid-twentieth-century Boston. As noted above, in cities like Boston, white Catholics' parish commitments contributed to the persistence of racial segregation in urban neighborhoods. But by 1976, many whites had already abandoned Egleston Square. Holding out for a white homebuyer was unlikely, whether the homeowner had wanted to or not. In Martin's story, we see how his interaction with the homeowner strategically played one impulse against another, leveraging her parish loyalty against any hesitation she might have had about selling her home to a mixed-race couple. Almost two decades later, Martin did convert to Catholicism. It was just as well— he already attended Mass with his family and had served on the Parish Council for years.

FIGURE 2. Liturgical dancers from the Inner City Catholic Youth Group prepare for the Roxbury Black History Month Mass at St. Mary of the Angels, February 1, 1998. From left to right: Keena Villard, 13, of St. Angela's; Tyjuana Flores, 15, of St. Joseph's; Nneka Oleru, 15, of St. Mary of the Angels; Karmissa Rolle, 17, of St. Angela's. ©Lisa Kessler 1998.

Making Homes

While some people come to St. Mary's because they live within or near its territorial boundaries, or once did, others have based their belonging on different factors. The voluntary nature of their arrivals suggests that they remain bound to St. Mary's for reasons that have little to do with geography. In both Mass communities, parishioners described staying because they were immediately invited into involvement and leadership. Claudia, a prominent parish leader born in the Dominican Republic, first came to St. Mary's in the 1980s after moving into the Academy Homes complex with her husband and kids. A passerby had to direct her there—like apparently everyone else, she had no idea that the half-underground building a mile up Columbus Avenue from her apartment was a Catholic church. She stayed because other Spanish Mass parishioners immediately recruited her to represent the Spanish-speaking community on parish committees. "Just [my] second Sunday [here], they asked me to be on the Parish Council," she recalled. "And almost right away, like maybe the following Sunday . . .

they came and said, 'We are missing one of the readers. Can you read [at Mass]?'" She felt so nervous, she recalled, that "I thought people heard my heart bumping [through the microphone] instead of my words. But it was great. I never felt strange, like a stranger. Ever." At her previous parish, she explained, "I was just one more parishioner. That's it. But St. Mary's was welcoming."[43] These days, Claudia no longer lives in the neighborhood, but she still belongs to St. Mary's. Occasionally, conflicts or frustrations cause her to attend Mass elsewhere. Despite these temporary hiatuses, she always returns to St. Mary's in the end. Her friendships with members of both Mass communities, forged through decades of involvement on the Parish Council, keep her coming back.

Claudia invited others. "My sister and I started coming every Sunday," Ximena recalled. "We used to sit in the back of the church, always. Never in the front of the church. And just one day, Claudia asked me if I want to be a Eucharistic minister. And I said okay." Soon, Ximena was involved in everything. She started bringing communion to elderly and homebound parishioners, giving her the chance to visit neighbors in their homes. She became a lector, then a Sunday school teacher. She joined the Spanish community's Christian formation group, served as a Confirmation sponsor, helped run the parish bazaar, assisted with church accounting, and supported liturgy planning. Eventually, she became a leader in the parish's once-thriving family ministry, planning annual summer bilingual retreats for St. Mary's families.

Marisol, another Spanish Mass parishioner, had a similar experience. Marisol sang in the choir, and she and her family were involved in many other aspects of parish life. Like Claudia almost three decades earlier, Marisol joined St. Mary's around 2009 because she moved into the neighborhood. Right away, she was drawn in by the sense of shared authority. "It didn't seem like there was a 'boss,'" she said. "Everyone was one." When I asked her how she would describe St. Mary's to someone who had never been there, she responded:

Well, in the first place, I would call on them to get involved. Because if you get involved, you're basically going to stay here. Sometimes we see the Mass as something that we have to "fulfill." We come to Mass and we leave. But when people start contributing—as a lector, or helping with the [Eucharistic] cup, or helping around the church, they tend to stay. . . . When you have a commitment to the community, you feel more and more glued to it. You can't get unglued very easily. And that is what happens at St. Mary.[44]

The tendency to involve new parishioners in positions of leadership was not only or even primarily about retention. Nor did it seem to be driven by a desire to place people of color in visible leadership positions to attract a more diverse membership base, a strategy common among some diversity-seeking congregations.[45] As chapter 3 will explore, St. Mary's vigorous, sometimes controversial tradition of lay leadership had roots in the local reception of Vatican II, and in a particular way in the advent of the Parish Pastoral Council structure. The stories that these generations of lay leaders shared with me about their early years at St. Mary's suggested that the community treated leadership not as a position to be earned but as the right and duty of all the faithful—even the non-Catholic faithful. After all, Martin sat on the Parish Council for years before he ever formally converted to Catholicism. Following Vatican II, lay leadership at St. Mary's was principally about expanding boundaries, not enforcing them.

Not everyone agreed about the level of inclusion, however. Gina, a relative newcomer to the English Mass, lamented the trouble she encountered breaking into the established in-crowd of longtime lay leaders. She wondered aloud if it was because her fellow Euro-American parishioners—those whom she described as "the educated, middle-class white people"—were more preoccupied with empowering the involvement of parishioners of color. "I think the wish to be more integrated between groups and the wish to do good distorts, let's say, normal community building or community inclusion," she conjectured. Gina's explanation deserves careful unpacking, because it hints at dynamics that shaped relationships in the English Mass in ways that often went unnamed. First, she noted a temporal dissonance, a palpable difference in longtime parishioners' experiences of community at the parish compared to the experiences of newer members. Long-timers reminisced nostalgically about the friendships they had cultivated over decades. These relationships were solidified during moments of crisis, often under the leadership of a beloved priest—the neighborhood antiviolence work of the "Jack Roussin years" in the 1980s, for example, or the anticlosure protest in 2004. The community organizing and public witness demanded of parishioners during those years fostered strong bonds. A newer parishioner, Gina arrived during an uncharacteristically placid period at St. Mary's, and at a point in which the laity of her generation had already begun to hand over leadership to younger and—as she rightly observed—more diverse parishioners.

Intersecting with this temporal dissonance was a racial one. What Gina seemed to be hinting at was the disorientation that accompanied her experience of white racial decentering. St. Mary's was different from other Catholic and non-Catholic churches she had attended in the past, she noted, in large part because of its diversity. And yet the very diversity that drew her to the parish was also the source of her frustration. I sensed that she felt betrayed by her fellow white parishioners who were more concerned with what she termed "doing good"—that is, consciously including people of color and Spanish speakers in leadership—than with investing in "normal community building." Her disorientation was likely magnified by the fact that at many U.S. parishes, white inclusion and racial and ethnic siloing are "normal community building." During our conversation, I felt aware that, because I was also an "educated, middle-class white person" and relative newcomer, Gina was disclosing to me feelings and impressions that she likely would not have felt comfortable articulating to a parishioner who was a person of color. She perceived natural kinship between us that she did not necessarily associate with the broader St. Mary's community.

Finally, Gina's description of intra- and interracial dynamics drew attention to what might be termed the side effects of ecclesial solidarity. For Gina, parish life at St. Mary's felt more like a project than a celebration. In her perspective, white people at St. Mary's were *trying too hard*. Relationships felt burdened by an excess of intentionality. I asked Gina if feeling left out ever made her think about leaving St. Mary's. After all, she, like many others, had started coming because she was invited by a friend, not because she lived nearby. If parish involvement generally kept people connected, would dissatisfaction over her perceived exclusion drive her away? "Uh-uh," she responded, shaking her head. "No. I can only be away for a week or so, then I'm just drawn back. It feels like this . . . this is real life. This is reality, what we have here. It's not like church as separate from every other part of life."[46]

In a way, Gina's devotion to St. Mary's reminded me of Gayle's, even though, to Gina, Gayle probably represented the kind of gatekeeping white do-gooder she had come to quietly resent. For both women, there was something about the "real life" of St. Mary's—racial, cultural, and ideological dissonances and all—that felt to them like a more authentic expression of whatever church was supposed to be. On some level, both women were there out of a desire to worship in a community over which they did not possess control, where they could feel the world pressing back on them, where they were not the ultimate arbiters of belonging.

Gina was not the only parishioner whose hedged articulation of racial discontentment seemed to contrast with the depth of her commitment to the parish. A handful of others approached conflict in ways that fell outside of the deliberative "St. Mary's way." While newcomer Gina was discreet about her dissatisfactions, others were more blunt. In the English Mass community, confrontations would begin with some ostensibly minor, incidental complaint—the sacristy had been left in disarray, someone assigned a responsibility at Mass had failed to show up—and occasionally devolve into rants about entire communities or decades-old antipathies. Then other people would get upset back, and eventually someone would storm out. Among Spanish Massgoers, the most painful conflicts I witnessed surfaced over disagreements about moral and spiritual issues and clerical allegiances. Whereas conflicts in the English community often seemed like flashes in the pan, rifts in the Spanish community appeared deeper and more personal and took longer to heal.

In both cases, however, shared commitment to the labor of the parish covered—though not entirely—a multitude of wounds. Indeed, most of the conflicts, it seemed, could be traced back to rival convictions about the identity and mission of the community. Many of those who were most invested in the parish—and most ready to fight about it—were also those who had lived in Egleston Square through decades of violence and struggle and had worked hard to preserve the few resources to which the church and neighborhood had access. Yet theirs was not the "we built this parish"-style territorialism often at the root of conflict in changing communities. Even parishioners whose families had belonged to St. Mary's for a half century would have arrived when the church was home to a mixture of races and ethnicities and backgrounds. They didn't build the parish either, and they knew it. Even the most vocal complainants were accidental evangelists for St. Mary's. As we see in the next chapter, well-established structures of intercultural solidarity meant that individual prejudices and grievances, even the most persistent, did not ultimately dictate parish practices.

The Parish as Way Station

St. Mary's was a place of porous borders. To belong was to choose to be in between. The internal diversity of both the English and Spanish Mass communities, as well as the tradition of collaboration between the two, made the parish a rare place of friendship and solidarity across difference, even as it posed practical challenges. St. Mary's bridged these divides in unexpected ways. Though Boston is a small city, its transportation lines do more to keep people in their places than to connect them. I learned this the hard way. Without a car, traveling from St. Mary of the Angels to Boston College meant an hour-and-twenty-minute commute on public transportation: I would catch the bus to Jackson Square station, where I would board the Orange Line train to Back Bay, where I would get off and walk to the Copley station on the Green Line, where I would wait for a B-line train, which I would ride to its final stop. Roxbury and Brighton were just five miles apart. Sustaining a community that bridged social, class, and generational divides meant that people arrived at Mass in a host of ways, often on foot, by bus, bike, carpool, or municipal senior shuttle. Once I finally got a car, I learned that those of us who drove to Mass could expect to receive a phone call from Gayle or another leader on Sunday morning asking if we wouldn't mind picking up one of the parish elders on our way. English and Spanish Mass attendees even carpooled with one another, the one arriving early, the other staying late. St. Mary's bridged other divides, too. Sacramentally, a parish is a site of mediation between believers and God. In post-"Spotlight" Boston, however, the distance be-tween people and God was nothing compared to the distance between people and the institutional church. For parishioners like Michelle, the community she found at St. Mary's acted as a middle space between the God she loved and "the church" she resented. In many ways, the parish was a bridge, touching both sides of a divide (which is to say, affirming real difference where it existed) and creating space for the possibility of togetherness in the middle.[47]

Boundaries and borders form a key category in both Latinx theologies and postcolonial theories of culture. Extending Gloria Anzaldúa's notion of the borderland as a place where the distance between cultures, races, and classes "shrinks with intimacy,"[48] Sophia Park suggests, "The borderland can be a place within metropolitan centers for the meeting of cultures rooted in class, gender, and ethnicity. . . . [The] borderland signifies the in-between space where two or more cultural or political elements are joined."[49] The city is another kind of borderland, one in which encounter and transformation occur at the site of this joining. Rather than impermeable markers of division, borders are dynamic sites of negotiation and, as postcolonial theorist Homi Bhabha posits, of local cultural production. Referencing Martin Heidegger, Bhabha argues that boundaries are "the place from which something begins its *presencing*."[50] In other words, boundaries are beginnings, not end points. Without idealizing border space, Bhabha and Anzaldúa both suggest that the condition of in-betweenness discloses the possibility of encounter and solidarity and, on the basis of these relationships, the emergence of something new. It is in this sense that theologian Michael Nausner, drawing on Bhabha, proposes "reimagining [the] homeland *as* a dynamic borderland, that is, not necessarily in opposition to those I cannot yet imagine as belonging to this land."[51] Ecclesiologically, tracing the migrations that made the place of St. Mary's raises the need for conceptions of church that are attentive to change, ambiguity, and the tension between mutuality and particularity.

In a church marked by social and cultural transformation, reimagining the parish as a sort of borderland offers a generous vision of ecclesial belonging. Yet Anzaldúa's emphasis on mestizaje raises the relevant tension of whether and to what extent encounters among peoples necessarily result in cultural and ontological fusion. In a borderland, can particularity persist, or do all gradually become one, sublimating distinctive cultural practices and identities into hybrid forms that inevitably bear the mark of domination? Anzaldúa's borderland theory is better understood as a kind of second reflection on the reality of encounter across difference rather than as a normative template for it. What should we make of the third spaces that such encounters produce? Can anything good come out of Nazareth (Jn 1:46)? Rejecting dualistic understandings of existence and belonging—the idea that, to avoid illegitimacy or confusion, one must be either this or that, here or there—what makes borderland spaces distinctive is the gradual emergence of something vital and unpredictable in the space where cultures and peoples meet.[52] In other words, as Gregory Fernando Pappas contends, betwixt and between is "a real place to be."[53] What distinguishes "borderland parishes" like St. Mary's from Hoover's "shared parishes," then, is the presence of this third space. In shared parishes, cultural subgroups see themselves as boundaried communities—in between them, there is little ground on which to stand. In a borderland, however, shared practices give rise to interstitial belonging even as they enrich and encourage particularity.

For theologian Roberto Goizueta, borders function as "not merely a geographical but, more profoundly, a theological category, a place that makes present the glory of God."[54] This to say, the borderland can be understood as *locus theologicus*, a privileged site of divine solidarity and revelation.[55] Understanding a border in this way—not as a syncretistic burden whose ambiguities and impurities must be resolved for the sake of orthodoxy, but rather as a space in which a people's search for God in history takes new and unexpected forms—requires what Goizueta calls a Christological "transvaluation of the border."[56] Far from the geographical, political, and religious center of Jerusalem and dominated by the Roman Empire, Jesus's Galilee marks a paradigmatic theological periphery. As Goizueta states, "The Galilean borderland frames Jesus' life, death, and resurrection; it is from whence he came and where he is going."[57] Incarnate on the border, in Jesus the glory of God is revealed in "that godforsaken place from which nothing good has ever come."[58] Sr. Margaret, a religious sister who had worked at St. Mary's on and off since the 1980s, once told me that in her early days there, even the other sisters in her community looked at Roxbury as a kind of local Galilee: "[People] have got this prejudice, a racism," she recalled with disgust. "It's set up right there, and could anything good come out of Nazareth? *Could anything good ever come out of Roxbury?*"[59] That God would make a home in this marginal place is evidence, Goizueta contends, that "God chooses what the world rejects."[60] Recovering the ecclesiological significance of difference requires centering reflection precisely at the site of difference—both the sources of rupture and the moments of embrace. It requires, in other words, a theological option for the borderlands, for the in-between spaces where God has revealed Godself to dwell.

The welcome ritual at the end of Mass at St. Mary's each week mapped the expectation of exodus and return onto the community's ecclesiologi- cal self-understanding. Situated in a place fashioned out of interwoven mi- grations, life at St. Mary's was a litany of transitions, of welcomes and good-byes. Yet there was also something durable behind these shifting cur- rents, an abiding sense of story for which everyone who arrived there became responsible. This was the paradox at the heart of St. Mary's— stability and change. Approaching the parish through the metaphorical lens of the borderland helps to unpack the complex relationship between these forces. Parishioners' stories of arrival and belonging reveal both the power and insufficiency of the territorial parish model. In one sense, the territorial stability of the parish model enabled St. Mary's to bear the flu- idity of a century of near-constant cultural transition. Its fixed boundaries required it to become a space of convergence in order to survive. If the parish could have followed its early Euro-American parishioners to the suburbs, it might have done so. But the role of the parish is, first and fore- most, to stay put—to remain "stably constituted," in the words of the Code of Canon Law. St. Mary's basement-level doors stayed open, ready to wel- come whoever showed up next.

In another sense, however, attending to parishioners' stories of bound- ary crossing offers a gentle indictment of exaggerated Catholic anxieties about "parish shopping." Driven from spiritual homes by church closure, ideological alienation, racial homogeneity, and a host of other factors, the ecclesial migrants who ultimately settled at St. Mary's crossed parish boundaries seeking new life and a place to belong. Those who undertook these interparish migrations viewed their journeys as more forced than voluntary—as acts of spiritual survival. For some, St. Mary's was a refuge, the one parish where they felt like they could stay Catholic; for would-be converts like Martin and Florence, St. Mary's was the first place that had ever made them want to call themselves Catholic. For parishioners like Yamaris, carpooling across town on Sunday mornings was about seeking a space of inclusion in the church, claiming the right to liturgical partici- pation and to be treated like someone who belonged there. For others, like Gayle, finding St. Mary's was propelled in part by the opposite impulse: a recognition that faithfulness to the Gospel required seeking out discom- fort, eschewing the lure of racial and ideological familiarity for a commu- nity that more clearly imaged the breadth of the people of God. When parish belonging is determined territorially, residential segregation and parish segregation are mutually reinforcing. For some white parishioners, faithfulness to the Gospel required crossing parish boundaries, defying the hegemony of Boston's religio-racial status quo.[61] Viewed in light of these journeys, parish choice appears to be less about the triumph of consumerism over the virtue of local belonging, as it is often characterized in Catholic theological and pastoral discourse,[62] and more about the longing for a basic level of inclusion and justice—a yearning for home. As Carmen Nanko-Fernández rightly notes, borders are rarely the final destination.[63] Like the streetcar barn that was the site of its earliest liturgies, and like the elevated rail station whose construction brought waves of change to Egleston Square, St. Mary's was a way station, ready to welcome those who were there for the first time, and those who had been away for a while and returned.

3 Receiving Vatican II in Roxbury

January 17, 2012

In a Boston winter, nightfall begins in the middle of the afternoon. It is barely six thirty, but the city is already dark and icy as people shuffle into the parish house. Claudia pushes open the door, and for a moment, the sounds of Columbus Avenue clamber inside with her. Wind-blown leaves scrape against concrete; cars honk and bus brakes screech, and in the distance, a low police siren echoes. Claudia makes her way inside, pushing her hip against the heavy wooden door to coax it shut. Unwinding her scarf from her shoulders, she adjusts the grocery bags in her arms and blows warm air into her pressed fingertips and begins to thaw.

Originally from the Dominican Republic, Claudia arrived at the parish almost thirty years ago. She didn't remain an outsider for long. St. Mary's had begun offering a Spanish Mass in 1971, a decade before she moved into the neighborhood, but Spanish-speaking parishioners were still underrepresented on the Parish Pastoral Council. She seemed like a natural leader, someone bold enough to advocate for the concerns of the Puerto Rican and Dominican parishioners before the council of English speakers. Even though she was new, parishioners persuaded her to join the council. She had been a leader in the parish ever since, known for her ability to work with almost anyone and for throwing parties that brought everyone together, regardless of language.

Claudia greets me in the kitchen with a kiss on the cheek. On the counter, somebody has arranged a plate of crackers and cheese cubes. I fish a half-full box of cookies from a cabinet, left over from a baptism celebration the Sunday before. Claudia pulls a grocery store vegetable tray and an extra large bottle of red wine from her bag and adds them to the countertop buffet. The coffeepot is on, crackling and sputtering, the aroma filling the parish house like an embrace.

We are gathering for the monthly meeting of the Parish Pastoral Council. Living in the parish house means that I'm on council, too, though I mostly listen. Established after Vatican II, parish pastoral councils are among the only structures in the Catholic church for the incorporation of lay voices into parish governance. Parish councils are consultative, not authoritative; they exist to advise the pastor—at least, that's what canon law says.[1] At St. Mary's, authority seems to flow in the opposite direction. I set my paper plate of cheese and baptism cookie and my Styrofoam cup of Merlot on the corner of the long meeting table and take a seat on a metal folding chair. Around the table, I count six Spanish Mass parishioners, six including me from the English Mass, plus an Irish American religious sister, a Chilean Jesuit deacon, and the parish maintenance manager, who has a Boston accent straight from central casting.

Tonight's agenda is a page long. The archdiocese has announced a plan to cluster St. Mary's together with two neighboring parishes into what it is calling a collaborative, assigning them all a single pastor to share. It is not a merger—each parish will keep its own church building and maintain its own finances—but the decision has put people on edge, dredging up the ghosts of closures past. On top of that, Lent is approaching, which means that somebody needs to plan the parish Mardi Gras party, and the liturgy point people are looking for lay volunteers to coordinate each of the bilingual Holy Week masses. The Social Justice Cluster has a full report, and the Finance Council representatives have a budget dilemma to resolve. "There's no way we're getting out of here on time," the council member next to me mumbles, raising an eyebrow. I have to laugh. In my five months at St. Mary's, I don't think I've ever gotten out of anything on time.

The pastor, Fr. Luis, is running late. No matter. Gaby, a young, cool professional originally from Tijuana who cochairs the council, calls us to order. Every meeting begins with a prayer, followed by the reading of the parish mission statement. One council member recites it in English, and another follows in Spanish. The mission statement is posted on the meeting room wall, printed in block letters on a laminated poster:

Saint Mary of the Angels is a multicultural and multilingual Catholic community of believers in Jesus Christ and His message. We strive to live our faith in joyful worship, providing spiritual nourishment, a welcoming and inclusive environment and sense of family in all our activities, and committing ourselves to promote justice in our neighborhood and broader world.

La Parroquia Santa María de los Ángeles es una comunidad Católica multicultural y multilingüe de creyentes en Jesucristo y su mensaje. Nosotros procuramos vivir nuestra fe en alegre adoración, proveyendo alimento espiritual, un ambiente agradable e inclusivo y un sentido de familia en todas nuestras actividades, y comprometiéndonos a promover justicia en nuestra vecindad y el mundo más amplio.

Parishioners crafted the current mission statement in 2001 as part of a parish self-audit process that culminated with an official archdiocesan visitation. The previous mission statement read like an awkward relic of post–Vatican II ecclesiological anxiety: "While we see community as the full People of God, we also recognize the need for a responsive, organized and professional program of Catholic Christian ministry."[2] The community saw the parish audit as an opportunity to consider anew what they were about and hoped to become. Parishioners spent a year in small groups deliberating every word and phrase of the new statement.[3] Now, reciting it in Spanish and English is a ritual that begins every meeting. Parishioners know the mission statement by heart, like a creed. In many ways, it is a creed, giving the community shared language to hold itself accountable to its vision. When they composed it, they both codified and created a parish culture. Now, whenever a new event or initiative is proposed, parishioners begin by evaluating it against the mission statement: *Is it planned for a time when everyone can come? What about parishioners who work long hours? Who will translate? Who can give rides to elders who don't drive after dark? Is it joyful? Spiritually nourishing? Is it welcoming to children and youth? Does it help people to know Jesus? Does it promote peace in the neighborhood?*

"Does anybody have any reflections?" Gaby asks us, looking around the table. The reading of the mission statement is always followed by an invitation to name where we've seen the mission in action in the life of the parish.

"¿Algunas reflexiones?" fellow council member Ramón repeats. At this and every meeting, every comment is translated from English into Spanish or Spanish into English, usually by Ramón. Translating is hard work, and beads of sweat are already forming across his forehead.

Martin, the other Parish Council cochair, speaks up first. "Pauline's funeral . . ." he starts. Nods and murmurs fill the room. Last week, a longtime parishioner died unexpectedly. Pauline's funeral Mass felt like a homecoming: The church was full, and the music—a selection of her gospel favorites—was soul stirring, at once mournful and jubilant. Martin pauses to let Ramón translate. Members have adopted a stop-and-start verbal cadence, naturally timing their sentences to account for these frequent bilingual punctuations. He continues. "It really felt like, this . . . this is who we are."

"Esto . . . esto es lo que somos."

———————

"Vatican II happened in Rome," writes historian Massimo Faggioli, "[but] the council was transacted . . . largely by the Church's margins."[4] In Boston, St. Mary of the Angels is the margins. It is a poor parish serving a largely working-class community, situated in the heart of a Boston neighborhood that bore the brunt of political and ecclesial divestment propelled by redlining and white flight. Architecturally and figuratively underground, the parish has spent the better part of fifty years hovering on the brink of closure. But marginality also has its benefits. In a hierarchically structured church with clearly defined roles and power relationships, occupying the peripheries affords a community a certain degree of freedom.

St. Mary's is also a parish *of* margins. When Vatican II rendered the church's boundaries more porous, it supplanted parochial isolation with a vision of salvation in and with, not from, the world. For a parish that was defined by the boundaries it encompassed, this ecclesiological revisioning was transformative. For parishioners, "reading the signs of the times" for themselves in the wake of Vatican II gave rise to parish practices of solidarity both *ad extra*—between church and neighborhood, Catholics and non-Catholics—and *ad intra*—between generations, middle-class and poor, lay and ordained, English-speaking and Spanish-speaking, and between and among parishioners of different races, ethnicities, and backgrounds.

Yet, as the first part of this chapter will demonstrate, the spirit of lay agency and local solidarity at St. Mary's was not entirely the product of Vatican II. Laity had been "reading the signs of the times" at St. Mary's from the beginning, decrying the pastoral neglect and abuses of power they were already suffering. Archived letters written to the chancery by St. Mary's parishioners throughout the 1920s, '30s, and '40s document their demands for justice and increasing dissatisfaction with their own powerlessness. Yet without parish or diocesan structures in place to authorize lay voices, and without any apparent archdiocesan commitment to the increasingly neglected area, parishioners had to engage in creative, tactical resistance drawing on a limited repertoire of possibilities. Vatican II empowered laity by creating the ecclesial conditions and structures necessary for this spirit of agency and resistance, already simmering below the surface, to flourish.

In chapter 1, I argued that a major unfulfilled trajectory in the reception of Vatican II was its vision-in-germ of the parish as a school of solidarity. The second part of this chapter continues the constructive response to the question of community in difference by contrasting two attempts at solidarity propelled by Vatican II. The first was a 1965 initiative by Boston's Richard Cardinal Cushing to provide pastoral intervention to "inner-city" parishes through a missionary program called the Roxbury Apostolate. Despite the archdiocese's attempt to revive the Roxbury parishes it had long neglected, the program appears to have been undone by its own idealism and undermined by the capricious nature of institutionally led solidarity "from above." The second was the establishment of the St. Mary's Parish Pastoral Council around 1969. Seizing the postconciliar ethos of openness and collaboration, laity leaned hard into their newfound power in order to place their struggling parish into a relationship of costly solidarity with the increasingly marginalized community it served.

"Sincerely Yours, Disgusted Parishioner": Lay Dissent Before Vatican II

Charles A. Finnegan was appointed pastor of St. Mary of the Angels in 1916. Stingy, erratic, and authoritarian, Finnegan was a constant source of ire for parishioners and neighbors alike. Letters addressed to the chancery from local Roxbury merchants, community members, and even assistant priests at the parish detail a decades-long litany of grievances. In a 1933 letter, a former parish janitor accused Finnegan of withholding his tools after Finnegan fired him in retaliation for filing an insurance claim against the parish after being injured on the job.[5] An organist wrote to

the chancery with a list of Masses for which Finnegan had apparently refused to pay him.[6] A local undertaker wrote to complain that Finnegan
had denounced him from the pulpit, accusing him of overcharging for his
services.[7] Assistant priests who were sent to serve St. Mary's alongside
Finnegan regularly wrote to William Henry Cardinal O'Connell begging
for reassignment. In 1935, one wrote to complain that he was laid up in
bed with a cold because Finnegan refused to set the church thermostat
above fifty-five degrees.[8] In another, a young assistant priest pleaded for
a new assignment. He didn't want to be perceived as a "quitter," he clarified, but Finnegan's penchant for control left him without any meaningful work to do.[9] In 1949, a veteran priest penned a request for transfer for
the first time in twenty years. "Conditions here are anything but conge-
nial," he stated.[10]

But none were blunter about Finnegan's pastoral failures than his parishioners. In a 1928 letter, a St. Mary's parishioner named Charles
O'Connor wrote to the cardinal to lament that Finnegan "allows no one
to have a difference of opinion, and an expression of an opinion would
bring forth his immediate resentment." The people of St. Mary's "endure
him," O'Connor wrote, "because they could do nothing else." While con-
ceding that Finnegan did the essentials—administering sacraments to the
dying, offering Masses for the dead—O'Connor concluded that "[t]here
seems to be no bond of sympathetic co-operation between Pastor and
people—and people and their Pastor—nor can there be." O'Connor begged
the cardinal's forgiveness for the letter—"a peculiar and unusual course"
for a layman, he acknowledged—but underscored that writing it was a last
resort, meant "to call attention to a condition that is not healthy and will
not get better and may result in an open breach that may cause grave
scandal."[11]

The following year, a parishioner identifying himself as J. C. McCuller
penned a less apologetic note. McCuller began with a blunt question: "Do
you expect the present generation to respect the Priesthood when Pastors
show us differently[?]"[12] Accusing Finnegan of being "only a minister,"
McCuller, like O'Connor, conveyed a certain recognition that the prevailing
understanding of the role of clergy was insufficient. The priest should be
more than a sacramental dispenser, both men seemed to say; the wall of
separation between the priest and his community was a detriment to both.
An equally scathing indictment came in another letter to the chancery

almost a decade later. Calling the situation at St. Mary's "an injustice," the anonymous writer begged Cardinal O'Connell to launch an investigation of the "tyrannical" Finnegan. The letter is signed, "Disgusted Parishioner."[13]

Finnegan's evident disdain for the laity was more than a personality flaw. In a parish that was marginalized and underfunded from the day it was established, these abuses of clerical leadership splintered Egleston Square's already fragile Catholic community. According to a 1942 letter from parishioner Helen L. Mullen—the only such correspondence on record signed by a woman—Finnegan's weekly hour-long tirades from the pulpit against the evils of birth control were so explicit that she was embarrassed for the young altar boys who had to hear them. Even when other priests were celebrating the Mass, Finnegan would materialize at the point of the homily, ascending to the ambo and launching into his weekly invective against whatever social ill or personal grievance was freshest in his mind. Finnegan was infamous in Egleston, Mullen reported; his rants were the talk of the town. By driving people away from St. Mary's, he was also undermining the life of the community:

> The parish is so small that I doubt, if everyone attended, the revenue would be adequate, but he is losing it every week instead of gaining it, for a very great number of the parishioners go to other churches just to hear Mass in peace and quietude. I know I would arrange my budget to give him a dollar a week if I could be sure he would stay down off the pulpit and let the other priests talk now and then. Surely they must know how.[14]

Like many of her fellow parishioners, Mullen had begun to boycott St. Mary's, crossing parish boundaries in search of a less dysfunctional spiritual environment. "I will send him my 'support' at Christmas and Easter and for the yearly collection, but I'll go to another church to hear Mass the way it seems to me it should be heard," she concluded. "And a lot of other persons will continue to go to the other churches."[15] Faced with a tyrannical pastor and a seemingly unresponsive chancery, the laity's only recourse was to withhold the most valuable asset they had: themselves.

Parishioners also lamented the state of relationships between the parish and the world around it. Egleston Square's Catholics seem to have felt a responsibility to be good neighbors on account of their minority status, an instinct evidently not shared by their pastor. Writing on behalf of "the people in Roxbury," McCuller lamented his embarrassment over Finnegan's parsimony toward their neighbors: "Think of the feeling our Jewish neighbors have for us when our Pastor buys fourteen and fifteen cents worth of stew meat from one of their nearby markets," he wrote. ("This has been witnessed by the writer," he added, perhaps preemptively exonerating himself from accusations of hearsay.[16]) For his part, Finnegan made no effort to conceal his disdain for his neighbors, once describing Egleston Square's growing Jewish population as "an invasion."[17]

Laity in the pre–Vatican II period are commonly portrayed as engaging in parish participation with passive compliance—the so-called "pay, pray, and obey" approach. But as this record of correspondence suggests, St. Mary's parishioners evinced unwillingness to do any of the above, at least not without a fight. The world of early-twentieth-century Catholic Boston was one characterized by clear delimitations of power, highly circumscribed hierarchical relationships, and well-defined parish boundaries. Unable to appeal to formal ecclesial structures of lay authority or theologies of ministry that would have supported collaboration, parishioners had to be tactical in their resistance, creating space for dissent within fixed, preexisting structures and with the resources and possibilities available to them.[18] They withheld money, crossed parish boundaries to attend other churches, and took the bold, insubordinate step of voicing their need for intervention to a cardinal archbishop who would come to be known for his princely, dismissive air.[19]

Yet despite their risky dissent, laity were still at the mercy of archdiocesan authorities to change their situation. Cardinal O'Connell, for his part, evinced little concern about the situation at St. Mary's. Instead of addressing parishioner laments, O'Connell apparently forwarded their letters to Finnegan himself, who responded by lashing out at his congregation.[20] Assistant priests who raised concerns had better luck than the laity did. Often, they were relieved of their assignments and transferred to other parishes. Records show that many lasted only a few months before they were driven out by Finnegan's bullying.[21] Finnegan would remain pastor of St. Mary's until 1953—thirty-seven years in total. By the time he was finally replaced, the parish was on the brink of ruin. "Many years of indifference, lack of pastoral direction and indifference to Mass and the Sacraments have left the district in a sorry plight," Finnegan's successor

Rev. James P. Donovan wrote. The stately parish house was crumbling, the church's finances were in shambles, and participation was marginal.[22]

Interpreted in an ecclesiological light, the letters of lament penned by parishioners throughout the 1920s, '30s, and '40s decried the barriers to solidarity both *ad intra* and *ad extra* within the power structure of the pre–Vatican II parish. Descriptions of their "tyrannical" pastor expose both the spiritual and practical dangers of the overly calcified boundary between clergy and laity. The letters hint, too, at the ambiguous role of a territorial parish in a mostly non-Catholic urban neighborhood, suggesting the fruitlessness of a defensive stance against the world and other faith traditions in a religiously pluralistic context. The following decade would bring the Second Vatican Council. With it came the clarion call to respond to the signs of the times, the compelling ecclesiological image of the church as the people of God, the explicit incorporation of laity into the mission of the church, a renewed understanding of the church's presence in and for the world, new structures of collaborative leadership, and a pervasive sense of creative hope in the future. But the experiences of these early parishioners suggest that some of what was revolutionary about Vatican II was as much a response to dynamics already active at the parish level as it was the introduction of something new. Put another way, Vatican II created the conditions for the spirit of lay participation already simmering below the surface to become ecclesially and ecclesiologically meaningful.

Vatican II and the Roxbury Apostolate: Solidarity with the City

> Sister Marie Augusta [SND, of Emmanuel College] told us once why some Christians can be racists without realizing they are wrong. "When you don't know, it doesn't bother your conscience." . . . We have come to know, and our consciences are bothering us.
>
> "The Roxbury Report," 1964[23]

By the early 1960s, white residents of Roxbury had begun to move en masse to the suburbs, taking jobs, industries, and tax revenue with them. The white parishioners who remained at St. Mary's were aging. Meanwhile, younger African American families and growing communities from Puerto Rico, Cape Verde, Trinidad, Cuba, Haiti, and elsewhere had settled in the neighborhoods around Egleston Square. In Roxbury, people of color faced a matrix of oppression exacerbated by the siphoning effect of suburbanization and decades of redlining.[24] As Massachusetts State Representative and Boston community activist Mel King later put it, "[The] systematic denial of jobs, housing, education and political representation by the Boston power structure came to full development in the creation of the 'ghetto,' for the image of the ghetto allowed the ruling elite to blame the Black community for what they had systematically imposed upon us."[25]

Viewed as the epicenter of urban decline, Roxbury came to be seen by city officials and archdiocesan authorities alike as the consummate Boston "ghetto," the notorious problem child of "inner-city" Boston.[26] "Blighted" neighborhoods around Roxbury were the targets of 1960s-era urban renewal projects, some of which did more to displace poor Black residents than they did to meaningfully rejuvenate the area.[27] Exacerbating Roxbury's decline was the prospect of a massive, eight-lane highway project slated to cut directly through the heart of Egleston Square. To clear land for the Southwest Expressway, the city had begun to displace residents by eminent domain, most of whom were low-income minorities and immigrants. Precarious neighborhoods were torn apart as homes were razed. Neighborhood activists from Roxbury, Jamaica Plain, Hyde Park, and the South End—St. Mary's parishioners among them—united in 1969 to stop the catastrophic highway project. But damage had already been done.[28] Destabilizing Roxbury neighborhoods had also further destabilized its parishes.

For the church in Boston, the city's increasingly gaping racial divide was also a geographical and parochial one. As a Boston Redevelopment Authority report later observed, "As the wave of suburbanization . . . swept over the country, Boston [was] sorely impacted, but Roxbury was devastated."[29] Middle- and upper-class white Catholics were to be found increasingly in suburban parishes, while predominantly poor Black and Hispanic Catholics were disproportionately concentrated in urban centers and worshipped in underresourced inner-city parishes like St. Mary's. For some archdiocesan leaders, the racial divide had become a source of major pastoral concern, even as ecclesial dynamics contributed to the rift. Virulent racism was a persistent feature of the Boston Catholic landscape. In 1964, Cardinal Cushing issued a statement on Pentecost imploring Boston

Catholics to eradicate racism from their parishes, neighborhoods, and hearts. To pastors, he wrote:

> I say we are facing an evil of enormous dimensions; this evil has crept into some corner of every parish. There are those kneeling each week at the Lord's table whose heart is turned against the just appeals of the Negroes here in our own Archdiocese. Occupy the front lines in this battle against evil. From your pulpit and in your schools, in parish meetings and in your contracts with men everywhere, work constantly to erase the evil of race hatred and the subtler evil of hard-hearted indifference![30]

Later that summer, Cushing issued another statement: "The time for polite talking is done. The racist Christian is a contradiction."[31] Cushing often took bold public stances against racism, decrying the hypocrisy of white Catholics who participated in the sacraments on Sunday yet spent the rest of the week with their backs turned to their neighbors of color. He once bluntly reminded believers that the consequence for the sin of racism is hell: "The price of segregation here below," he warned, "may well be segregation for all eternity from the company of the elect."[32]

Yet despite Cushing's fervent appeals to Catholic social doctrine to denounce racial injustice, and despite the efforts of organizations like Boston's Catholic Interracial Council (CIC), white Catholic attitudes on race remained virtually unchanged. In 1965, the CIC wrote in a report that "the majority of Negroes is now convinced beyond any doubt that the majority of white Catholics, lay and cleric, is against them." Black Catholics "find themselves facing a crisis of faith by reason of the fact that the white voters of Boston, overwhelmingly Catholic, seem to have locked the door to the ghetto and thrown away the key."[33] Indeed, racist upheaval over bussing-based school integration that would define the following decade would be led largely by white Catholics.[34]

It was clear that the Boston Catholic church's racism problem would not be solved by powerful words, nor by prayerfully waiting for white Catholics to have a change of heart. What was needed instead was a structural commitment to city parishes and their people. In the summer of 1964, the archdiocese sent a group of seminarians to participate in a monthlong inner-city immersion at St. Joseph's Parish in Roxbury. During their weeks in the city, the men worked for community organizations like the newly

established Massachusetts Freedom Movement, conducted a parish census by visiting parishioners in their homes, and led voter registration
drives. In the evenings, they heard lectures from local leaders, organizers, and educators, including Mel King and David S. Nelson, president of
the CIC. The seminarians collected their critical reflections on the experience in a report to Cushing.[35] The Roxbury Report, as they titled their
conclusions, detailed the urgent need for a pastoral approach to the inner
city grounded in a more prophetic stance against racial and economic
injustice and greater cooperation between parishes and local community
organizations. In language that prefigured *Gaudium et Spes*, the report
read:

> Social action demands involvement, some direct, concrete commitment
> as an expression of concern and fellowship with the world Christ has
> redeemed. For many reasons, the Church in our society seems often to
> have overlooked its mission by refusing to become involved in the civic
> community. In a pluralistic society, selfless community service is an ob-
> ligation of churchmen. Our neighbor, the object of the Second Great
> Commandment and the Beatitudes is he who has a need, be he Chris-
> tian or not, nearby or not, of one's class or not.[36]

What the Roxbury Report advocated for was both a comprehensive revaluation of the world and a reconsideration of the church's mission in that
world. Indicting the institutional church for its neglect of the inner city,
a neglect based in part on the fact that most African Americans in Boston
were not Catholic and therefore not objects of the church's concern, the
report declared that the church's mission of salvation necessarily entailed solidarity between both the church and the world, and among persons and communities of different races, cultures, classes, and religions.
As Ormond Rush puts it, "The council's theology of mission is a theology
of ecclesial presence in the world."[37] The Roxbury Report, like the con-
current Second Vatican Council, espoused a vision of salvation that regarded God at work in the transformation of human society toward the
realization of a "genuinely human life" (GS 26). *Gaudium et Spes*, promulgated the following year, would declare the church's support for social
movements that take up the work of promoting the common good (GS 41,
42). It would cast public work as salvific work and its primary agents, the
laity, as partners in the church's mission of salvation.

Most striking was the Roxbury Report's examination of the fraught relationship between suburban and urban parishes, a proxy for describing the relationship between white Catholics and Catholics of color. The report states:

> The evils of poverty and discrimination do not flow from the fact that people in the suburbs have property while people in the inner-city do not. The evil is that one community excludes the other, that the so-called Christian in the suburb denies his neighbor in need, who happens to be in or from Roxbury, the right to attain the level of human decency he has attained. This is what we mean when we say the sickness of Roxbury is the sickness of the suburbs.[38]

In essence, the report contended that the fundamental problem was white Catholics' refusal of solidarity to their Black and Brown neighbors. Placing the church's neglect of Roxbury in historical perspective makes the irony of this neglect particularly striking. Most parishes in Roxbury, like St. Mary's, were established during a period of nineteenth- and early-twentieth-century church-building fueled by a steadfast commitment to providing for the spiritual and social needs of immigrant Catholics. The commitment to the poor and working-class faithful was so all-encompassing that it was practically excessive—so many parishes were built that some, like St. Mary's, never served that many parishioners. But as the Boston Irish seized postwar opportunities for upward mobility, so did the church. Once African Americans began moving into the city, the church, like many of its white faithful, made a preferential option for the suburbs.

The Roxbury Report concluded that racial injustice in Boston parish life could only be addressed by a systemic ecclesial recommitment to the city. Later that summer, Cushing sent letters to the pastors of Roxbury parishes stating that the problems facing their communities—"the encroachment by industrial firms, the razing of considerable housing, the relocation of many of your parishioners"—were more than any one of them could handle on their own.[39] In August 1964, just before departing for Rome to begin the third session of Vatican II, Cushing announced his intention to create a missionary apostolate for "the renewal of the life of the Church lived in its inner-city parishes."[40] He put out a call for priest-volunteers "ready to give their all to the poorest of the poor."[41]

When Cushing returned from Rome that November, he immediately convened the group that would become known as the Roxbury Apostolate. The third session of Vatican II had produced the Dogmatic Constitution on the Church, *Lumen Gentium*, as well as the Decree on Ecumenism. Both of these documents, in different ways, encouraged Catholics to think more expansively about the church's boundaries, imagining the church primarily as a community of cooperation in mission rather than as a rigid hierarchy. No doubt fresh in Cushing's mind was *Lumen Gentium*'s emphasis on the duty of bishops "to instruct the faithful to love for the whole mystical body of Christ, especially for its poor and sorrowing members and for those who are suffering persecution for justice's sake" (LG 23). *Lumen Gentium*'s solidaristic, socially oriented vision of salvation cast the cultivation of community as an urgent dimension of the church's mission. In this way, the Roxbury Apostolate is a case study in the immediate local reception of the council's ecclesiological vision.

The Roxbury Apostolate would begin in three parishes: St. Philip, St. Joseph, and St. Mary of the Angels. Each would be assigned a pastor, a parish administrator, and a deacon from among the volunteers. At an early preparatory meeting, the men were given a reading list that included not only Karl Rahner's *The Christian Commitment,* but also Martin Luther King, Jr.'s *Why We Can't Wait,* Dorothy Day's *Loaves and Fishes,* Michael Harrington's *The Other America,* and local Roxbury Episcopal priest John Harmon's "The Church and the City: The Need for a New Theology."[42] The bibliography, filled with works by non-Catholics, African Americans, and women, offered a glimpse of the profound cultural shift underway in the church at the time.

Reflecting the changing perception of the parish as a community, one of the main questions the apostolate volunteers grappled with in the months leading up to the start of their ministry was how to "[form] a parish community from the many ethnic, age and economic groups in the area."[43] Indeed, at stake in the Roxbury plan was not only the immediate needs of the inner city but also the larger structural question of whether the parish, as it existed, was adequate to respond to the exigencies of the times. If, as the Roxbury Report concluded, the problem was a lack of interracial and interclass solidarity, then the question was whether the parish structure was equipped to foster the kind of solidarity necessary to address the injustices dividing the church. Under conditions of profound social inequality and searing racial injustice, could a parish ever be a community?

The question was a topic of intense debate. According to minutes of the first apostolate preparatory meeting, some present argued that the parochial structure was inadequate and should be abandoned. The lack of contact between priests and laity, the disconnect between priests' standards of living and that of the people, and the perception of the rectory as the priests' private mansion rather than as a community resource all fortified the wall of separation that divided clergy from laity. Moreover, "since parish lines do not reflect the structure of the community," parish boundaries impeded rather than enhanced the church's ability to serve and unite the community in an integral way. Others voiced support for the existing parish structure. Most of this support was circumstantial: People already felt bound by a sense of loyalty to their parishes, loyalty that would be disrupted with the introduction of a new system of belonging. Parish infrastructure—church buildings, schools, rectories—already existed. In a resource-strapped situation, why reinvent the wheel? Moreover, proposing a new structure would also pose needless canonical challenges. Finally, some argued, to abandon the parish system in the inner city could invite the resentment of other priests, who might view the entire project as either irrelevant or exclusivist.[44]

Ultimately, they settled on a middle way. The Roxbury Apostolate would work within the existing parish structure while fostering cooperation over parish lines, "making sure that the nature of the parish is such that it serves the needs of the people."[45] Clergy selected for ministry in Roxbury were instructed to begin by immersing themselves in the lived realities of the people of their parish—to "read the signs of the times"—and to allow a stance of solidarity to guide their pastoral approach. They were to adopt a standard of living equal to that of their mostly impoverished parishioners.[46] Rectories would become open-doored "parish houses," spaces for community gathering and welcome, breaking down boundaries between clergy and laity and between church and community.[47]

The goal of the Roxbury Apostolate was to revitalize parish structures by cultivating an organic, porous relationship between the church and the world, between the parish and the neighborhood. Apostolate priests were urged to work ecumenically and to collaborate with one another across parish lines, recognizing that the "church in the inner city is part of a complex urban structure."[48] They were instructed to empower the laity, working to ensure that parish leadership reflected that of the local community: "Who are the neighborhood leaders to whom people go for advice[?] These should be the Church's lay leaders."[49] They were urged to support local credit unions, cooperatives, and workers' unions, to involve themselves in civic affairs, and to advocate publicly on behalf of their people. Mercy and understanding were key. As the men were reminded at their final meeting before taking up their new posts, they should not "[expect] a person to let us take care of his 'psyche' while there are rats in his children's beds."[50] They were advised to approach their new roles with open minds, prepared to embrace unconventional and experimental pastoral solutions such as storefront pastoral centers in the name of serving their people. Above all, they were to treat the laity with humility and a spirit of collaboration, overtly rejecting the paternalism that had long characterized their role: "We must be mobile, open to change, open and willing to change ourselves."[51]

On February 23, 1965, Fr. Henry F. Barry (not to be confused with Fr. Henry A. Barry, St. Mary's first pastor of the same name), Fr. Lawrence Perry, and Deacon Thomas Corrigan moved into the parish house and set about heeding their mandate to read the signs of the times. They established a summer camp to offer relief to working parents and an escape for Egleston Square's kids. Parishioner Florence, whose children attended the summer camp in those days, remembered with a chuckle that every Monday, Barry would round up the neighborhood kids and take them for ice cream at the Howard Johnson's down the street.[52] Given the broader ecclesial backdrop of their 1965 arrival, another one of their initial tasks was to renovate the church sanctuary in line with Vatican II's liturgical reforms. Fr. Perry drew up the renovation plans himself; given the parish's limited budget, most of the construction was completed by parish volunteers who worked as carpenters and painters.[53]

Barry wrote to the chancery for permission to replace the church's pipe organ with a small electric one "sufficient for our basement church." He later received permission to sell off an antique chandelier hanging in the parish house to help the church pay its bills.[54] In 1967, arsonists twice broke into the church and set it on fire, forcing the priests to lock

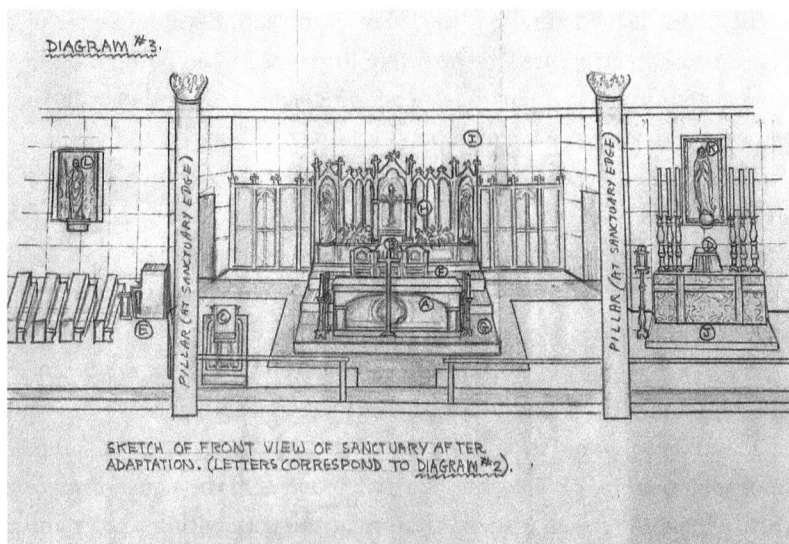

FIGURE 3. Renovation plans for the St. Mary of the Angels sanctuary drawn up by Rev. Lawrence Perry in response to the liturgical changes following Vatican II, 1965. St. Mary of the Angels Correspondence File, Roman Catholic Archdiocese of Boston.

it during the week. Barry converted the front office of the parish house into a simple chapel, welcoming parishioners into the rectory for daily Mass.[55] Weekday Masses and communion services are still celebrated there today. At some point between then and now, a former pastor used shoe polish to paint the amber windows with a mosaic of the Beatitudes swirling over the Boston skyline: *Blessed are the peacemakers; Blessed are the poor in spirit; Blessed are they who suffer persecution; For theirs is the kingdom of heaven.*

What became of the pastoral experiment in Roxbury is not clear. I did not come across any evaluative reports or follow-up records of the Roxbury Apostolate in archdiocesan archives. What is clear is that the archdiocese's commitment to solidarity with the inner city was short lived and, as such, did little to address the systemic asymmetries of power and resources that marginalized Catholics of color in Boston. Cushing's successor was Portuguese American bishop Humberto Medeiros, whose storied commitment to racial and economic justice was emblematized by his iconic 1972 pastoral letter "Man's Cities and God's Poor." Despite the scope of this commitment, parish conditions in Roxbury declined. By the

FIGURE 4. The window of the parish house chapel, painted with shoe polish by a former pastor. Photo by the author.

early 1970s, reports from area priests suggest that the state of affairs at St. Mary's was as bad as it had ever been. The open rectory—so ideal sounding in the rosy glow of Vatican II—had become a serious problem as boundaries dissolved completely. The parish was badly understaffed and plagued with clergy infighting. In 1972 and '73, St. Mary's priests were robbed at gunpoint four times in six months. Scared for their own safety and ground down by parish dysfunction, clergy isolated themselves from the neighborhood.[56] In communications sent to Cardinal Medeiros throughout the summer of 1976, clergy in Roxbury collectively lamented the lack of "sensitivity . . . given to the validity of inner city ministry."[57] According to notes from one meeting of the Roxbury clergy, a priest at nearby St. Joseph's Parish complained that the inner city seemed to be where bishops sent "displaced" priests.[58] Updates from St. Mary of the Angels were not included in the communications because by then, it did not have any full-time clergy at all. By the time Fr. Jack Roussin arrived at the parish in December 1976, he was met by eight parishioners at Mass and a Sunday collection totaling $8.80.[59]

Why did the Roxbury Apostolate ultimately fail to make lasting change at St. Mary's? As an archdiocesan initiative, it was propelled by the spirit and rhetoric of both the War on Poverty and the Second Vatican Council and was informed largely by impressions of life in Roxbury from the white, mostly-outsider seminarians and priests who served there temporarily. (Until the mid-1970s, Boston only had one African American priest).[60] While Apostolate organizers encouraged volunteer priests to eschew paternalism toward their parishioners, preparatory meeting minutes nevertheless evince how deeply engrained such attitudes were. The "Negroes, Puerto Ricans, Cubans, and others" of Roxbury were portrayed as powerless, inarticulate, and uneducated, living in filth, reliant on welfare, products of broken homes, and tragically deprived of the virtues of a stable Christian family life. Meanwhile, while the archdiocese's Roxbury initiatives also included a parish-sharing program that partnered inner-city parishes with wealthy suburban ones for financial and charitable support, they demanded virtually nothing of suburban whites, the group whose resistance to interracial solidarity was identified as the problem in the first place. Furthermore, because the pastoral program was introduced "from above," it was predicated on the chancery's authority to install priests in parishes and withdraw them at will. While the program was implemented with an ostensibly genuine desire to do good for Roxbury, the fact remained that archdiocesan support for the upstart program could be withdrawn as swiftly as it was given. Given that I found no traces of follow-up on the program in RCAB archives, this seems to be exactly what happened. Concern for the crisis-state of Roxbury parishes continued, but the sense of urgency and spirit of hope-filled solidarity emblematized by the apostolate faded away. In a hierarchical institution characterized by frequent personnel change, even the worthiest pastoral initiatives can atrophy when the individual who pioneers them is transferred to another post, or when budgetary constraints demand (or offer a convenient excuse for) their dissolution. Thus, while it would be easy to look at this period in St. Mary's history as a hopeful but ultimately unsuccessful experiment in the parish-level implementation of Vatican II's vision of solidarity, what the story of the Roxbury Apostolate actually suggests is the failure of a certain genre of solidarity that relies primarily on transitory institutional goodwill.

The Parish Pastoral Council: Solidarity in the City

The fleeting success and ambiguous end of the Roxbury Apostolate invite a shift in focus to the grassroots. How did the laity in Roxbury receive the Second Vatican Council's message of solidarity? At St. Mary's, the tradition of lay dissent fomented during the unhappy Finnegan years laid the foundation for what became a radical turn to lay leadership after Vatican II. The source of this change was the advent of the parish pastoral council. Vatican II recommended the incorporation of laypeople into parish leadership in an advisory capacity, particularly with respect to its pastoral and apostolic work. *Apostolicam Actuositatem*, the Decree on the Apostolate of the Laity, laid the groundwork for structures of cooperation and collaboration between clergy, religious, and laity:

> In dioceses, insofar as possible, there should be councils which assist the apostolic work of the Church either in the field of evangelization and sanctification or in the charitable, social, or other spheres, and here it is fitting that the clergy and Religious should cooperate with the laity. While preserving the proper character and autonomy of each organization, these councils will be able to promote the mutual coordination of various lay associations and enterprises. Councils of this type should be established as far as possible also on the parochial, interparochial,

and interdiocesan level as well as in the national or international sphere. (AA 26)[61]

Lay-ordained collaboration was also implied in *Lumen Gentium*, which advised pastors to "willingly employ [the] prudent advice" of the laity and to encourage them to "undertake tasks on their own initiative" (LG 37).

Following Vatican II, the Archdiocese of Boston released guidelines urging parishes to form pastoral councils "for that uniting of hierarchy and laity which the council sees as absolutely necessary."[62] Some of the initial details were hazy; the structure and purpose of parish councils would be reinterpreted, clarified, and eventually codified in the 1983 revision of the Code of Canon Law.[63] But at St. Mary's, parishioners aching for a sense of agency perceived an opening and ran through it, establishing a Parish Council of their own. The fourteen-person council included six laymen, five laywomen, and the parish's deacon and two priests. Members were mainly Irish, Italian, and African American. During the spring and summer of 1969, the Parish Council made a series of bold decisions to place the struggling parish into a relationship of costly solidarity with the marginalized people and neighborhoods it served.

On March 16, 1969, a typewritten letter landed on the desk of Fr. William Calter, the parish administrator at St. Mary's. As it turned out, the letter was from his own Parish Council. Their chairman, Darrell Simpson, wrote to inform Fr. Calter that the council—apparently without the presence of Calter himself—had voted to transfer the parish's bank accounts from the First National Bank of Boston to the Unity Bank and Trust Company of Roxbury. The move, Simpson explained, would demonstrate solidarity with the Black community in and around the parish:

> As you know, the Unity Bank and Trust Company is the first black operated bank in our city. It is a community bank, serving the needs of the community. The transferal of our parish funds to this bank is a small but eloquent expression of attitude on the part of the parish and the church. In actively supporting the bank, we show an interest in the community and its people, who are parishioners.[64]

"Please inform the diocese of our decision," the letter concluded. This was not a request.

Fr. Calter did as the Parish Council directed. Composing a letter to the chancery to request the transfer of funds, he attached a copy of the Parish Council's letter to his own. At the chancery, the letters set off alarm bells. The amount of power that clergy at St. Mary's had apparently ceded to laity was unfathomable. "I believe there are two problems here," began an internal memo from the archdiocesan chancellor to Cardinal Cushing. "It is my understanding that the council is not policy making, but it is rather advisory in nature. If it is policy making, then we have no choice but to agree. I question whether it is policy making for this would place the Cardinal in a subordinate role." The second problem was financial: Unity Bank and Trust charged higher fees than the parish's current bank did. The decision would cost the cash-strapped parish money that it barely had. Cushing ultimately granted the request, but only under the condition that Calter advise the headstrong Parish Council as to their proper place in the administrative structure of the parish—that was, outside of it.[65]

The council persisted, undeterred by Cushing's rebuke of the authority they claimed. They had begun their work by rethinking their community's economic commitments; now they shifted their focus to its liturgical life. That spring, at the behest of St. Mary's Spiritual Development Committee, the Parish Council voted unanimously to request archdiocesan permission to celebrate the Sunday Mass on Saturday evenings during the summer, "on the basis of pastoral experiment." The anticipatory Saturday liturgy was an outcome of Vatican II whose implementation was still under development at the time. For the people of St. Mary's, offering Mass on Saturday evenings instead of Sunday would address a "pastoral-liturgical problem which seems very evident during the summer season each year"— that was, "the unfortunate conflict between Sunday Mass participation and legitimate recreation outside the city on the one day when this is possible." The council explained:

> We realize that this conflict exists in many parishes; yet we realize that most of our people do not have the pleasure of a summer cottage or the luxury of weekends away from home. Economically, this is out of their reach. The only opportunity for any relaxation away from the oppressive pace and heat of the city is a day trip on Sunday.

If Saturday Mass were not possible, the council proposed an unconventional work-around: Perhaps, they suggested, the parish could begin the

Sunday liturgy at midnight.[66] When they didn't receive a reply, Fr. Perry phoned the Chancellor, who responded that he "considered it somehow inappropriate that the letter should come from the Parish Council rather than from the Parish Administrator."[67] Cushing dismissed the inventive midnight Mass idea, but at the council's urging, he applied to the Holy See for the dispensation necessary to celebrate the Sunday liturgy on Saturday evenings.[68] When the Vatican finally granted the dispensation, it gave Cushing the authority to allow the accommodation to any parish in the archdiocese that requested it. In postconciliar Boston, then, the first Saturday evening Masses were celebrated because working-class, city-dwelling laypeople insisted that they deserved a day of leisure and rest.

The biggest fight the council took on during the summer of '69 was for funds to construct a desperately needed parish hall. That May, the Parish Council sent yet another letter to Cardinal Cushing, this time accusing the archdiocese of mismanaging the parish's accounts. According to financial records dating back to the 1930s, they argued, St. Mary's should have had more than $150,000 to its name. But now, parish records indicated a balance of only $6,000, plus $15,000 worth of debt from church roof repairs in 1968. "As you no doubt realize, your Eminence," they wrote, "the whole inner-city church is in serious physical and financial shape. We do have real needs here at St. Marys [sic]."[69] Complicating matters was Calter's apparent reluctance to pursue the matter with the archdiocese himself. Circumventing their priest, the Parish Council appealed to the Archdiocesan Commission for the Promotion of Parish Councils for support. After a hearing, the Commission ruled that St. Mary's Parish Council had the right to present their concerns to Cushing. In a stunning show of support for lay authority, the commission chair concluded, "Accordingly the veto of Father Calter is overruled by a unanimous vote of the members present."[70] Buoyed by their success, the Parish Council sent a renewed request to Cardinal Cushing along with a copy of their "verdict." The reply was swift and blunt. It is the pastor's job to administer the parish, Cushing wrote. Parish Councils were formed to advise, not govern. Moreover, he stated, the Commission for the Promotion of Parish Councils had no authority whatsoever to hear an appeal like theirs and never should have done so in the first place. To grant this kind of power to laity, he concluded, would be to take away the administrative authority of the pastor. Their request for funds was denied.

The decisions St. Mary's fledgling Parish Council made in 1969 placed its parishioners into relationships of concrete solidarity with one another and the local community. The decisions were costly in more ways than one. As noted, moving the parish's accounts to the Black-operated bank resulted in a small but consequential financial loss for a parish so poor that it relied on subsidies from the archdiocese just to keep its lights on. But the Parish Council's decisions also cost the parish social capital. The laity's show of strength invited the suspicion of the archdiocese on whose support St. Mary's relied for its survival and placed the community at odds with one of its own priests.

The decisions were also about power—a demonstration of the laity's willingness to lead and a defiance of the hegemony of clerical authority that had so often proven unreliable. It is helpful to compare the Parish Council's matter-of-fact letters with the desperate missives that parishioners sent the chancery during the Finnegan years. By 1969, many parishioners' experiential formation in community activism was evident in the clarity and specificity of their demands, suggesting the influence of grassroots organizing on urban parish life during this period. Yet though the two sets of letters are distinct in both tone and context, in both cases the moral clarity of parishioners' calls for redress is evident. In both contexts, laity also evince an awareness that any fight for justice in and for their parish fell primarily on them. What set the latter demands apart, ultimately, was the presence of a structure whereby the laity could claim a voice in parish governance. As chancery officials were quick to point out, and as subsequent ecclesiastical interpretations of parish councils made clear, St. Mary's laity were exercising authority that they did not technically possess. Parish councils were to function more like advisory boards for priests than as boards of directors. Yet in a church that previously accorded laity no formal role in the direction of parish affairs, the parish pastoral council—even in its advisory capacity—felt like a real opening, a seat at the table. It was not so much a case of using "the master's tools to deconstruct the master's house," as Audre Lorde warned against, but rather something more tactical: using the master's tools to open the house's doors as wide as they could go without falling off the hinges.[71] Despite the dismal conditions of the ensuing years—conditions that arose from extreme institutional neglect—this solidarity became the early Parish Council's greatest legacy and eventually, as we will see in the final chapter of this book, the singular cause of the parish's survival.

Arising fundamentally from Vatican II's reaffirmation of the baptismal priesthood of all believers (LG 10), the introduction of the parish pastoral council into parish life made the voicing of lay concerns not only structurally possible but also ecclesiologically meaningful. Whereas the Roxbury Apostolate's well-intentioned attempt at cultivating solidarity was fleeting because it came "from above," it is not entirely accurate to say that the St. Mary's Parish Council helped to foment interracial solidarity "from below." Vatican II—the consummate example of ecclesial change from above in the modern era—created the conditions and structures whereby laity at St. Mary's could exercise power "from below." Their use of that power was tightly circumscribed by structures and norms of ecclesial authority at the parish, diocesan, and Vatican curial levels. Vatican II was also responsible for the theological language and ideas that implicitly and explicitly framed the Parish Council's decision-making processes: *Gaudium et Spes*'s call to read the signs of the times (which was influenced by Joseph Cardijn's "see, judge, act" method, itself an intervention "from below"); *Sacrosanctum Concilium*'s emphasis on deep continuity between liturgy and life; *Lumen Gentium*'s image of the church as the people of God; and the impetus toward pastoral experimentation and creativity encouraged by its historical consciousness and expansive notions of mission and salvation. In reading St. Mary's as a case study in the practical reception of Vatican II's vision of solidarity, it would be too simplistic to speak of an "ecclesiology from below" without recognizing how institutional forces both ignited and regulated the conditions for lay leadership at the grassroots level, even in the most unconventional ways. In the story of St. Mary's, we glimpse the complex, contentious, and ultimately iterative relationship between the "above" and "below" of post–Vatican II parish life and activism.

Conclusion

When I first started asking parishioners about the sources of their friendships at St. Mary's—especially their friendships with parishioners of other races, ethnicities, and life situations—I expected them to wax poetic about the beauty of worshipping in such an inclusive community or receiving the Eucharist alongside believers from all walks of life.

Instead, they talked about Parish Council meetings.

Amelia, the white English Mass parishioner who "migrated over to St. Mary of the Angels" after a disappointing leadership transition at her former parish, had served on the council for years. "I go to Parish Council [and think], *Oh, I love all these people!*" she laughed. "You know, so it's the same tired issues. But I still love all these people." I asked her what about it was so special for her. "It's sort of the power of the laity persisting through all the ups and downs and transitions of pastors," she explained.[72] While parish leadership is typically associated with its priests, clergy have been the least consistent dimension of life at St. Mary's. Instead, the Parish Council has been a source of stability and continuity through decades of flux. When, more recently, St. Mary's received a pastor many initially viewed as regressive and divisive, one member commented to me, "Well, we'll just have to teach him what it means to be part of St. Mary's." There was a strong awareness that the laity, not the clergy, were the primary bearers of the community's story. On a fundamental level, parishioners understood the Parish Council as the guardian of their church's history and tradition, their own local magisterium.

The Parish Council's persistence has also been the source of deep friendships across difference. Claudia, the longtime council member from the Dominican Republic, echoed Amelia's love for her fellow parishioners. When I asked her whom she felt closest to at the parish, many of those she named were longtime English Mass attendees. "We worked together for so many years," she explained, specifically referencing the community organizing that the council undertook in 2004 to save St. Mary's from closure. The theme of solidarity arising from moments of crisis was an undercurrent in many parishioners' stories. "This is the group that I—for any problem that happen to any of the parishioners—I can just call and say, *Listen, we have to sit down and resolve this. Okay?* So I feel like I have a closeness with them."

When Claudia was first tapped to represent the Spanish community on the council in the 1980s, she nearly quit. As an English language–learner, she had a hard time understanding the accents of some of her African American counterparts. "The first three times that I went to a meeting, I came out with a *terrible* migraine headache," she recalled with an exasperated sigh. A religious sister on the council begged her to stay. The sizeable but relatively more nascent Spanish-speaking community rightly felt unrepresented in parish decision-making, but for a variety of reasons—the power imbalance between the two linguistic communities, differing models of authority, scheduling conflicts—leaders were having a hard time persuading Spanish Mass parishioners to come to the meetings. From then on, Claudia recalled, "I was always in every meeting. Because I wanted to know what was going on. And that's why I always said, 'If you don't come to the meeting, you don't have the right to complain when the Anglos try to do something. Because you're not there to say no.' And that took a long time—a long, long time."[73]

Today, unlike when Claudia first arrived, the Parish Council roster is mostly balanced between English and Spanish Mass parishioners, and every meeting is held bilingually. The council is always led by two cochairs, one from each Mass community. Compared to overall parish demographics, however, members of the shrinking English Mass community remain overrepresented in leadership, indicating the persistence of barriers to participation even in communities highly committed to inclusion. At the same time, it was striking to me how many parishioners I talked to had served on the council at some point. As I observed, laity at St. Mary's treated leadership not as a position to be earned through seniority, specialized training, or proximity to clerical power but rather as the right and duty of all the faithful, a notion reaffirmed by Vatican II's emphasis on the priesthood of all believers. As Claudia's story (not to mention my own inclusion on the council) illustrates, the Parish Council was composed not only of highly involved, longtime parish "insiders," but also of newcomers. Like Claudia, Gaby had been invited to join and soon cochair the group on one of her first Sundays at St. Mary's. Parish Council meetings were important sites of encounter and negotiation in the life of the community, a space where the parish mission was both constructed and lived out.

Though the meetings involved only a small cross section of parishioners, the centrality of the Parish Council in the life of the St. Mary's community made its opening reflection ritual consequential for all. Discussions at Parish Council meetings often turned heated. Disagreements were common. The interruptions required for translation were a constant reminder of the borders of language and life experience across which parishioners were working. The mission statement, the product of protracted parishwide discernment, offered common language to a community otherwise defined by difference—a place in between from which to begin. When members shared reflections on the mission statement, they were engaging in the work of reception—in this case, the intertwined receptions of both the community's own "creed" and of Vatican II's ecclesiological vision, transacting the council's outcome at the parish level. These reflections became part of the community's story about itself, created and recreated around the meeting table each month.

4   Passion of the Neighborhood

Life in a poor community is always political.

Fr. Jack Roussin, St. Mary of the Angels Parish Administrator and Pastor, 1976–92[1]

The passion of the neighborhood is our passion, and it's the passion of Jesus. His passion was not for an historical moment. His passion was for eons, and for whoever was to come. So we have to enter into that time and distance kind of thing, beyond area, and beyond now. . . . I think in terms of kingdom, and I think in terms of what Jesus did, in his historical life. And how he did it. And how he was totally frustrated. And how it ended. And very often, that's how it ends with us. The thing is never completed totally. I think the aspect of the walking in the neighborhood, it's believing in the neighborhood to begin with, when I walk, and praying for the people that I know I don't know, with the idea that Jesus did this at one point, and we are that reach—of the hands to the heart. It's that whole song that we sing: "*Open my eyes, open my ears, open my heart.*" It's a mutual thing that happens on the walk.

Sr. Josephine, Neighborhood Way of the Cross organizer[2]

March 29, 2013

Encaminémonos a llevar nuestra cruz.
Now let us begin our walk with the cross.

We surface from the basement sanctuary up a concrete stairwell and onto Columbus Avenue, bubbling up and covering the city pavement like an underground spring. A parishioner named Javier leads the procession. A short, gray-haired Puerto Rican man dressed in jeans and a black jacket, he carries a large cross on his shoulder. The cross is made of

FIGURE 5. A parishioner shoulders the cross as participants gather in the center of Egleston Square's main intersection, April 6, 2012. Photo by the author.

cardboard, but it's large and bulky and looks convincingly enough like wood. A slim crown of thorns encircles its top. Behind him, the crowd winds down the block, spilling off the sidewalk and into the busy street.

The crowd is diverse, multigenerational, and eclectic. An interracial couple in their thirties hold hands and, to the delight of everyone around them, the leash of a friendly, curly-haired dog. Another woman walks a bike. Victoria uses a cane to briskly navigate the uneven pavement. A small crowd of Dominican American teenagers bunch together at the fringe of the procession, hanging on each other's arms and resting their heads on each other's shoulders. A van filled with parish matriarchs who can no longer walk the route rolls steadily along beside us.

A breeze rattles a row of blossoming cherry trees, sending a shower of pale pink petals down on our heads and shoulders and swirling around our shoes. Late March in Boston is usually damp and chilly. But today, the sun is shining, the sky a thin blanket of iridescent gray. As we walk, a young Dominican woman at the front of the procession begins to sing. The clear, mournful notes resound from clangy speakers tethered to the bed of a pickup truck, echoing off the brick facades of the apartment buildings that line the street:

Madre, óyeme, mi plegaria es un grito en la noche.
Madre, mírame, en la noche de mi juventud . . . [3]

I recognize many people in the crowd as parishioners, but there are just as many faces I've never seen. A longtime parishioner identifies some of them for me: a neighboring Baptist pastor, a well-known local Jewish leader, a Congregationalist minister. As we process, she continues to whisper introductions: *See that officer over there? He was a youth group kid. He got involved with the gangs back when he was a teenager, but then Father Jack helped him turn it around. See that young woman? Her family's lived on this block forever.*

Despite its ostensible solemnity, there is a busyness to procession, a kind of buoyancy. Walkers greet one another with warm embraces. Some spot friends across the crowd, waving in exaggerated, smiling silence. Children dart around walking feet, leaping onto the concrete half-walls and courtyard edges that line the sidewalk. As we pass, neighbors step out of their apartments and lean against railings to watch, sometimes striking up conversations with those on the fringes of the crowd. Above us, children make faces and wave, flattening their noses against third-story windows. We are enveloped by an urban symphony of honking horns and the vibrating bass of car radios and the percussive crunch and shuffle of our own footsteps. Columbus Avenue is a cacophony, even by Boston standards. It is a thoroughfare to a nearby hospital; ambulance sirens hang in the air at all hours of the day and night. At the end of the block, Columbus meets two other streets in a confounding, lopsided asterisk of an intersection. Within this ecosystem of brick and concrete, the cross and river of walkers are an interruptive sight. Traffic slows as curious drivers look on. One car rolls to a stop beside us. Its driver lowers the passenger-side window and calls out, "What's going on?"

"It's la caminata. The Viacrucis," a woman next to me calls back in an amalgam of Dominican-accented English and Spanish. Today is Good Friday. The people of St. Mary's are walking the Way of the Cross.

We come to a stop on the lawn of Berea Seventh Day Adventist Church in Dorchester. The church is situated in a renovated house at a busy intersection about a half mile up the road from St. Mary's. Two months earlier, a thirteen-year-old African American boy named Gabriel was shot in the stomach by a drive-by gunman as he walked to meet his mother for Fri-

FIGURE 6. Parishioners sing as they walk the 2012 Way of the Cross down a neighborhood street near St. Mary's, April 6, 2012. Photo by the author.

day night church choir practice.[4] He survived the random attack, but the shooting churned up fears of a return to the kind of violence the community had worked so hard to overcome. Today, Gabriel's church represents Jesus's three falls, a combination of traditional Stations III, VII, and IX. We are greeted by Gabriel's mother Shirley and Berea's pastor, Rev. Nigel G. David, Sr. The crowd has grown since the procession began, and we spill from the sidewalk onto the street, between parallel-parked cars and into the bus lane.

Standing under the cross, two women from St. Mary's pass a microphone back and forth, alternating between English and Spanish:

Jesús cae tres veces.
Jesus falls three times.

The readers pause and the crowd recites a verse of the traditional St. Alphonsus Liguori Stations of the Cross devotional text, which is printed in booklets handed out at the beginning of the walk:

Like a lamb led to the slaughter or a sheep before the shearers, he was silent and opened not his mouth.

Good Friday
Stations of the Cross
St. Mary of the Angels
Catholic Church

March 25th, 2016

Marzo 25, 2016

Viernes Santo
Vía Crucis
Santa María de los Ángeles
Iglesia Católica

FIGURE 7. The Good Friday Way of the Cross program booklet, handed out at the beginning of the ritual, contains the prayers, reflections, and song lyrics used during each station. This one is from 2016. Photo by the author.

Many genuflect. Our knees graze the cool, cracked concrete of the sidewalk.

> Te adoramos, O Cristo, y te bendecimos. Porque por tu santa Cruz redimiste al mundo.[5]

The women continue to read, their words echoing over the busy intersection:

> The instruments of torture—whips, crown of thorns, cross—all blood-letting, caused a weakened Jesus to fall, then fall, then fall again. Each time he got up to pursue his terrible journey to Calvary. How? We can't even imagine. We stand in front of Berea Seventh Day Adventist Church. This was the destination of Gabriel just a short time ago and today we remember his journey. As Jesus fell that first Good Friday, so Gabriel fell a few months ago, shot by unknown young people in a drive-by car. As we walk, let us recall recent deaths by peers in our neighborhood, and promise that we will get up, get up again and get up continuously by living non-violent lives, by reaching out to younger neighbors and to the families of victims and perpetrators alike. We pray that there will be someone there for all recuperating Gabriels as well as for those who have acted violently when the realization of what they have done to another human being grips them with feelings they can't handle. We pray in gratitude for all the members of the Seventh Day Adventist Parish and Roxbury neighbors who so lovingly support Gabriel and his mother as both his physical wounds and the wounds of memory continue to heal.[6]

When they finish, they pass the microphone to Gabriel's mother, Shirley. She thanks the crowd for coming and offers an extemporaneous prayer of thanksgiving to God. Then she pauses, closes her eyes, and begins to sing. The looks on the readers' faces suggest that this part was not in the script. Her voice crackles faintly with tears. It's stunning, arresting. Next to me, a Black woman hums along to the gospel melody. Others join in with murmurs of "Amen" and "Yes." When she concludes the song, everyone breaks into applause. A few people come forward from the crowd to embrace her.

The procession continues. Leaders hand off the cross to the shoulder of an older Jamaican man. The singing begins again, though the truck-bed sound system cuts in and out:

Pueblo mío, ¿Qué te he hecho?
¿En qué te he ofendido? Respóndeme . . . [7]

After about ten minutes, a Dominican mother who lives just down the block from the parish takes the cross from the man and continues the procession. We make our way down the street to a short-term respite care facility for people experiencing homelessness. After years of community-led advocacy to renovate the shuttered facility, its reopening is finally on the horizon. Outside the building, a woman from New Orleans who found herself in Boston after Hurricane Katrina describes the joy that washed over her as she was recently handed her first set of house keys. Her story of everyday resurrection signifies Stations V and VI: Simon and Veronica Aid Jesus as He Walks.

Open my eyes, Lord,
Help me to see your face . . . [8]

We turn and head down School Street to the next station, where Jesus encounters the Women of Jerusalem in front of the Rafael Hernández School, the public, bilingual elementary school across the street from St. Mary's. Its legendary longtime principal, Margarita Muñiz, was a Cuban immigrant, prolific educator, and pillar of the Egleston Square community. During the darkest days of Roxbury's gang epidemic, one parishioner told me, she would open the doors of the school every weekend and keep them open late into the night, providing the children of the neighborhood a safe space away from the violence of the streets. She permitted local cops and X-Men gang members to meet there for Saturday morning basketball games aimed at quelling neighborhood violence. Principal Muñiz died of cancer in November 2011. A fourth-grade boy from St. Mary's, the son of Dominican immigrants and a student at the school, steps into the center of the semicircle formed by the crowd. Next to him, his friends hold the cross together. Taking the microphone, he unfolds a piece of paper from

FIGURE 8. With help from an adult, students from the bilingual Rafael Hernández School carry the cross together to the steps of the school, where a station commemorates the death of Principal Margarita Muñiz, March 29, 2013. Photo by the author.

his pocket and begins to read, first in English and then in Spanish. Confidently, he relates his gratitude for the education he receives at his school and the pain he and his classmates felt after the loss of their beloved principal.

Perdona a Tu pueblo, Señor,
Perdona a Tu pueblo, perdónale, Señor . . . [9]

Turning a corner and starting up the block back to the parish, we stop for a final time on a corner outside of a brick apartment building. When I lived in the parish house, I passed the building at least twice a day but knew almost nothing about it. Today, I learn that, for decades, a beloved Puerto Rican abuela had called one of its apartments home. She was well known to everyone on the block, who saw her as a symbol of stability in good times and bad. She died recently, surrounded by her seven children and many grandchildren. Today, some of her family members gather under the cross as two of her grandsons, young men possibly in their early twenties, take the microphone and tell us about her life through tears. Their

FIGURE 9. Family members of a recently deceased neighborhood matriarch help to carry the cross from the corner of her apartment to the parish lawn. In the background, the round Walnut Park Apartments tower is a Columbus Avenue landmark, March 29, 2013. Photo by the author.

words enfold her death into the darkness of the final stations: Jesus Is Stripped of His Clothes, Nailed to the Cross, Dies, and Is Laid to Rest in the Tomb.

> *Were you there when they crucified my Lord?*
> *Were you there when they crucified my Lord?*
> *O sometimes it causes me to tremble! Tremble! Tremble . . .* [10]

As we start back up Columbus Avenue to St. Mary's, a grandson helps to carry the cross. Returning to St. Mary's, we stop for the final time on the parish lawn. As leaders offer a closing prayer, members of the youth group walk among us with Styrofoam cups of soil and plastic bags of seeds. They direct us to plant our seeds along the nubby concrete-and-iron fence facing the street. When we return to the parish lawn for the Pentecost potluck fifty-two days later, the seeds will have shot up into towering sunflowers, symbols of new life. After the prayer and planting concludes, leaders invite us into the parish kitchen

FIGURE 10. Walkers process up School Street as residents of Spencer House, an affordable senior living community, watch from the patio, April 6, 2012. Photo by the author.

for a warm lunch of bread and fish soup that Ramón—widely recognized as one of the best cooks in the church—has prepared in giant stockpots. After we have walked for more than two hours, the simple, meatless Good Friday meal tastes exquisite. This evening, some of the walkers will return to the darkened church for the bilingual Good Friday liturgy. But attendance there will pale in comparison to the multitude now pressed into the kitchen and hallways of the parish house for soup and stories.

A Migration in Miniature

The Stations of the Cross is a traditional Roman Catholic devotion in which a series of fourteen tableaus mark successive moments along Jesus's journey to crucifixion, from his condemnation to death (Mt 27:15–26; Mk 5:6–15; Lk 23:17–25) to his entombment (Mt 27:60; Mk 15:46; Lk 23:53–54). Devotees meditate on Jesus's passion and death by ritually recounting and retracing his final steps, pausing to pray and chant or sing at each station.

Though the Via Crucis (Way of the Cross) in its modern form dates to around the fifteenth century,[11] it is part of a genre of devotion that has existed since the early church. The nun Egeria, whose detailed record of her journey from Europe to Jerusalem in the 380s marks the earliest known account of Christian pilgrimage, describes a stational procession from Gethsemane to the place of the crucifixion.[12] Stational liturgies like the one in which Egeria would have participated demonstrate a deeply rooted genealogy of reverence for the particularly urban context of Jesus's suffering and death. This early precursor to the Via Crucis conveys a sense that, for Christians, the crucifixion means something not only theologically and spiritually but also spatially.[13] City streets are to the end of Jesus's life what the stable is to his birth. The stations pay subtle homage to the Roman cityscape of the incarnation's final preresurrection gasps.

Underlying the Stations of the Cross is a spiritual imagination of mutual companionship and divine-human solidarity in the midst of suffering. On one hand, by attending with such granularity to Jesus's final hours, Christian devotees spiritually accompany Jesus in his torment. On the other, by walking the Way of the Cross, participants' everyday sufferings are recast as quotidian passions in which Jesus is a faithful companion on the journey.[14] Unlike Jesus's first disciples, Christians today have the benefit of knowing the rest of the story: This is a struggle that ends in resurrection, making the sorrowful way at the same time a hopeful one. Even so, while one occasionally encounters interpretations of the stations that include a fifteenth chapter indicating Jesus's resurrection from the dead, the traditional fourteen conclude with Jesus lying dead in the tomb. By resisting the urge to compress the Triduum sequence, wrapping it up with a satisfying paschal resolution, and instead urging devotees to dwell patiently, almost tediously, in the particularities of Jesus's agony, the stations and their attendant rituals accent suffering as a site of divine-human solidarity. God is near not only in the defeat of death on Easter morning but also, somehow even more intimately, in the torture and abandonment that preceded it.[15]

From its late-medieval origins, the Stations of the Cross devotion was translocal and imaginatively contextual. Sarah Lenzi argues that the ritual developed in parallel in both Europe and Jerusalem. In Jerusalem, the Via Crucis emerged as a pilgrimage practice sometime in the fifteenth century. Meanwhile, the specific fourteen-station order seems to have originated in devotional manuals in Europe. The European station sequence was eventually adopted as canonical in the Holy Land, at which point the two devotional trajectories merged. What is important to observe, in other words, is that it was largely the European form of the devotion that was mapped onto the Jerusalem-based one.[16] It would be natural to believe that the Jerusalem Via Crucis was the original, "authentic" version of the ritual, given its geographical context. That the stations actually emerged a continent away from the Holy Land testifies to their transportability. Put simply, Christian communities have been reading their own storied geographies into the footsteps of Jesus's final hours for centuries. To call what happens in Roxbury every Good Friday a *contextualization* of the Stations of the Cross, then, is not quite accurate, if that term implies unidirectional translation. Rather, the Via Crucis has always been an exercise in local theologizing.

Most modern Roman Catholic churches bear some depiction of the fourteen stations, typically in the form of reliefs or paintings hung around the sanctuary walls. The stations that line the inner walls of St. Mary of the Angels evince both the "before" and the "after" of Vatican II aesthetic culture. Fourteen large white plaster reliefs surround the sanctuary, beginning with Station I ("Jesus Is Condemned to Die") and concluding with Station XIV ("Jesus Is Laid in the Tomb"). Below each statue, someone has taped two laminated pages—one captioned in English, the other in Spanish—from what appears to be a 1980s-era Lenten edition of a Catholic social justice publication. These small posters portray Jesus's suffering in the weary faces of Mexican migrants, each set recalling the station's theme with a different scene of desperation and persecution. The contrasting sets of stations mutually interpret one another. The posters transpose the pristine-looking suffering depicted in white into the register of present-day injustice. The reliefs, meanwhile, bind the trauma of migration to the foundational Christian story of Jesus's death on the cross. Indeed, liberation theologians have drawn compelling parallels between Latin American migrants' often perilous transnational journeys and the Via Crucis.[17] Yet the lower set of stations intimate, but do not exactly reflect, the immigration journeys of many St. Mary's parishioners. While many hail from Latin America and the Caribbean, I do not know of any who crossed the U.S.-Mexico border on foot. It is not clear who hung the posters or when, but in any case, the presence of this second set of stations likely says more about the social justice commitments of the English Mass community than the specific migration histories of Spanish Mass community members.

Yet cities are borderlands, too. As we have seen, parishioners from both Mass communities arrived in Egleston Square and at St. Mary's through migrations of many kinds. Crossing national, geographic, cultural, racial, parochial, and denominational boundaries, they have made a spiritual home in the in-between space of St. Mary's. What's more, in our conversations, many described their migrations to St. Mary's in a variety of soteriological terms: There, they encountered the parish that saved their faith, that kept them Catholic despite disillusionment and institutional betrayal, that reunited them with the sounds and customs of their homeland at a moment of wrenching homesickness. I have described the parish as a way station for a pilgrim church, an ecclesial community encompassing hybridity and difference formed by intersecting migrations. At a parish in which nearly everyone can describe the displacements and wanderings that first led them there, the Roxbury Neighborhood Way of the Cross is a migration in miniature. This common journey annually reaffirms the bonds of solidarity among parishioners, neighbors, the remembered dead, and all of them with God. As this chapter will suggest, it is a journey that annually makes and remakes the community—a practice of memory, hope, solidarity, and ultimately, salvation.

According to parish records, parishioners initiated the multilingual Way of the Cross in the 1970s as a public, ecumenical form of liturgical protest against neighborhood violence.[18] Winding through the streets, the stations are places—street corners, storefronts, apartment buildings, community organizations—where suffering, death, and new life have visited Egleston Square throughout the prior year. Taking a different route every year, the procession invariably crosses neighborhood boundaries, gang territories, and parish lines as it weaves together the stations into a single path, as though embroidering a new map on top of an existing one. The short pilgrimage from station to station intentionally leads participants through streets they walk daily, unearthing the dangerous memories hidden just beneath the concrete facades of quotidian city life.[19] At the same time, the ritual's "devotional kinesthetics"[20]—its stops and starts, genuflections and signs of the cross, silences and songs and bilingual recitations—heightens the experience of embodied community among its diverse participants.

This chapter weaves together text, photography, and song in a phenomenological analysis of the urban Way of the Cross as a practice of ecclesial solidarity. Tracing the emergence of the ritual, I retrieve the story of Hector Morales, a teenage parishioner killed by police in 1990 whose spontaneous funeral procession through the streets of Roxbury took on the form of an organic Via Crucis. Today, the Good Friday journey continues as a protest against violence and an invocation of divine presence in the midst of everyday dyings and risings. In it, memories of migration and struggle converge in the present, recast in the paschal vernacular of suffering, death, and resurrection. By crossing neighborhood boundaries, parishioners reconfigure their relationships with local space and one another while actively defying structures of injustice. Resisting interpretations of ritual as a form of narrow meaning-making or as the bearer of a singular, all-encompassing ecclesial culture, I contend instead that the Roxbury Way of the Cross can be understood as a form of practical action that affirms solidarity in difference. By sharing the cross, passing it from shoulder to shoulder throughout the three-hour journey, parishioners and neighbors practice a theological vision of salvation grounded in and oriented toward the collective.

A History of the Roxbury Neighborhood Way of the Cross

"Really Bringing the Church to the Corner"

Despite the good intentions of the Archdiocese of Boston's Vatican II–era Roxbury Apostolate, by the 1970s, St. Mary's had fallen back into disrepair. For parishioners, ecclesial neglect was compounded by increasingly dire municipal and economic abandonment of neighborhoods like Egleston Square. Residents frequently complained of a lack of basic sanitation services. Until 1992, no bank had a branch anywhere near the neighborhood. As white backlash to bussing and other integration efforts compounded the effects of white flight, inner-city Catholics effectively became segregated from their white, suburban counterparts. Combined with structural issues of poverty and lack of investment in education and youth services, Egleston Square's status as both a public transportation hub and as a cultural, ethnic, racial, and religious crossroads contributed to the steady rise of gang violence. Parishioners, many of them well-known community activists, campaigned tirelessly for peace in the neighborhood and for education, jobs, and opportunities for its youth. Through the Parish Council and other lay ministries, they also continued to serve as the backbone of St. Mary's, perpetually fending off threats of closure and sustaining one another despite near-total archdiocesan abandonment. Yet with each passing year, the intertwined fates of Egleston Square and St. Mary's became increasingly dire. It was nearly impossible to keep a priest at St. Mary's, as many refused assignments to the inner city.[21] As neighborhood violence spiraled out of control, parishioners found themselves planning the funerals of more and more young people.

In 1976, the arrival of new leadership marked a fresh chapter for the people of St. Mary's. What they needed was a priest who would commit to the place—who would see himself as a member of the community and not just as an administrator biding his time until he could plead his way into a better assignment. Rev. John J. Roussin—"Father Jack," as he was known—was born in Lynn, Massachusetts, a mostly working-class town half an hour's drive north of Boston. He entered seminary in 1968, in the possibility-laden afterglow of Vatican II. The first-line reception of the council's vision—its notion of a more porous boundary between church and world, its spirit of liturgical accessibility, its call to read the signs of the times—shaped his approach to priestly ministry. As a deacon, he developed a love for Spanish-language ministry, teaching religious education, and working with the mentally disabled. On the eve of his ordination to the priesthood, Jack asked for an assignment in the city, somewhere he could use his Spanish and work with people on the margins.[22] His superiors had just the place in mind.

Fr. Jack arrived at St. Mary's just before Christmas to find a church in shambles. The final communication on record from the priest who preceded him described a situation of unpaid contracts, linguistic confusion, decrepit buildings, armed robberies, and general chaos. The letter concluded with two words and four exclamation marks: "Total Disaster!!!!"[23] Jack was greeted by near-empty collection baskets and eight Mass attendees in a parish that theoretically served seven hundred families.[24] The front door of the parish house was boarded up with plywood, and paint was peeling in sheets off its aluminum siding. Inside, the house was flooded and overrun with cockroaches and rats.[25] The first thing Fr. Jack did was to repair the dilapidated building. He persuaded a friend at the fire department to condemn the crumbling front porch, forcing the archdiocese to pay for its reconstruction.[26] The house was the parish's only gathering space beyond the basement sanctuary—the church building didn't even have bathrooms. Making the parish house more hospitable was an important sign of renewal for church and neighborhood alike.[27]

Earnest, friendly, and wickedly funny, Fr. Jack was a believer in what Sr. Margaret, his longtime pastoral collaborator, called "shoe leather ministry."[28] He was convinced that the role of a priest was to empower the laity to do the work of the Gospel and that the church's task was to meet people where they were, in the messy complexities of their ordinary lives. Once, in a letter to the chancery, he expressed frustration with institutional approaches to inner-city ministry that seemed to regard the poor primarily as charity recipients. The people of Roxbury don't only need food pantries and used clothing donations, he wrote. They, too, want good liturgy and religious education just as much as Catholics in the suburbs do. They want to be agents of their own religious formation. At that point, roughly 50 percent of St. Mary's parishioners were Black, 40 percent were Hispanic, and the remaining 10 percent were Asian or "elderly White." Eighty-five percent lived on a fixed income. In a parish that served people from forty-three countries, most of them immigrant or refugee families, Fr. Jack ensured that liturgies and pastoral services were offered in English, Spanish, Lao, French, Haitian Creole, and Portuguese.[29] According to a profile of Fr. Jack that ran in the *Boston Globe*, he even commissioned a transliteration of the Mass into Lao to better serve the parish's Kmhmu refugee community. He invited girls to be altar servers years before it was officially permitted by the archdiocese.[30]

In Fr. Jack's ministerial vision, the youth held pride of place. As gang violence in Egleston intensified, he became a fixture on the streets, cultivating deep relationships with the neighborhood's young people, including members of the increasingly problematic X-Men, a local gang made up mostly of Puerto Rican teens from around Egleston Square. He and Sr. Margaret invited them to the youth group, which gathered dozens of teenagers from the parish every Friday night to go bowling or to the movies. St. Mary's youth group became a crucial in-between space, extending belonging across the blocks that demarcated gang boundary lines. "I had [at least] two [young people] . . . [with] whom we were involved as a parish here on both sides of the violence," Sr. Margaret recalled. "People who were *affected* by the violence, people who *did* the violence."[31]

Two of these youth were William and Hector Morales. As children, the brothers moved from New York City to Roxbury with their mother. The Puerto Rican family was poor and often on the brink of eviction. When they were teenagers, William and Hector joined the St. Mary's youth group. Around the same time, in part to help alleviate the burden of his family's poverty, William also started selling drugs. He quickly gained status on the block, ascending to leadership in the X-Men. I had heard many stories about William—by then a respected community leader—before finally meeting him at the Roxbury Way of the Cross in 2013. A few weeks later, we sat down for a conversation about St. Mary's during the 1980s and '90s. He described his friendship with Fr. Jack during those years:

> By the time I was sixteen, the gang epidemic in Boston got really ugly. . . . Father Jack was [always] coming out to the block. And Father Jack was a smoker. So his thing was that he was always reaching out to us not by inviting us to the church but by really bringing the church to the corner. So that meant that he would spend many nights out here on the corners with us while we're in the middle of— we're hustling drugs and doing stuff. He knew we smoked, so he'd bring an extra pack of Newports, share a cigarette with us, and have a conversation. He never projected his message, ever using Jesus or God or saints or anything. He knew how to sort of change the tone a little bit to just, if anything, kind of ignite our conscience a little bit about what it is we're doing and why we're doing it. And then to really start saying, "You know, you're thinking of *now*. What's the long term? I mean how long do you think you're gonna do this and get away with it?" So it was a very different thing. He developed a deep relationship with some of the most hardcore guys in this block. And they all had his respect. They're like, "If he says something, we respect it."[32]

Fr. Jack was a bridge. His approachability, down-to-earth sensibility, and his own relative youth—he was only thirty when he was assigned to St. Mary's—gave him credibility on the block. At the same time, in culturally Catholic Boston, his status as a priest—a role he sometimes downplayed, rarely appearing in clerics outside of Mass—made him a trusted partner among neighborhood leaders, local politicians, and the police.

Negotiating the borderline between the X-Men and local authorities was delicate work. In January 1990, some gang members threw a Molotov cocktail onto a parked police cruiser from the roof of a tenement down the street from St. Mary's. Residents feared that the firebombing would signal a point of no return in the already explosive situation in Egleston Square. In an effort to secure a semblance of peace for the neighborhood, Fr. Jack hosted weekly meetings between the X-Men and civic leaders in the parish house. Gang members wanted jobs and a place to hang out. Local authorities demanded the X-Men stop tagging the elementary school. They reached a series of compromises. Fr. Jack helped to secure city funds to hire the teens to do summer community work. As long as the graffiti

FIGURE 11. The day after Boston police killed Hector Morales, neighborhood youth gather in front of the mural that Hector helped to paint, November 25, 1990. Jim Mahoney, the *Boston Herald*.

stopped, Principal Margarita Muñiz agreed to open the school gym on Saturday mornings for basketball games between the teens and police. The most important development was an artistic one: The Egleston Square Neighborhood Association hired muralist Roberto Chao to work with the X-Men to paint a huge mural along School Street. The finished product was a montage of Martin Luther King, Jr., Malcolm X, and Puerto Rican heroes like Roberto Clemente, Willy Colón, and independence activist Pedro Albizu Campos. The faces appeared underneath the Puerto Rican flag and fists emblazoned with the words "LATINO POWER." Alongside them, light blue bubble letters broadcasted a tensive mix of territorialism, unity, and hope: "WE ARE ALL IN THE SAME GANG"—"STOP THE VIOLENCE."[33]

The Emergence of a Ritual

As neighborhood violence intensified, so did efforts to build peace. The Good Friday Neighborhood Way of the Cross ritualized this community peace work. A timeline parishioners compiled for St. Mary's centennial celebration indicates that the first Good Friday walk through the streets of Egleston Square took place in 1974, though I could find no further details of that inaugural event. Longtime parishioners remember the ritual as it exists today taking shape later, sometime during the 1980s. In either case, the performance of the Stations of the Cross through the streets of Roxbury reflected the ecclesiological sensibility of a parish always pushing beyond its boundaries. "Jack was a strong believer that church needed to be in the streets," Sr. Margaret remarked, noting that in those days, the basement church was barely noticeable beneath the 1908 "temporary" flat roof it still sported, by then held together by some four hundred patches. "You had to look hard to see us if you were going by."[34] As it had in the early days, St. Mary's basement status still loomed large in parishioners' imaginations as a symbol of the community's humility, resilience, and subversive spirit. Propelled beyond itself by the insufficiency of its facilities, St. Mary's was a community convinced that the real presence of Christ extended beyond the parish walls, beyond the Eucharist, beyond the closing hymn at Mass.

The purpose of the Neighborhood Way of the Cross was to speak out against the violence and suffering on the streets of Egleston Square. "It was kind of small the first couple years," recalled Martin, the African American community leader who moved to Egleston Square with his wife in the 1970s. It was "another way of our going to the community, taking ourselves to the community, saying we were in solidarity with trying to make the neighborhood an inviting place, a safe place."[35] Fr. Jack led the procession dressed in billowing liturgical vestments. Behind him processed Sr. Margaret and a dozen robed altar servers carrying banners and torches and a stark crucifix portraying a Black Christ.[36] One swung a thurible, perfuming the streets with incense. The procession's liturgical aesthetic was strategic: Fr. Jack did not want the large crowd to raise alarm, potentially inciting the very violence they were there to decry. According to Sr. Margaret, Jack "want[ed people] to know that today is Good Friday, and we're out here to make a statement. And we made hard statements in those days."[37]

The stations led walkers along the path of Egleston Square's own passion. "Every year we'd go different places," Martin recalled. "If there was a tragedy, we would stop there. Or a block, an intersection where there was a lot of drug trafficking, we would stop there. And in some cases, guys would be on the street, obviously dealing drugs." Others recalled different memories. There were stations in front of liquor stores known for selling alcohol to minors and on corners where young people's lives had been cut short in drive-by shootings. Once they stopped at the site of a low-income housing complex destroyed by arson where some parishioners had lived: Station X, Jesus Is Stripped of His Garments. Another year, they prayed in front of the local police station.

On the walk, suffering and hope were interlaced. Stations V (Simon Helps Jesus Carry His Cross), VI (Veronica Wipes the Face of Jesus), and XIII (Jesus Is Taken Down from the Cross)—brief glimpses of humanity in the story of an execution—were usually signified by Egleston agencies and organizations performing local corporal works of mercy: feeding the hungry, assisting the elderly, building affordable housing, caring for the poor and sick, mentoring youth, calling for justice, working for peace. The geographical route formed by the neighborhood stops didn't always line up sequentially with the traditional fourteen stations. In those cases, the order of the stations would be amended, or several would be combined into one stop. The fragmentary, circuitous journey toward hope in Egleston gave rise to a nonlinear passion.

Soon St. Mary's organizers began inviting other churches, both Catholic and Protestant, to join them on the walk. Each congregation walked a Way of the Cross through its own neighborhood before coming together for a concluding ritual. One year, participants were each handed a rock to carry as they walked, symbolizing "the hardness that's in our neighborhood," Sr. Margaret explained. After processing through their own nearby streets, "we all met down at the Ruggles Street Station, and we planted a tree. Each community that came had endured violence. And so we came with that." The tree planting symbolized their prayer for "new life to come for all people. We had large gatherings, very large groups walking. And then we all planted our rock[s] around [the tree]. We needed to use [them] to build up and not to destroy."[38]

Another year, members of each church brought carnations to represent the number of young people killed from their respective neighborhoods. "There were thirty-something from here, and seven or eight from there," Sr. Margaret recalled. "We had about forty-six or so carnations [altogether]. And at Jackson Square [Station, where the groups came together], we measured off a gravesite and put the carnations on the grave site in memory of the kids that were killed that year."[39]

Crossing Local Borders

In a community where gang territorialism defined geographies of belonging, movement across neighborhood borderlines was both a political and theological act. "You know, when you've got gang-related issues, you don't cross over into another area," Sr. Margaret explained. "And so [the Way of the Cross was a way of saying], *No, we are coming together as one.*"[40] In Boston, gangs coalesced residentially around particular neighborhoods and housing projects. Within this milieu, Egleston's borderland status made it a battleground. A number of bus lines intersected at Egleston Station, making it a common stop for anyone traveling between Roxbury, Jamaica Plain, Dorchester, or Mattapan—including members of rival gangs. "Every other city gang member needed to come through Egleston in order to get to places," Will Morales recalled. He continued:

Can you imagine if you're at war with different people in the world and they needed to come through a terminal to get home? While they're waiting for their ride home, they would do their damage, and then take somebody else's place. And so we felt the threat of the gang epidemic as a result of the fact that people kind of came through here. And we also began to respond to that threat very quickly. We wanted to protect our neighborhood, protect our families, protect our own friends, protect our own investments. We didn't want people to just come in here and take over.[41]

As we have seen, local territorial boundaries had long shaped the lives of Roxbury's young people. During the early twentieth century, bitter rivalries between Jewish and Catholic youth, whose perceived ownership of neighborhood space was exacerbated by congregational and parochial membership, were part of daily life in Egleston Square. As the area became more racially and ethnically diverse, the nature of these invisible boundaries shifted, along with their attendant rivalries. But the challenge of ministry in a community defined by its own internal divisions endured. Welcoming residents of rival neighborhoods as well as Jewish and Protestant neighbors into the ritual was a gesture of defiance against this history of division.

In this way, too, the churches' selection of MBTA (Massachusetts Bay Transportation Authority) bus and subway stations as meeting points for the conclusion of the Way of the Cross was theologically significant. The stations symbolized the living connections between neighborhoods even as they recalled the story of Roxbury's complicated past. Since Egleston's earliest days as a streetcar suburb, transportation lines had been an ambivalent force, a source of both unification and division, development and destruction: the turn-of-the-century streetcars that welcomed German and Irish immigrants to Roxbury, the elevated Orange Line whose shady tracks spurred eager growth and parish building followed by stark divestment, the homes razed for the abandoned Southwest Expressway project that would have decimated the neighborhood, the bus lines that continued to crisscross and converge in Egleston Square even after the Orange Line tracks had come down. The Stations of the Cross mounted around the periphery of a church sanctuary convey the gathered assembly's sense of being contained within the memory of a journey, surrounded by the story of suffering and the hope of resurrection. If MBTA stations were Stations of the Cross, then the city, too, was a church.[42] The bus and subway lines that traversed the city, dotted with their familiar litany of stations, mapped the stational liturgies of everyday life, ordinary ways of sorrow and hope that traced the cartography of the community's passion.

Hector Morales and the Passion of the Neighborhood

By the fall of 1990, hope for Egleston Square felt increasingly tangible. The gang diversion projects of the summer had set community relations on a promising path, if a controversial one. Some accused Fr. Jack of coddling gang members and felt that the mural—a source of such pride for the teens—glorified gang membership. Others were upset that the mural appeared to mark Egleston as Puerto Rican territory, erasing the presence of the many other cultures who called it home.[43] Nevertheless, Saturday morning basketball games and community projects meant that the X-Men and police officers now knew one another by name.[44] The situation seemed to improve so much that a headline on the editorial page of the *Boston Globe* boldly proclaimed "An Egleston Square Comeback."[45]

The comeback proved fleeting. In the collective memory of Egleston Square's passion, one station marked a breaking point. Hector Morales, Jr., William's younger brother, was a soft-spoken teenager who loved chess and art and had taught himself to play five instruments. Unlike William, Hector found little appeal in the X-Men. Deterred by his brother's high profile in the gang, he assiduously avoided the entire scene. But several unprovoked attacks from members of a rival gang left him shaken and defensive. After William was imprisoned on drug trafficking charges, Hector took his brother's place on the block.

On the night of November 24, 1990, two plainclothes police officers approached Hector and a group of X-Men who were hanging out on the corner of Washington and School Street. The officers had reportedly been tipped off to a planned shootout between Hector and a member of a rival gang and had come to preempt the encounter. Hector and the officers knew one another well; by most accounts, the tone of their approach was tense but not aggressive. In a moment of decision-making that no one, in the chaotic days that followed, could quite explain, Hector pulled out a 12-gauge shotgun loaded with birdshot and fired at the two officers. They returned fire, hitting Hector four times. The officers sustained minor injuries. Hector died at Boston City Hospital three hours later.[46]

Egleston erupted. Rumors flared that the officers had shot Hector as many as a dozen times, even after he was down. Some claimed Hector begged the officers not to kill him, pleading with them to think of his mother.[47] The chaos unraveled into a standoff between police and gang members, the two groups poised for confrontation on opposite sides of Washington Street. Fr. Jack ran down the block to the scene, persuading Sr. Margaret to join him. "He said [to me], 'You're in youth ministry. You have to walk those streets and the kids have to see you here,'" she recalled.[48] They convinced the young men to stand down. In the combustible days that followed Hector's killing, Jack and other community leaders worked to maintain peace in the neighborhood. At one of several hastily organized community meetings in the aftermath of the shooting, Hector's mother Clara got down on her knees, sobbing, and in Spanish, begged the X-Men not to avenge her son's killing.[49]

Fr. Jack issued the same plea. He encouraged the young men to interrupt the cycle of violence with lament, rather than resorting to revenge. Recalled William:

> When the guys were thinking about retaliating, and just going all out, and figuring, *Hey, my boy gave his life for us, we should give our life up for him and make a sacrifice*, it was Father Jack who was the only one who had the deepest relations with these guys and was able to convince them to mourn first. And if you mourn first, and then you still have those feelings, and you feel like you have to do it, then do it. I mean, he wasn't encouraging it. He was just saying that you're skipping the mourning process. 'Cuz he knew that if they mourned, and they experienced loss, then something might inhibit that thought process about what their next steps are gonna be.

It is worth pausing to consider the significance of Fr. Jack's suggestion. Within a community wounded by ongoing violence, Fr. Jack recognized that the ritualization of mourning held a unique capacity to interrupt and transform cycles of revenge. In Egleston Square, acts of violence typically prompted response in various, mostly carceral forms: retaliation, prosecution, prison time, policing, and so on. But there was rarely time or space for reflection. Even more seldom were Egleston's youth called upon to become agents in the process of naming, mourning, and transforming the cycles of violence that threatened their lives. By urging Hector's friends to pause and grieve his loss—and the lost loved ones, opportunities, and dreams of their own that his killing symbolized—Fr. Jack invited the young men to claim a sense of moral agency.

True to William Morales's description of him, Fr. Jack managed to draw the neighborhood teens into the practice of faith not through heavy-handed sermons but through simple invitations to pause and sit with their reality. In this case, he invited them into the long tradition of lament. Ethicist Maureen O'Connell defines lament as an act of truth-telling that evokes social consciousness and moral responsibility and opens a public space for transformative compassion. In scripture, lament conveys "the groaning and suffering of a people, 'sometimes too deep for words' (Rom 8:23 and 26)."[50] As Walter Brueggemann writes, laments "bring public expression to those very fears and terrors that have been denied so long and suppressed so deeply that we do not know they are there."[51] Crucially, such raw expressions of grief defy the temptation to ascribe tidy theological meaning to suffering. Lament attempts neither to explain suffering nor to provide facile closure. Though lamentation often assumes the form of theodicy—we hear in the petitioner's cries the psalmist's ancient echo, *Why, God?*—what the practice of lament ultimately evokes is not meaning-making but accompaniment.[52] In Hebrew Scripture, Job's friends torture him as they grasp at theological explanations for his unspeakable losses (Job 15–25). They perform the work of friendship best in the moments before they attempt to decipher the metaphysical causes of his misfortune and instead dwell with him in his grief: "[T]hey raised their voices and wept aloud; they tore their robes and threw dust in the air upon their heads. They sat with him on the ground for seven days and seven nights, and no one spoke a word to him, for they saw his suffering was very great" (Job 2:12–13). Here we glimpse solidarity born of accompaniment.

The young men took Fr. Jack's advice. Two days after the shooting, some of Hector's friends fashioned a cross out of sticks and hung it on the side of the building above the place where he was shot.[53] That night, they crowded into St. Mary's with some two hundred other mourners for Hector's wake. His casket was draped in the Puerto Rican flag. As they filed up the aisle to pay their respects, they signed their names on the casket.[54] The next day, three hundred fifty people pressed into the wooden pews for Hector's funeral. They overflowed the tiny church, spilling up the steps and onto the sidewalk. According to William, the crowd included members of rival gangs, who had declared a truce in order to mourn together.[55] The Mass began with a candlelight procession from the spot on School Street where Hector had been shot and continued up Washington Street and Columbus Avenue to the parish. Some marchers held signs, like the one nineteen-year-old Luis Rivera carried:

HECTOR MORALES DIED FROM VIOLENCE IN OUR STREETS
REVENGE IS NOT THE ANSWER
ONLY PEACE AND LOVE
MORE JOBS FOR OUR YOUTH[56]

As the funeral mass concluded, pallbearers carried Hector's casket on their shoulders up the steep stairway of the basement church. They did not stop for the hearse. Instead, they made a right turn down Columbus Avenue and, as William described it, "just kept walking":

> They were supposed to take my brother's body out of the church and into the hearse, and the guys took it and marched it down the street. The funeral [director] was afraid, because they didn't know how to tell the guys, "You can't do that. You can't do that." They were so afraid. So Father Jack said, "Just do this: Take the [hearse] to School Street and Washington and wait for us there. Get there quick."
> And so Father Jack actually had to put himself out front . . . because this is not something that was planned, and then *lead* that group of kids, because they didn't know where they were going to take the casket. They would have just continued to walk. They probably would have walked all the way to the cemetery with it. And then he said, "We'll just bring it right here to School Street and Washington," because my brother was killed right here on the corner.[57]

In silence, mourners fell into a procession behind the casket. Hector's funeral had become a spontaneous Via Crucis. Led by the dead on the shoulders of the living, parishioners, neighbors, and rivals walked side by side down the middle of the city street to the corner where Hector had been shot. Across the street was the mural Hector had helped to paint that summer. Three days earlier, it had read "STOP THE VIOLENCE." But after Hector was killed, someone took white spray paint and scrawled over the

word "STOP." Now, hauntingly, the wall proclaimed, "THE VIOLENCE—
JUST BEGUN!" Above the image of Malcolm X, somebody had sprayed,
"Hec."[58]

William, who was still in prison at the time, watched news of Hector's
death unfold on television. Some feared William would try to avenge his
brother's death by stabbing a prison guard. To his surprise, however, the
prison warden made a suggestion similar to the one Fr. Jack offered the
X-Men: He proposed that William plan a memorial service for his
brother. "He allowed my mother to come, members of the family to
come," William recalled. The incarcerated men who showed up to the
service signed over canteen slips to help Clara Hernandez with Hector's
funeral expenses.[59] In retrospect, it is difficult to know quite how to interpret this striking detail. Was it a poignant glimpse of holy generosity
in an unexpected place? An act of reparation? Or a chilling testimony to
the self-feeding cycle of violence, imprisonment, and death? In any case,
as it had on the outside, lament transformed retribution, coaxing violence into prayer.

Hector, nineteen years old when he died, was one of seventy-three
young people killed in Boston that year. The 1990 death toll represented
a 230 percent increase in youth homicides over a three-year period and
marked the apex of gang-related violence in Boston.[60] Hector's shooting
occurred after years of unheeded calls for investment in resources for Egleston Square's youth. Occupying front-page headlines for weeks and in-
voked by city authorities and journalists for years afterward, the incident
became a notorious case study in the consequences of protracted inner-
city disinvestment.

That spring, on Good Friday 1991, the Neighborhood Way of the
Cross followed the same route Hector's impromptu funeral procession
had taken: up the parish steps, down Columbus Avenue, to the corner
of Washington and School Street. At the place where her son was shot,
Clara stood before the crowd and spoke of her anguish. Evoking the
pietà, Clara's arms held the empty space of her sons' absence: One was
dead, the other in prison. That year, the corner marked Station IV: Jesus
Meets His Mother.[61]

Later that fall, in response to community leaders' overwhelming demands for youth resources in Egleston Square, the Greater Boston YMCA
opened a branch in the abandoned sign factory on whose brick wall the

FIGURE 12. Fr. Jack Roussin leads the Good Friday procession past the mural Hector Morales helped create to the corner where he was killed, March 29, 1991. John Hill, the *Boston Herald.*

X-Men had painted their mural. It was the same corner where Hector had been murdered, where his mother had cried on Good Friday, and where, almost a century earlier, the first St. Mary's parishioners had celebrated Mass in their improvised sanctuary inside a streetcar barn. In 1997, several years after he was released from prison, William Morales was named the Executive Director of that YMCA. Eight years after that, the building that housed the YMCA was ceremoniously renamed. That Good Friday, William stood on the corner of Washington and School Street outside of the Father Jack Roussin Community Center. This time, he spoke of resurrection.

The Urban Via Crucis and the Contested Politics of the Passion

What does the Way of the Cross mean to St. Mary's and the people of Roxbury? In order to understand its significance, we must first look at the broader genre of urban Good Friday devotion to which the ritual belongs. The public performance of the Stations of the Cross holds a privileged place in the devotional ecologies of many urban communities marginalized by structural injustice. In some cases, these rituals are similar to the one in Roxbury, with stations that change each year to draw attention to particular sites of injustice within the community. In others, the locations of the stations are less important than the public nature and aesthetic drama of the passion performance itself. While diverse in context and history, these Ways of the Cross have several things in common. First and foremost, they foster an affective connection between participants and Jesus Christ, often implicitly inviting participants to view their own "crosses," their burdens and struggles, in union with Jesus's agony. Second, they ritually unsettle dichotomies between public and private, sacred and profane space, living and dead, and participant and observer. In his study of Good Friday at San Fernando Cathedral in San Antonio, Texas, Christopher Tirres argues that the spiritual and moral power of these practices stems from their capacity to become sites of integration and boundary transgression. When distinctions between past and present, "us" and "them" are ritually collapsed, Tirres suggests, participants are moved on a moral level through feelings of deep solidarity and empathy.[62] Finally, by portraying a community's existential struggle in the semiotic language of the crucifixion, these public Ways of the Cross evoke moral clarity by naming ongoing situations of injustice as modern-day crucifixions, orienting public imaginations toward the need for liberation.

Because of its migratory and public character, the urban Via Crucis takes on additional moral weight and aesthetic force in migrant communities. For this reason, analyses of the ritual have become a centerpiece of Latinx theologies. In a particular way, scholars like Tirres have emphasized the epistemological significance of the popular liturgies of Holy Week at San Fernando Cathedral. Cuban American theologian Roberto Goizueta, whose book *Caminemos Con Jesús* has become a classic of the genre, suggests that when the people of San Fernando ritually walk with Jesus to his death on Good Friday, they reveal a relational theological anthropology of accompaniment grounded in a preferential option for the poor.[63] For the Mexicano community in Chicago's Pilsen neighborhood, similarly, the annual Via Crucis has functioned both as a practice of lament in the face of structural injustice and as a prophetic act of resistance to forces of domination and assimilation. That ritual was first organized by Pilsen's St. Vitus Parish in 1977 after a massive Christmas Eve fire in a nearby apartment building killed ten children and two mothers, all of them parishioners. A week later, a second fire on New Year's Day killed five more. Parishioners pointed to substandard housing, municipal neglect, and a lack of Spanish-speaking firefighters as major contributors to the disasters.[64] Organizers planned the route to highlight parallels between Jesus's undeserved suffering and local sites of injustice. At each station, songs and reflections transformed the neighborhood into a "spiritual topography."[65] In her evocative account of Pilsen's Good Friday, Karen Mary Davalos describes the Via Crucis, which continues to draw annual crowds of over ten thousand people, as a "counterdiscourse to white public space . . . [that] articulates a vision of equity and justice."[66] Praying in the streets, participants sacralize public space even as they openly subvert the "material barriers, physical dangers, and social inequalities [that] constitute the architecture of domination."[67] In so doing, the space created by the ritual becomes a site in which participants actively contest and renegotiate the power relationships that structure their lives.

As the Great Migration transformed African American religious life, Black Catholics also adopted the public Stations of the Cross as a communal practice of devotion and religio-racial identity work. From 1937 to 1968, the community at Corpus Christi Catholic Church, a prominent Black Catholic parish in Chicago's South-Side Bronzeville neighborhood, annually reenacted the Living Stations of the Cross in the church's sanctuary. For Black Catholics in Chicago, many of them converts to the faith, the Living Stations in Bronzeville were a "self-making performance," distinguishing them from their evangelical Christian counterparts and drawing them closer to Christ. In his analysis of Corpus Christi's Living Stations, Matthew Cressler argues that Catholicism's devotional bodily disposition of restraint and self-discipline, embodied in the stations' pantomimed stops and starts, became an important religious signifier for the South Side's Black Catholics during a period of geographical migration and metropolitan cultural renaissance.[68]

While part of this devotional lineage, the Egleston Square Way of the Cross also differs in significant ways. The clearest distinction is in the extent of its diversity. In San Antonio, Pilsen, and Bronzeville, the Via Crucis is (or was) bound up with the struggles and journeys of specific cultural communities. While rooted in the place of Egleston Square, the Roxbury Way of the Cross is thoroughly defined by cultural, linguistic, and religious pluralism. The ritual's prayers, reflections, and songs alternate between English and Spanish. While Catholic in form, the stations often include Protestant churches and interfaith organizations. Similarly, the speakers invited to offer prayers or reflections at each station represent an ecumenical cross section of Egleston locals. Though the cross is passed primarily among parish members, the procession also attracts an interreligious cadre of neighbors and community leaders, including those from area Jewish communities. The most important marker of belonging in the ritual is neither baptism nor church affiliation but rather local commitment.

Second, the St. Mary's Way of the Cross is not a passion play.[69] To varying degrees, the preceding examples are all period pieces. Each features detailed costumes and sometimes elaborate theatrical sets: whip-wielding Roman centurions; a bloodied, thorn-crowned Jesus; veiled women portraying Mary and the anguished women of Jerusalem. At San Fernando Cathedral, the ritual concludes with a graphic dramatized crucifixion as a parishioner-actor portraying Jesus is tied to a cross and hoisted high above the square for all to see, flanked by two other crucified men representing the thieves Dismas and Gestas. In Roxbury, by contrast, there are no costumes or character roles. While the station's titles, the traditional Liguori prayers ("We adore you, O Christ . . ."), and the thorn-encircled cross tie the practice to the past, the ritual is staged firmly in the present day.

Moreover, and most importantly, no one person represents Jesus or his tormentors. Instead, the cross is passed from parishioner to parishioner, changing hands at each station, sometimes even midprocession. In typical passion reenactments, a male parishioner portrays Jesus, other men his torturers, and female parishioners his mother Mary, Veronica, and the women of Jerusalem. Most everyone else represents the crowd, the mass of bystanders who garner a bad reputation throughout the Holy Week liturgies. The crowd is portrayed as capricious and easily persuadable, singing "Hosanna in the highest!" on Palm Sunday and hissing "Crucify him!" on Good Friday. In Roxbury, any distinction between Christ-figure and crowd is fleeting and fluid. Parishioners of any gender or age could be asked to step into the role of Jesus next. The reflections read at each station draw intricate parallels between past and present, naming Christ's presence in both modern-day crucifixions and in local works of mercy and healing. But among participants, no one takes up the cross in isolation. Dressed in jeans and tennis shoes, parishioners shoulder its bulky frame together. In this way, the ritual transposes the crucifixion—and, implicitly, notions of sin and salvation—from an individual register into a communal one. We will return to this point in the next section.

Ritual and Contestation

Discerning the contours of meaning of a passion staged against the backdrop of social reality is a high-stakes task, and a complicated one. As public sites of religious, cultural, and political negotiation, each of the aforementioned urban Ways of the Cross reveals the contested politics of the passion. In Pilsen, the Via Crucis signifies resistance to domination, yet it takes place within a context of patriarchy that it can do little to challenge, making its vision of justice and equality an "ambivalent [one] for women."[70] At Corpus Christi in Bronzeville, the Living Stations attracted two distinct groups: the African American parishioners who planned and participated in the ritual, and the white journalists and worshippers who turned out in droves to gaze upon Christ's suffering portrayed by Black bodies—as Matthew Cressler describes it, "white voyeurs [who] sought out 'authentic' experiences in working-class communities."[71] The ritual's Black and white participants did not simply differ in their interpretations of the Living Stations. In many ways, they experienced entirely different events with disparate meanings. Similarly, Wayne Ashley's account of the public Stations of the Cross at a predominantly Puerto Rican parish on the Lower East Side of Manhattan in the 1990s narrates the conflict between parishioners and the parish's progressive Euro-American priest. Priest and faithful clashed when the former began repurposing the Good Friday devotion to make provocative political statements on progressive social issues without regard for the Puerto Rican community's devotional traditions or their very different set of social concerns.[72] Here, too, we see a single ritual interpreted in ways that are not merely different but barely commensurate.

Rather than functioning as a conduit of unified, collective meaning-making, ritual is often the site of contestation, compromise, and a superabundance of diverse and often disparate experiences. Ritual conceals even as it reveals. It privileges some stories over others, heals certain wounds while ignoring other ones. It speaks with a fractured voice. These internal excesses and conflicts of meaning are true of virtually any ritual, even the most circumscribed, and is certainly the case on the streets of Roxbury every Good Friday. In a community defined by cultural, linguistic, generational, and theological difference, the Via Crucis's embodied vernacular of actions, places, and symbols serves as a common language. But in this shared semiotic language, the ritual tells many different stories at once. As participants walk, they carry with them their own memories, motivations, beliefs, and identities, all of which indelibly shape their experiences of the passion journey.

Predictably, then, the St. Mary's Way of the Cross has hosted its share of disagreements. Martin recounted a conflict that arose one year between the English and Spanish Mass communities over the question of how closely the ritual should imitate Jesus's suffering. "As the parish become more multicultural—it was always English-Spanish—but as the Latino population grew and was more involved, the walk took a different flavor," Martin explained. One year, some Spanish Mass members insisted that the Good Friday procession adopt a more overtly pious, reenactment-like character. "We always carried the cross, but there was one year some of the people wanted to reenact [the crucifixion], like the Romans. So these guys were wearing, like, helmets and looking like that. You know, there are places that do that. And acting like Christ, and stumbling and falling. A very *dramatic* dramatization."[73]

The change only lasted one year. "I think as a group we . . . yeah, it's not . . ." Martin said, trailing off. For some Latinx parishioners, a Via Crucis that visually recalled Jesus's suffering felt poignant and appropriate to the spiritual significance of Good Friday. For Martin and other longtime parishioners (including some Latinx long-timers), however, the graphic passion reenactment evoked discomfort and a visceral sense that such expressions were not "us." The performance felt contrived. For those who had been present at its inception, the Neighborhood Way of the Cross was both a memorialization of Jesus's passion and a protest against violence in the present day. When the heavy-handed aesthetics of reenactment threatened to outperform the walk's local significance, the ritual seemed to lose some of its original purpose and power. In listening to Martin narrate the conflict, I sensed that what he was getting at was not only a feeling that the change betrayed the ritual's protest-oriented roots. Flattening the ritual into a reenactment decontextualized and dis-placed it, constricting its capaciousness and, in turn, the ability of many different people to read their own stories into it. Yet rejecting the change also meant saying no to the contributions of a group of newer Latinx parishioners, a move that conflicted with the parish's mission of inclusion.

The short-lived controversy illustrates one challenge of ritual in contexts where competing visions are at play and the unique tensions such differences raise in a community that makes welcome a central part of its mission. Judgments about ritual forms can become a proxy for a host of other conflicts over inclusion, integration, and ideology. As I noted in chapter 2, longevity often proved the most potent source of division in the parish. Long-time parishioners, whose experiences of St. Mary's were rooted in the searing 1980s and '90s and the legacy of Fr. Jack, had an experientially different understanding of the parish's identity than those who arrived later on. As new migrants settled in and around Egleston, they joined a parish suffused with a sense of its own story, posing a challenge for integration. Such was, or seemed to be, one source of the feeling of tepid welcome that English Mass newcomer Gina articulated in chapter 2. The question of ownership over parish identity and ritual practice was an issue I encountered at St. Mary's from long-timers in both the English and Spanish Mass communities. Whenever a newcomer—including a new priest—attempted to make changes that departed from the long-established, often idiosyncratic "St. Mary's way," they would frequently be met by objections that such changes were simply not "how we do things." Of course, practices taken for granted as indelible parts of the quasi-institutionalized bricolage known as St. Mary's tradition were once themselves inventions, ad hoc responses to crises or practical needs.

Martin ultimately interpreted the Way of the Cross disagreement in a positive light. Reflectively, he regarded the incident as evidence of conflict's constructive possibilities:

I think what it showed was the challenge of working in a multicultural setting, because you have to honor and respect all of the cultures that are part of it. And we're still struggling with that, in a way. . . . And those [struggles] are good, in a way, because it forces people to talk about the issues and come up with solutions. Because I think what you sometimes get is kind of, *Why don't they want to do this? Why do they want to do that? We've always done it this way![74]*

Indeed, despite the soft hegemony wielded by the parish's storied past, ritual *was* frequently the site of compromise. Gayle, who helped to lead the bilingual Lenten Retreat, once described to me how the planning process for the annual event—an important one for the parish, attracting nearly equal numbers of English and Spanish Mass retreatants—was always the fruit of intense intergenerational and intercultural negotiation. One year, Dominican parishioners proposed a new format for the retreat's sacrament of reconciliation service. Before going to confession, they suggested, retreatants should write their sins on slips of paper, then use a hammer and nails to pound the paper slips into a large, wooden cross. The ritual would symbolize the pain that human sin caused to Jesus, bringing retreatants face to face with their own fallenness and their need for repentance. Spanish Mass leaders were excited about the proposal. Its affective spirituality resonated with their sense of Lenten piety. English Mass leaders were less enthusiastic. They feared the ritual would cast God as an angry judge out for revenge rather than as a loving, forgiving parent. They wanted the service to accent hope, not sin. Eventually, the planning team arrived at a compromise. The reconciliation service would feature the cross-and-nails ritual. However, after everyone had gone to confession, retreatants would remove the papers from the cross and throw them into the fireplace. Then, on new slips of paper, everyone would write their hopes and place those on the cross where their sins had been. "It's kind of symbolic of taking each one of our theologies and trying to bring them together," Gayle said. "I think what happens is that there's a lot of listening. And there's a lot of leaving one's ego at the door. On everybody's parts."[75]

Besides Martin, no one who spoke with me about the Neighborhood Way of the Cross mentioned the year of conflict, nor any other serious dissatisfaction with the ritual's current or previous form. It seemed that debates about the "real meaning" of the Via Crucis were settled. Indeed, in our conversations, participants confidently elaborated on its significance. As it turned out, virtually everyone I talked to described something different.

For some, like Spanish Mass choir member Marisol, the ritual was a journey of memory, reconnecting them with the Holy Week processions of their childhood homelands. Growing up in the Dominican Republic, Marisol recalled,

> My grandmother used to do the Via Crucis on her own with her grand-children. She went from house to house. She wasn't walking in the street with a big cross or anything. She had just a tiny cross that she carried, decorated beautifully with colored paper, and she had the little books to read each station. I was little. She put all of us grandchildren behind her and brought us with her to all of the houses, knocking on [doors]. . . . She liked it. She said she it was her own Via Crucis, all over the neighborhood. Her alone. We loved her so much.[76]

Now, when Marisol's preteen children ask her why they have to attend the Way of the Cross every year, she tells them the story of her grandmother. Similarly, Parish Council translator Ramón connected his annual participation in the walk with cultural and religious remembering: "I think it's been a way to connect to my root of being Catholic in South America, specifically in [my home country]—as a way to connect to the past, the tradition of the past . . . not only of the past when I was growing up but also to the tradition of Jesus Christ two thousand years ago."[77] For Marisol and Ramón, walking the Way of the Cross collapsed both geography and time. Participating became an act of traditioning, carrying the past into the present as a source of hope for the future.[78]

For others, the Way of the Cross was primarily about reinscribing a sense of local commitment to Egleston Square and its people. Walking through the streets took on an almost sacramental quality, the river of footsteps an efficacious sign of local solidarity. "I think that it helps me to kind of come back to reality about where I live, because it's my home, it's my neighborhood," explained Olivia, who moved a few blocks away from St. Mary's with her partner after a months-long search for the "right" parish. "To have the stations in our neighborhood is really powerful for me. Like this place that I live really, every day, lives the Stations of the Cross. And whether we recognize it or not, it's happening. People are living their own Way of the Cross in our neighborhood. So, I also think that it gives me an entrance—a way of interacting with our neighborhood that, because I've only lived there two years, I wouldn't necessarily get access to."[79] As a newer, white resident, Olivia mentioned occasionally feeling like an outsider in Egleston. Walking the Via Crucis each year gave her a sense of intimacy with her neighbors, making her feel more united to the community and its story.

Still other participants were drawn by an inarticulable sense of spiritual obligation to accompany Jesus in his final hours. Omar, a first-generation Cuban immigrant, described feeling compelled by tradition: "To walk around the neighborhood on Good Friday, it's . . . how do I say . . . I've been doing it for many, many years. Since I don't have to go to work [that day], I feel like I gotta come over here and do this."[80] Ximena, the bilingual lay leader who helped to coordinate religious education, echoed the motivation. "It's something that I have been doing all my life, since I was maybe three, four years old. All my life, with my parents," she explained. "I have to walk. I have to go. It's like I need to do it. It's part of my religion and it's part of my beliefs, to follow all those [stations] of Jesus. It's something that I . . . I don't know how to explain, but I feel like I have to go."[81] One year, a few weeks before Easter, Ximena and her sister received word that their brother had been murdered in their home country. They were unable to return for the funeral, so that year, Ximena's home became a station in the Via Crucis. The two women decorated Ximena's front steps with flowers and sacred imagery and welcomed their fellow parishioners and neighbors in the rain.[82] In the end, the community with whom Ximena accompanied Jesus in his hour of need joined her in hers.

In a parish where seemingly everyone has come from somewhere else, the Way of the Cross is a shared journey. What enables this Good Friday migration to cultivate the sort of space that opens toward solidarity has much to do with the intersection of its Christian and urban semiotics; linguistic and cultural inclusivity; aesthetic simplicity; porous, public boundaries; and the moral urgency and relevance of the neighborhood passions to which it attends. These points of commonality—the elevated cross, the recognizable narrative arc of the passion story, the muscle-memory peripatetics of Catholic devotional movement, the familiar streets and buildings and homes, the well-known local events—become middle spaces of encounter across difference and thus shared referents for memory and hope. Walking the journey together transforms this parish of migrants into a migrant parish, a pilgrim church.

Of course, in a migrant parish, long-standing rituals migrate, too. Rather than being remade wholesale, as the group of newer Spanish Mass members attempted to do one year, the Via Crucis is more often gradually reimagined from the inside as its ever-changing community of participants practices alternate interpretations. The ritual is home to many stories at once. Some of these stories have nothing explicit to say about nonviolence or social justice. Others have little to do with Gospel accounts of the crucifixion, at least on the surface. Instead of debating what the Way of the Cross "really means," participants like Marisol, Ramón, Olivia, Ximena, and Omar simply read their own memories and understandings into it. By bringing their pasts, devotions, cultural contexts, and theological commitments to bear on the ritual's significance, new parishioners continually renegotiate its meaning from the inside. As the late ritual theorist Catherine Bell writes, "[A] person's involvement in ritual activities . . . is never an indiscriminate openness to what is going on. A participant, as a ritualized agent and social body, naturally brings to such activities a self-constituting history that is a patchwork of compliance, resistance, misunderstanding, and a redemptive personal appropriation of the hegemonic order."[83] In other words, to acknowledge the complex politics of the passion performance is to recognize the theological agency of its practitioners. Ritual is a site within which power relationships and ecclesial identities are ever being reworked, however subtly and surreptitiously.

From Theodicy to Solidarity

Foregrounding the moral and theological agency of the hundreds who show up to process through the streets of Egleston Square every Good Friday helps us to appreciate more clearly how a such a ritual participates in the formation of community. It is tempting to regard Christian practice as containing, and thus imbuing participants with, a particular, predefined set of beliefs and worldviews. According to this perspective, ritual forms individuals into a community of faith primarily by consolidating group identity.[84] In the wake of collective trauma, we grow even more inclined to speak of ritual's value in this way—that is, as a communal meaning-making activity, a way of making sense or seeking closure.[85] Understood within this frame, the question the Way of the Cross would appear to answer is, *What does the Christian tradition tell us about what all of this suffering means?* To be sure, it hints at answers: *These victims of poverty and injustice are the crucified people of today.*[86] *Like Galilee, Roxbury is just the kind of out-of-the-way margin where God might pitch a tent. Resurrection is both an eschatological reality and a social one, sprouting up in small, hidden ways all the time through acts of neighborly love. Peace is the way of Christ. Violence is an affront to God. Confronting our pain is more important than seeking revenge. Christ is on the side of the poor.* Undoubtedly, these were some of the "hard statements" Sr. Margaret spoke of when she recalled the many ways that the people of St. Mary's took to the streets during the worst of the gang years.

Yet while part of the ritual's work clearly involves interpreting Egleston Square's struggle in light of the Gospel, collective meaning-making is an incomplete way of framing the solidarity ritualized in its streets every Good Friday. Participants do not emerge from the final station of one mind. (And, as Gayle's recollection of the Lenten Retreat reconciliation service disagreement suggests, no ritual could possibly bring all parishioners to theological or ideological agreement.) Even if it were somehow achieved, interpretive consensus would not be the source of the ritual's power. Indeed, part of the enduring power of the Via Crucis tradition is its resistance to superficial meaning-making. While the Roxbury stations incorporate instances of everyday healing and rebirth, the traditional ritual concludes not by celebrating Jesus's resurrection but by mourning his death. In other words, as the quintessence of Good Friday, the Way of the Cross resists the sort of satisfying closure that the jump to Easter morning might offer. Thus, while it is possible to frame the Roxbury Via Crucis as a communal practice of interpretation, its many layers of internal diversity and the agency of its participants suggest that it is also more than that.

"Solidarity is produced by people acting together, not by people thinking together," writes anthropologist David Kertzer.[87] In other words, as Jewish cultural anthropologist Don Seeman puts it, ritual is "generous."[88] Seeman, drawing on Emmanuel Levinas, argues that in moments of collective trauma, the purpose of lament and other ritualized responses to suffering is not to exegete its meaning, domesticating pain through the imposition of cognitive order or distilling from it some edifying spiritual or civic lesson. Instead, transposing the question of ritual's power in the midst of pain from a hermeneutical key to a phenomenological one, Seeman argues that lament functions primarily as a "ground of intersubjectivity."[89] By effecting embodied presence, ritual makes space for empathy, accompaniment, and relationship where these may once have felt impossible. Ritual sets the table for presence: the presence of God, the presence of others, the presence of the dead. What mattered after Hector Morales's murder was not only or even primarily what the Way of the Cross *said* about the community's struggle, but what it enabled parishioners and neighbors to *do* under such conditions.[90] In the face of ongoing violence, and across ethnic, linguistic, generational, political, and gang divisions, the Good Friday procession gave parishioners and neighbors a way of joining with one another. It offered them an embodied itinerary for walking a common journey. Solidarity, not theodicy, is the work of the Via Crucis. Thus, the implicit question the ritual poses to participants is not primarily, *What does Jesus's passion teach us about what it means to suffer,* but rather, *With whom are we saved?*

Solidarity, Salvation, and the Shared Cross

"We adore you, O Christ, and we bless you. / For by your holy cross you have redeemed the world." These lines from the Liguori text of the Stations of the Cross are such a normative part of the Good Friday devotion that even at St. Mary's, they are recited verbatim from the traditional script. In many ways, they serve as the ritual's thesis statement: *Jesus saved humanity from sin by his death on the cross; therefore, Christians honor him by following him in his passion.* Reading these words aloud on the streets of a community whose own passion is on wrenching display makes questions about the relationship between crucifixion and salvation inescapable.

Sarah Lenzi traces the devotional lineage to which the Via Crucis belongs to the eleventh-century rise in pietistic practices centered on Jesus's bodily suffering, a turn often associated with the atonement soteriology of Anselm of Canterbury.[91] The Liguori text's use of the economic metaphor of redemption to signify salvation—a term that originally denoted the act of buying the freedom of an enslaved person by paying off their debts—suggests a transactional imagination hovering behind the ritual's operative soteriology. According to the logic of redemption, sin is framed as a kind of debt to God. By dying on the cross, Jesus pays humanity's unpayable debt with his own life. Being both human and God, and thus having accrued no sin-debt of his own, Jesus is the only person in history capable of paying this debt.[92] The cross, then, is the mechanism by which Jesus makes this payment—the bank at which he cashes in his life. Moreover, by framing adoration as something that is owed, the text suggests that walking the Way of the Cross is one way that Christians today make payments toward another kind of debt: that of gratitude to Christ for his unmerited, redemptive sacrifice. Within the logic of the ritual's traditional staging, then, there is no need for a Station XV: The cross has done the saving.[93]

The traditional stations frame salvation as a quasi-economic transaction that occurs between the first and second Persons of the Trinity and individual humans, who secure their salvation by professing personal belief in Christ's atoning sacrifice. Yet this framing leaves unaddressed the role of other seemingly vital actors. What role do human relationships, social structures, and concrete practices serve in the economy of salvation? What is the role of the church? The community? The Holy Spirit? Similarly unaddressed are a host of follow-up questions: Was Jesus born for any purpose other than to die? If it is only the cross that saves, is the resurrection merely a receipt of this transaction? And if, again, it is the cross that saves, then in what sense should we regard human suffering as worthy of veneration? If innocent suffering pays the debt of sin, then what is the moral status of those who cause the innocent to suffer? What, ultimately, does following the Via Crucis entail for the life of a community already bearing its share of crosses?

As Nancy Pineda-Madrid has convincingly argued, such theologies of the cross ultimately fail to take adequate account of the role of the community in the work of salvation—both the positive primacy of social relationships in a life of faith and the negative, crucifying reality of social injustice. At worst, by appearing to locate salvation entirely in Jesus's suffering and death, such theologies seem to have little to say to those who suffer injustice today. In the Gospel of Matthew, Jesus warns his would-be followers of the high cost of discipleship: "If any want to become my followers, let them deny themselves and take up their cross and follow me. For those who want to save their life will lose it, and those who lose their life for my sake will find it" (Mt 16:24). Lest anyone labor under the impression that faithfulness to God offers a life of comfort and security, Jesus neatly dispels them of that fantasy. Yet, as Pineda-Madrid rightly contends, the notion that self-denial and submission are the price of admission into the kingdom of God has proven dangerous. The symbol of the cross has been used to justify highly individualized understandings of the Christian life and to excuse, even valorize, innocent suffering. The false idea that faithfulness to Christ demands silent assent to violence and abuse has been wielded as a weapon of domination, perpetuating the suffering of women, Black Americans, migrants, and other marginalized persons and communities.[94]

As they walk the Via Crucis together, the people of Egleston Square perform a crucial shift in this imagination. To understand how, let us return to where we began, with the procession's opening words: "*Encaminémonos.* Now let us begin *our* walk with the cross.*" Eschewing the typical centering of a singular Christ-actor in favor of communal sharing of the cross transposes the passion story from an individual register into a collective one. Refusing to idealize suffering qua suffering, the Egleston Square ritual instead portrays the crucifixion less as a soteriological necessity than as a historical one—that is, as the painful propensity of a society living under the weight of empire to execute the poor and vulnerable and those least able to defend themselves.[95] Indeed, the obvious injustice at the heart of the local sufferings to which the Roxbury stations witness each year guards against the urge to romanticize Jesus's agony. During the procession, the invitation to carry the cross comes unexpectedly and without warning, in some way evoking the cruelty of circumstance and the reminder that in life, anyone can find themselves forced to bear a burden they did nothing to deserve. Yet no one is made to shoulder the cross for more than the distance between two stations. Walking side by side, parishioners and neighbors share its weight. The cross in the streets becomes a symbol of divine presence—a God who has suffered in solidarity with a people who have suffered. In turn, the public, communal presence that the cross effects corroborates the Liguori text: "*For by your holy cross, you have redeemed the world.*" Salvation comes not in the torture of the cross but in the sharing, which points in its own way toward the hope of resurrection.

Solidarity is a soteriological category. That is, to speak of solidarity is to make implicit claims about the nature and locus of salvation. Solidarity takes as its orienting truth the recognition that, in the words of Martin Luther King, Jr., "We are caught in an inescapable network of mutuality, tied in a single garment of destiny."[96] Solidarity calls forth the recognition that all struggles for justice and liberation are interconnected, giving rise to unlikely partnerships. The privileged, meanwhile, learn to view structures of sin and domination not as problems to be dealt with by their victims but rather as forces that dehumanize their beneficiaries as well and thus degrade the entire social fabric of the community. In this way, solidarity is both an affective orientation and a sustained practice motivated from two directions: empathy for and indignation at the undeserved suffering of others, and the desire for personal conversion from apathy and complicity to responsibility, community, and love. On some level, undertaking the costly, inefficient, painstaking work of reorienting one's life and the social structures within which one exists toward the flourishing of the community only makes sense if one believes genuinely that her soul hangs in the balance. Ironically, this self-orientation serves the productive end of alleviating the privileged from the desire to play moral savior to the poor. Here, the oft-cited words of Aboriginal elder and activist Lilla Watson offer a helpful mantra: "If you have come to help me, you are wasting your time. If you have come because your liberation is bound up with mine, then let us work together."[97]

We can illustrate the point by recalling the Archdiocese of Boston's attempt to sustain the Roxbury Apostolate in the 1960s. While the initiative began with vigor, no amount of good intentions could shake the program's fundamental paternalism. Instead of attempting to address the cause of the inner-city parish crisis identified by the archdiocese's own Roxbury Report—white Catholic racism and refusal of solidarity to Catholics of color—the Apostolate instead opted to treat its effects, no doubt growing frustrated when the initiative failed to make lasting changes. However, when the St. Mary's Parish Council coalesced in the years after Vatican II, laity reoriented the parish's financial and liturgical practices to concretely bind the fate of parish to the good of its most racially, ethnically, and economically marginalized parishioners. Both initiatives were expressly motivated by solidarity. Which of the two achieved it?

In a community riveted by violence, ritual is an act of survival. Sr. Josephine put it this way: "We're family. We're brothers and sisters. And when we own one another's pain, we're able to do things that we never could do alone." Here, the soteriological practice of crossing neighborhoods, gang territories, and transportation lines becomes clear. In Egleston Square, such divisions have long signified territorialism and violence. Positioned on opposing sides of these boundaries, neighbors become enemies, agents of one another's destruction. Within an ethos of division, temporal salvation is construed as a zero-sum game achieved by protecting territory and eliminating neighbors-turned-rivals. Yet when community members unite to ritually cross these boundaries, weaving points of division into a common journey that ends in resurrection, they reveal to themselves the reality of their own interconnectedness. The Roxbury Stations of the Cross perform a common yearning both immanent and eschatological for salvation *in* community and salvation *of* the community. The fundamental intuition of solidarity is that there is no salvation outside of one another.[98] Uniting to resist structures of violence, domination, and dehumanization is an act of faith in a God whose own incarnation evinced the salvific power of solidarity with the victimized.[99] Reflecting now on Sr. Margaret's recollection of the "hard statements" parishioners made with the Via Crucis during the worst of the violent years, I am struck by a sense that their hardest statement of all was presence itself.

Conclusion

The journey with the cross annually constitutes and reconstitutes the community.[100] To make this migration in miniature is to become in some way a part of the people of St. Mary's. On my second of six Good Fridays at St. Mary's, Javier approached me in the street. Clasping me on the shoulder and bringing his voice close to my ear, he asked—or rather instructed—me to carry the cross next. I was surprised. It hadn't occurred to me that my presence in the ritual meant that I, just like anyone else, might be invited to participate in this way. The year Hector Morales was killed, I was a toddler in a middle-class family in the suburbs of Denver, Colorado. I never met Fr. Jack, who fulfilled his dream of joining the Missionary Society of St. James the Apostle and moved to Carabayllo, Peru, in 1993. After working to cofound Socios en Salud, a sister organization of Partners in Health dedicated to curing multidrug-resistant tuberculosis in Peru, he died of TB himself in 1995. I wasn't there when the archdiocese tried to shutter the parish in 2004 and the neighborhood rallied to its defense. None of these community touchstones were part of my personal experience. At that point, I had lived the story of St. Mary's for a year and a half. *Was this cross mine, too? Was it somehow presumptuous of me to momentarily assume this central role in the ritual?*

These are questions that occur to me now, in retrospect, but they did not arise at the time, at least not in a categorical way. Besides, there was no way I could have declined. No matter my intention, to say no to the cross would have meant saying no to the community. Javier and another man gently positioned the bulky cardboard cross on my shoulder. I nodded and felt my cheeks and neck grow warm as I started to walk. To be the center of attention, even for a moment, felt odd. I became intensely aware of my steps: *Am I walking too fast? Too slow? Should I stride to the front of the procession or remain in the middle? What should I do with my face? Should I look sad? Do I look too sad? Should I fix my eyes forward or down? Is this research? Can I write about this?*

In any case, it was clear to me then, and remains evident to me now, that whatever my reservations, walking the journey meant that I, too, was part of the community. And the ritual quietly transformed me, burrowing itself into my own urban imagination. I experienced the city differently after my first St. Mary's Good Friday. For weeks, every bus ride felt strangely like an act of anamnesis, its rhythmic stops and starts a liturgy of memory through the ordinary places of dying and rising that made this community I had grown to call my own. St. Mary's, I realized one rainy afternoon while waiting for the bus, was not unlike the MBTA station under whose smoky concrete eaves I was hunched with damp and grumbling neighbors, all of us breathing puffs of frosty vapor into one another's shoulders. The parish was a stop along the way, a meeting point formed by crossings. Few had arrived there from the same place or for the same reasons. What united them was this collision of presences: theirs, others', God's. They were there, shoulder to shoulder, willing enough to get on board, to bear with one another on the way.

5 Ritualizing Solidarity

When it's bilingual, you feel identified with the community. It makes you look into the future and say, "Well, everything will be [good] in the future and everyone will be together, because neither language nor race nor anything else will separate us." Only the Word of God will bring us together, to feel like brothers and sisters. Like a community.

Yamaris[1]

I think anytime you mix groups, it requires more work. People sometimes have to be consciously active in the role of mixing and getting along. . . . Sometimes, it's a cultural thing. And sometimes, it's a communication thing that, until you realize it's an issue, you don't even realize that there should be a conversation about it. Sometimes, you have to know what you don't know, or have conversations—get to really *know* one another—before you can meld well. And I think sometimes the melding doesn't happen because of fear. Oftentimes, one community either feels they're going to be overshadowed by the other, or their customs are going to be changed, dropped, whatever, if they become truly part of this bigger community. And they're afraid. They don't want to lose their identity.

Michelle[2]

April 1, 2012

On Palm Sunday morning, Mass begins at the playground two blocks away. On days like this—the liturgies of Holy Week, Pentecost, and other important church feasts—St. Mary's celebrates only one Sunday Mass, a bilingual liturgy to which parishioners from both language communities contribute in equal measure. Waving grassy palms in the air, we process slowly up the sleepy street to the church. We're led by two Jesuits, a French priest and a Chilean deacon. A trail of adult altar servers from the Spanish Mass follow behind, then the rest of us. As we approach the stone stairwell down to the church, the mounting echo of bongo drums punctuates the morning tranquility. We erupt through the doors to the shock of a feverish refrain, music meant to evoke the frenzy that surrounds Jesus's entry into Jerusalem in the Gospels: "*Hosanna Hey! Hosanna Ha! Hosanna Hey, Hosanna Hey, Hosanna Ha!*" singers call into the microphone. To the right of the altar, a joint choir made up of musicians from both Masses leads the raucous song. Everyone is dressed in red and waves palms above their heads to the beat of the music.

I am assigned a role in today's liturgy, so before making my way to the park, I had used a sweater to save a seat in a pew near the front. When I reenter the sanctuary with the procession, the sweater is nowhere in sight. I finally spy it bunched between two women sitting in the spot I had tried to reserve (laughably, it turns out). I awkwardly retrieve it and scan the church for another place to sit, sliding into a pew directly behind a pillar that everyone else avoids, for obvious reasons.

The Palm Sunday liturgy traditionally features a lengthy reading of the passion narrative, with celebrant and lectors voicing the parts of Jesus, the narrator, and other supporting characters. But for a multilingual congregation, the long, involved reading presents challenges. The parish has hymnals but rarely uses missalettes, making it hard for the assembly, who collectively read the part of the crowd, to follow along in another language and to anticipate their own lines. Massgoers receive the passion story again on Good Friday, first during the Way of the Cross and later from a bilingual cadre of lectors during that evening's liturgy. Seeking a different way to tell the story, the liturgy and religious education coordinators worked together to develop an alternative practice for Palm Sunday: In place of the Gospel reading, a group of parishioners performs a ten-minute passion mime in front of the altar. The silent, expressive performance, set to poignant instrumental music, offers a way into the story that doesn't require missalettes or translations.

I was caught off guard when organizers assigned me a role in the Palm Sunday mime. I was even more surprised when I learned what that role was: I would be playing Jesus. I demurred. I still viewed myself as a guest in the parish house, and I didn't want to alienate anyone by stirring up controversy, regardless of how fascinated I was by the idea of reimagining the narrative's gender roles. But I was persuaded when one organizer explained that young women had been portraying Jesus in the mime for a number of years. It was a way of acknowledging the crosses that the women in the community carried, she explained to me, citing issues like domestic abuse, workplace harassment, and the heartaches of motherhood. I admit that I was also compelled by the fact that the organizers and choreographers were Black and Latina women. I found myself more willing to accept the role knowing that it wasn't simply the earnest but misplaced brainchild of a fellow progressive white person. When the organizers announced the mime's cast at the next Parish Council meeting, however, the pastor—a newly assigned and short-lived diocesan priest also managing two other parishes—vetoed the plan. He maintained that the "more traditional" Spanish Mass parishioners would be uncomfortable seeing a woman play the role of Jesus, a claim that mime participants from the Spanish Mass rejected. Even if he were right, it seemed clear that he was using concern for Hispanic parishioners to avoid admitting that he was the one who didn't like the idea. The pastor wouldn't be presiding at that Mass or, for that matter, any of the other Holy Week liturgies at St. Mary's. Regardless, the power was in his hands. On one level, I was secretly relieved to have been released from the burden of the mime's central role. In a deeper way, though, the decision felt as revealing as it was theologically absurd: I was reassigned to the role of Peter. Apparently, as a woman, I could play the man who cut off somebody's ear and denied Jesus, just not the Savior himself.

The following year, I was given the cross to carry up School Street in the Good Friday Way of the Cross. Much later, I was struck by the contrast between the passion mime during Mass and the Via Crucis in the streets. Both were highly contextualized; both were lay directed and performed. But only in one of the spaces could anyone—a woman, a mother, a child, a gay man, a teenager—stand *in persona Christi*, in the person of Christ. The streets, it seemed, offered transgressive possibilities, the chance to imagine. Who were all those theorists who had long ago decided that the private realm was women's domain? In the streets, a woman could be Jesus.

———————

April 7, 2012

Six and a half days later, the Easter Vigil Mass begins at sundown on Saturday with a bonfire in the parking lot. As dusk falls around us, we follow the fragile light of the Easter candle around the block once again before descending into the darkened church. We spill down the stairs and fumble in silence for a pew, cocooned in the glow of the towering candle.

"La luz de Cristo," the Jesuit presider intones from the back of the church in French-accented Spanish.

"Gracias a Dio-os," we chant in response.

Processing up the center aisle, he repeats the refrain in English: "The light of Christ."

"Thanks be to Go-od," we call back through the darkness.

The priest carefully lowers the candle and turns to those seated nearest the aisles. Outside in the parking lot, ushers had passed around baskets of thin vigil candles. Beginning at the front of the church, people reach their candles into the Easter candle's flame and turn to share the light with neighbors. A luminous wave slowly spreads through the sanctuary. The church is full. I'm seated among friends, five of us pressed into a side pew built for three or four, staggering our hips to fit. The intimacy

FIGURE 13. Parishioners light one another's candles in the darkened church sanctuary during the nighttime Easter Vigil Mass, April 15, 2017. Photo by the author.

of the church feels dreamlike, a sea of faces cloaked in the oceanic glow of subterranean candlelight.

Gaby lights my candle, and I turn around to share the flame with the person seated behind me, an older woman from the Spanish community whom I know by face but not by name.

"Recibe la luz de Cristo," I venture, guessing at the Spanish translation of the ritual exchange.

"Gracias a Dios," she responds. Our wicks touch. Between us, a papery orange flame reaches toward the sky.

———

In previous chapters, I've examined embodied ritual as a site of solidarity in the local church. Observing how often parishioners drew from the lexicon of migration to narrate their journeys to St. Mary's—whether those migrations involved crossing parish boundaries, neighborhood divides, denominational identities, racial lines, or international borders—I proposed that we understand St. Mary's as a way station in an urban borderland. In turn, I've asked how ritual practice helped parishioners to perform this border work—to cultivate friendships, tell stories, exercise power, build peace, and, in a real way, to survive. The welcome/bienvenidos ritual during Mass announcements ritualized, and thus normalized, the acts of arrival, departure, and return. Reciting and reflecting on the parish mission statement at the beginning of Parish Council meetings ritualized both the slow rhythm of translated communication and an approach to authority that centered laity as agents of parish history and decision-making. And the Good Friday Way of the Cross through the streets of Egleston Square ritually reaffirmed the bond between parish and neighborhood, publicly mapping the presence of God in the community's everyday passions, deaths, and resurrections. This shared journey annually transformed a community of migrants into a migrant community. Laying bare their interconnectedness, the ritual performed a liberative intuition of communal salvation.

What should be clear from these examples is that ritual does not unify people by erasing their differences or making questions of power irrelevant. If anything, ritual magnifies and clarifies these distinctions and renders aesthetic verdicts. By the light of the Easter candle, difference becomes resplendent. Under the shadow of the cross, social inequalities become abhorrent. Ritual is where the work of solidarity begins, the means through which people who would not otherwise ordinarily find themselves in the same space practice being a community. In much the same way that the ritual of soccer practice trains individuals to become a team, ritual offers an embodied script, a set of movements and actions and materials and reference points through which people practice the work of togetherness and improvise common belonging.[3] This chapter will unpack this claim, placing the ritual world of St. Mary's into conversation with ritual theorists Catherine Bell, Émile Durkheim, Edith and Victor Turner, Selva J. Raj, Adam Seligman, and Robert Weller. Arguing for an expansive, ecological understanding of practice and a view of ritual solidarity distinct from the Turners' *communitas*, I propose that we view the bodily vernacular of ritual as the language of community.

Ritual Displacement: Getting Mixed Up on Purpose

For Catholics, Holy Week—the period between Palm Sunday and the Easter Vigil—marks the apex of the liturgical year, the point during which Christians commemorate Jesus's entry into Jerusalem, last supper, condemnation, crucifixion, and resurrection from the dead. The Holy Week liturgies are also replete with material and bodily enchantments: If one attends every Holy Week Mass and service, she will have dressed in red and waved palm branches aloft, washed someone's bare feet in a pan of water (at St. Mary's, everyone takes turns washing everyone else's), followed an intoxicatingly incensed Eucharistic procession through the aisles of the church, marched through neighborhood streets, bowed low to kiss a crucifix, gazed into a bonfire, raised a candle in a darkened church, and consumed the bread and wine of the Eucharist four times. Because of its aesthetic riches and the effort that planning such detailed liturgies requires of parishioners, Holy Week is a period of intense togetherness. Yet a conversation I had with English Mass lay leader Michelle revealed another reason why Holy Week is so important to the St. Mary's community. According to Michelle, the Palm Sunday procession—her favorite part of the week—pushes parishioners out of their comfort zones. She didn't mean this metaphorically: She was talking about physical pushing. Unlike Good Friday's Way of the Cross, in which a police officer bikes alongside the procession to stop traffic so that walkers can proceed down the middle of busy streets, Palm Sunday is a more modest affair. Ushers instruct walkers to remain on the sidewalk as they move from park to church. When the procession begins, the palm-waving crowd bottlenecks onto the narrow sidewalk. Spatially confined and propelled by the movement of the crowd, people surrender control over their places in the procession. Once they are inside the church, attendees are directed into pews quickly so that the liturgy can recommence. As I learned firsthand, relinquishing control over one's place in the procession also means spending the nearly two-hour Mass seated among strangers. After laughing at my seat-saving attempt, Michelle offered the following reflection:

> People don't worry. They get into the line wherever they get into the line and, you know, they work their way into the church. A lot of times people seem to have the attitude that "this is *my* pew." But on Palm Sunday, because of the way the procession goes, and the fact that some of the elderly and sick [who choose not to walk in the procession] may already *be* in the church in the pews, people often just end up processing into a pew, and whoever's in line together behind one another gets to be in that pew. Which is, I think, maybe the perfect way it should be.[4]

Michelle later admitted that, Palm Sunday aside, she sometimes feels a rush of indignation when she arrives late to Mass only to find someone sitting in "her pew." But every year, the Palm Sunday procession interrupts her territorialism, displacing her within a space over which she typically feels a great deal of control. She comes to Palm Sunday knowing that she's going to get mixed up.

Amelia, another lay leader from the English Mass, raised similar themes of displacement and relinquishment of control in a conversation we had around her kitchen table a couple of weeks after Easter in 2013. She thought back on her years of walking the Way of the Cross in a way that echoed Michelle's description of Palm Sunday:

> You know how the walk kind of flows, and people kind of move around and see different people? I never have the feeling that I have to walk with so-and-so. There's people that come past you or say hello to you. You just rub up against all different people, you know. And I love that about it. And it's not like you have to make small talk or anything. You can just kind of nod or whatever, acknowledge [them]. And there's just so many different kinds of people, people I'd never seen before.

Different ages. So there's something about just kind of coexisting with all those people. And you all have a singular purpose, you're all kind of looking forward, in a way. You're doing it together, and not having to . . . I don't know how to describe it. There's a kind of meditative quality about it.[5]

Holy Week's displacements were not just spatial or bodily. The Holy Week liturgies, which always included a minimum of two languages, also involved linguistic dislocations. Yamaris, who started attending St. Mary's after moving to Boston from the Dominican Republic in 2011, cited Palm Sunday as an example of how the shared experience of misunderstanding during bilingual liturgies gave her a sense of common belonging:

We identify with one another, because I don't understand all of the English, but there are other things I *do* understand. So you say, "Wait, now you're going to see." Yes, they'll say one of the parts in English, and then the other part in Spanish, and I—it unites us because we're all [in the same boat]. We're all looking for meaning in the Word and listening to the Word. But now and again, everyone is going to understand it one way, and maybe I'll understand it another way. But in the end, it has the same meaning. At least I think so.[6]

For Yamaris, the shared experience of incomplete comprehension at bilingual Masses made her feel a sense of camaraderie with other parishioners, Spanish and English speakers alike. It shifted the balance of power, leveling the linguistic playing field: Instead of one group understanding everything and the other almost nothing, everyone took turns being insiders to the meaning of the text. Full understanding was something they could only achieve together, as one body. Yamaris saw linguistic difference as a source of mutuality and interconnection. She took the long view: In the end, everyone was together, listening to the same scriptures, sharing the same space, and oriented toward the same God.

Yamaris spoke highly of her experience at bilingual Masses, but not everyone was so positive. I knew of a few English Mass parishioners who didn't participate in bilingual liturgies at all, and others from both Mass communities who attended but found them tedious. Some felt that they magnified differences rather than commonalities. Jael, a perennially put-together and perfectly coiffed Dominican mother and professional who was very involved in ministry at the parish, described bilingual Masses as "regular." I wasn't sure I understood what she was getting at, so I asked her to explain. Maybe they felt unusual for "los americanos," she said with a shrug, but for "los hispanos," having to adapt to someone else's language and norms was something they were used to. Ordinarily diplomatic, Jael was frank:

> We're here, and we bother to learn a little of the language, but those who are from here don't have to learn *our* language. So they can't do more [of the Mass] in Spanish than in English because [the americanos] are not going to understand, or they'll understand less.[7]

At bilingual gatherings, it was clear how far Spanish Mass members outnumbered English Massgoers. Nevertheless, Jael could see that despite their majority, there remained an expectation that the Mass would give equal time to Spanish and English. Ultimately, the primary onus to adapt remained on los hispanos.

Moreover, Jael felt that bilingual Masses accented the differences between the two communities, sometimes casting los hispanos in a poor light. With a hint of both sarcasm and exasperation, she admitted feeling "embarrassed because [the americanos] are *so* organized, and we are *not*." She laughed and raised her eyebrows pointedly as she continued:

> Take Communion—when we're going up to receive Communion—and we can't get organized, and [the americanos] are all *very* organized. I like that about them. If we could learn and adapt to the rule of going pew by pew . . . but—boom! [*she slapped the table*]—we get out of there fast and it's goodbye to the rules![8]

Communion marked the clearest moment of disjuncture between the two communities. When it came time to receive the Eucharist, English Massgoers would file into the center aisle methodically, pew by pew, from the front of the church to the back. Spanish Massgoers, on the other hand, would join the line at will, in no particular order. When the two communities came together, the process became a free-for-all. The chaotic Communion line was a visible sign of deeper differences in parishioners' approaches to moral issues and sacramental participation. Spanish Mass attendees, as far as I could tell, adhered more diligently to Catholic teaching instructing believers to refrain from receiving the Eucharist if they had not been to confession or were in a state of what the church defined as mortal sin. This was especially true of sins involving sex: It was fairly easy to infer that the kind of moral transgressions that kept people—especially women—out of the Communion line were things like living unmarried with a partner or being divorced and remarried. At Spanish Masses, it was common for only a portion of attendees to receive the Eucharist each week. Once, a Spanish-speaking priest had gone so far as to deny Communion to a faithful parishioner on account of her "irregular marriage" outside of the church. The scandalous moment made receiving the Eucharist even more fraught, at least when that particular priest was presiding. English Massgoers, by contrast, generally opted to receive the Eucharist regardless of the state of their mortal souls, and the Jesuits who usually presided at English Masses were not known for turning anyone away.

One might expect the sacrament of the Eucharist to mark the quintessential rite of unity between the two communities. Indeed, as previously explored, in bishops' documents and postconciliar ecclesiologies, the Eucharist is understood as the paradigmatic sign and source of unity among peoples. In practice, however, the Eucharistic ritual at bilingual Masses did more to accent divisions. Dissonant cultural and theological norms around receiving Communion reproduced stereotypes—in the eyes of Spanish Massgoers, the parish's English-speaking, predominantly U.S.-born Catholics were order obsessed and cavalier about church teaching on sin; to English-speakers, the Latinas/os seemed spontaneous and disorganized and submissive to clerical authority. Sharing in the Eucharist may have signified Catholic unity in a deeper, symbolic sense, but ironically, it was the point in bilingual Masses at which parishioners felt most foreign to one another.

For English speakers and Spanish speakers alike, then, bilingual liturgies were experiences of displacement, albeit in different ways. For many, the ritual dislocations that occurred in the process of planning and participating in the liturgies were welcome, if occasionally frustrating. While the acute discomforts—sitting someplace new, following along in another language, feeling disoriented during Communion—were temporary, such work had largely constructive long-term effects on intercultural relationships. The act of ritual displacement subtly renegotiated power, loosening claims of ownership over parish space, even among the most stubborn.

Additionally, many of the Holy Week rituals involved vulnerable bodily encounters with whoever happened to be next in line or seated nearby, whether friend or stranger. On Holy Thursday, after the priest and deacon washed the feet of twelve parishioners, everyone in the church would line up to wash and dry one another's feet using basins placed throughout the aisles. Though not instructed to do so, participants would invariably embrace after the washing exchange. During the veneration of the cross on Good Friday, everyone's lips grazed the same crucifix. At the Easter Vigil, flames passed in intimate exchanges among neighbors illuminated the sanctuary. And the processions through neighborhood streets on Palm Sunday, on Good Friday, and at the Vigil mixed people up, weaving them together in new and different ways as they walked.

At the same time, for Massgoers like Jael, bilingual Masses still reflected the inequalities of everyday life. The linguistic and spatial displacements Jael experienced there were no different than the challenges she faced constantly as an immigrant. In the end, and often in spite of their own best

FIGURE 14. At Holy Thursday Mass, twelve parishioners representing a cross section of parish cultures, languages, generations, and life experiences have their feet washed by a Jesuit deacon, April 13, 2017. Photo by the author.

intentions, it was the comparatively small English-speaking community that dictated the liturgy's linguistic parameters. Gender roles, too, remained circumscribed, as I experienced in my near turn as Jesus in the Palm Sunday mime. Liturgy discloses profound creative power, but such power is not limitless. It remains subject to the same social forces that shape life beyond it, even when it transgresses or subverts them.[9]

Ecologies of Practice

Parish Ritual Beyond Liturgy

When I began this project, I intended to focus the bulk of my attention on intercultural liturgical practice. After all, theologies of parish life—what few exist—understandably center the celebration of the Eucharist as the parish's raison d'etre. In a brief but compelling case for the theological significance of the parish, Karl Rahner underscores that the church becomes "event" in the local celebration of the Eucharist.[10] What Rahner calls the "placeness" of the community, its divinely charged local character, is a reflection of the incarnation of Jesus Christ, the presence of God made known in and to the local church in the priestly act of Eucharistic consecration. The intuition is fortified by Vatican II's declaration of the liturgy as the source and summit of the Christian life (LG 11). Given the centrality of the liturgy in the life of Catholic parishes, why have I waited until the penultimate chapter to discuss bilingual Masses? Does this reluctance to foreground the most fundamental, ubiquitous of all Catholic rituals suggest that the work of cultivating community in difference can only be done in unconventional ways? If so, does this diminish the realistic possibility of solidarity across difference within "ordinary" parishes?

These chapters have examined an array of rituals beyond the Mass because I quickly came to realize that in order to understand how bilingual liturgies "worked," it was necessary to look far beyond them. It was clear to me that for the people of St. Mary's, Christ was incarnate in the celebration of the Eucharist, and in a host of other places, too. Whereas Rahner associates the parish's "placeness" with the consecration of the Eucharist, the incarnational imagination governing liturgical practice at St. Mary's seemed to be less about momentary divine ingression into the world and more about the diffuse network of presences glowing around every street corner and table and pew. When parishioners spoke of encountering God, they pointed me to moments I would have almost certainly overlooked. Within the liturgy, they talked about the way the Spirit moved when the choir would break into their favorite hymn, or when a priest would deliver a homily that met the moment, or when parishioners would pass the microphone around the church during the community-led Prayer of the Faithful, offering up their own sorrows and gratitudes to God and one another. Some felt God's presence at the Pentecost potluck or on parish retreats or at ELI (Equipo Latino Ignaciano), a weekly Spanish-language faith-sharing group in the Ignatian spiritual tradition. One mentioned Gifts of Warmth, an annual winter clothing drive and visit to patients at Shattuck Hospital, a local safety-net medical center. Another woman described the holiness of the multicourse Sunday suppers that she and others would cook and serve, restaurant style, to elderly parishioners. So many people talked about the sacred role of coffee and donuts after Mass that it seemed to take on the status of a veritable second Eucharist. And then there were the meetings: parish council meetings, community organization meetings, finance meetings, choir practices, liturgy planning meetings, social justice cluster meetings, ad hoc meetings to problem-solve whatever new emergency had arisen that month. In the end it was not the liturgies alone that fostered solidarity but rather the collaborative labor that went into making them happen behind the scenes—the agenda setting, planning, rehearsing, debating, vacuuming, decorating, cooking, organizing, calling, volunteer recruiting, notetaking, record-keeping, walking, listening, fund-raising, evaluating, and cleaning up. This is not to dismiss the centrality of liturgy and sacrament for the community. Instead, it is to emphasize liturgy's enmeshment within a complex ecology of sensory, embodied, formative, and deeply ordinary practices, so many of which have gone underexplored and underappreciated in scholarly considerations of parish life.[11]

Following the people's lead, this book has sought to disrupt the tendency to view liturgy as the only form of parish life and ritual worthy of any real theological consideration. This tendency is, in its own way, a legacy of Vatican II. In consolidating Catholic worship around the Eucharist, the Council deemphasized devotional practices and material objects, which had represented vital realms of lay agency and spiritual creativity. As a result, theologians today find themselves in the odd position of making the case that a given Catholic practice is somehow "Eucharistic" or "liturgical" in order to justify its value as an object of theological concern. The implication is that such subjects are only worthy of serious consideration if one can prove their proximity to Eucharistic practice (and, by extension, to the exercise of clerical authority) or their resonance with a Catholic "sacramental imagination."[12] The Eucharistic consolidation of parish life and practice reflects a similar funneling of post–Vatican II ecclesiologies into the communion paradigm, as argued in chapter 1. As we noted there, communion ecclesiology locates unity-work largely in sacramental practice, invoking Christians' baptismal oneness-in-Christ and Eucharistic unity-in-diversity in order to dismiss critical questions of power in ecclesial communities as tangential to the "true" mission of the church. I suggested that this overemphasis on liturgical unity has not only militated against the church's ability to speak coherently about serious injustices in its midst; it has often served as a cover for them. By contrast, expanding our understanding of divine presence in the local church also empowers us to think more boldly about the nature of that church.

Broadening our ritual lens in parish studies further highlights critical, often class-based disparities in liturgical access. Without priests in residence, and with pastors who were also responsible for the administration of two additional parishes, St. Mary's could not offer daily Mass to its parishioners. Instead, during the week, laypeople led morning communion services in the small parish house chapel using hosts consecrated by the priest the Sunday before. Laity at St. Mary's may have been empowered to lead by a strong postconciliar spirit of the church as the people of God, but on a much more immediate level, they were also motivated by necessity. Clerical presence at St. Mary's had been inconsistent since at least the 1970s, making laity responsible for nearly every aspect of parish life and ministry. One Sunday, a scheduling error meant that a priest failed to show up to celebrate the English Mass. Instead of instructing everyone to go home, Sr. Josephine ascended the ambo and led the community in an impromptu Liturgy of the Word. When it came time for the homily, parishioners passed around the microphone and offered their own reflections on the day's Gospel reading. Parishioners' capacious understandings of religious practice and divine presence seemed to refute the clericalist and classist notion that lack of consistent access to clergy, and thus to the sacraments, meant that God was less fully present in their community.

Seeing Ritual Ecologies

What the ritual world of St. Mary's suggests is that every parish ritual, from the mission statement reflection at the beginning of Parish Council meetings to the spontaneous funeral procession for Hector Morales, is enmeshed within a larger *ecology of practice*. No ritual is an island. Rituals arise within and shaped by complex social, cultural, and political environments and are constellated within systems of myriad other rituals, practices, and traditions.[13] These fluid, changing, vulnerable relationships constantly shape and reshape what a ritual does and means for the people who practice it. Following the work of the late ritual theorist Catherine Bell, I regard ritual as a form of contextually situated practice—that is, as the strategic, social act of ritualization that takes place within the unfolding of ordinary life. For Bell, ritual should not be understood as a discrete, esoteric genre of cultural artifact but rather one of many forms of embodied practice through which individuals and communities negotiate power, relationships, space, and story. Like all forms of practice, rituals are inextricable from the lived circumstances under which they arise and are performed. The Good Friday Neighborhood Way of the Cross, described in the chapter 4, illustrates well Bell's notion of ritual practice insofar as its power relies explicitly on its embeddedness within the urban topographies, social landscapes, and imagined horizons of life in the particular place of Egleston Square. Rather than signifying or conveying preexistent meanings, values, or power relationships, ritualization is one strategy that members of communities use to negotiate these very meanings, values, and relationships. The outcome of this construction is both contingent (that is to say, not predetermined) and consequential.[14]

As Bell argues, abstracting rituals from their contexts, dusting off their messes and inconsistencies in order to analyze them with greater theoretical purity, ends up removing precisely the factors that most determine their functioning.[15] Studying rituals contextually thus requires taking stock of the broader communal repertoires of practice in which they are embedded. Consider again the Neighborhood Way of the Cross. While the ritual is evocative in its own right, an ecological view of that ritual recognizes it as one dimension of an ornate constellation of ecclesial, liturgical, social, and administrative work. This recognition foregrounds its relationship to the many other practices, large and small, that comprise the landscape of St. Mary's and Egleston Square. Indeed, the Via Crucis has been perennially embedded within a complex and ever-evolving local ritual ecology. After the killing of Hector Morales, for example, a number of other peacebuilding practices and spaces sprang up around the neighborhood; these, too, shaped the power of the Good Friday procession. These included the establishment of Greater Egleston Community High School, an alternative school for youth who had dropped out of school or been involved in gangs; the annual Hands Around Egleston Square community celebration; and, a decade later, the cultivation of the Egleston Square Peace Garden (these I describe in the final chapter). The Way of the Cross was also only one instance of the public presence that infused the whole of St. Mary's liturgical life. St. Mary's leaders were fixtures on the block throughout the year, especially in the worst of times, and the parish house was a critical neighborhood gathering space. This consistent presence underscored parishioners' convictions in the twinned destinies of parish and neighborhood. Such presence also legitimized the prophetic claims and bold commitments parishioners made on Good Friday. Were the Via Crucis the parish's single annual foray into the streets, it would still have been poignant, but its moral authority and transformational capacity would have been diminished. St. Mary's claims of solidarity become credible only when considered within the justice-oriented ecology of practice that parishioners labored over decades to create.

Besides being home to an array of often-overlooked internal practices, parishes are also enmeshed in broader, external networks of practice operating both locally and translocally. St. Mary's was affiliated with the Roxbury and Jamaica Plain parish "cluster," the Archdiocese of Boston and its Black Catholic and Hispanic Catholic networks, Boston's colleges and universities, neighborhood coalitions and development associations in Egleston Square and Jamaica Plain, and citywide and statewide political networks. St. Mary's was also constellated within networks that extended far beyond Boston: the worldwide network of Jesuit institutions and organizations; transnational apostolic movements such as the Spain-based Neocatechumenal Way from which the Spanish Mass drew musical repertoire and, in later years, priests; the Caribbean homeland parishes to which parishioners would periodically return, bringing back news, songs, and instruments; and the universal Catholic Church itself. Within this ecology, liturgy at St. Mary's was an open system, one shaped in profound ways by people's enmeshment in many other networks of practice.

At no point in the liturgical year was this enmeshment more evident than at the Easter Vigil Mass. Every Easter, a musician from the Spanish Mass choir would take to the ambo, classical guitar high on his chest, and lead the assembly in a vigorous, haunting rendition of the Pregón Pascual by Spanish composer Kiko Argüello. The Pregón (in English, the Easter Exsultet) is the long, evocative proclamation exalting Christ's defeat of death sung before the Easter candle while the church is still dark. During the refrains, everyone in the assembly lifted their candles and joined in, singing with such fervor that it sounded like a roar. After the first reading, the Creation narrative (Gen 1:1–2:2), the choir sang a buoyant merengue song composed, I eventually learned, by the pastor of a parish in the village outside of Santo Domingo where some of the musicians were from: "*Son un regalo de Dios todas las cosas. Todas las cosas, son un regalo de Dios . . .*"[16] After the second reading, a selection from Exodus (14:15–15:1),[17] the choir would break into the African American spiritual "Wade in the Water." And on it went, the liturgy an eclectic revue of community favorites: during Communion, Suzanne Toolan's folk-contemporary hymn "I Am the Bread of Life." At the liturgy's closing, a bilingualized worship song from the early '90s—"Celebrate, Jesus, Celebrate/Celebran, Cristo, Celebran"—was followed by a rousing postlude of Argüello's "Resucitó." To an outsider, it would be easy to see the Easter Vigil Mass as a musical sampler platter, culturally representative but aesthetically disjointed.[18] But that would be a mistake. With occasional variations, the choir would sing the same songs year after year, which meant that over time, the entire parish had developed a shared repertoire. English speakers belted out the infectious refrain of "Resucitó" by heart, while Spanish speakers clapped in time to the deep-blue notes of "*God's gonna trouble the water.*" Every Easter Vigil was like a choir practice for the whole community. Over many years, the songs of some had become the tradition of all.

Viewing parish rituals through an ecological lens alleviates a certain hermeneutical burden that arises in the consideration of the role that such rituals play within communities, especially those beset by violence or division. This burden results in the tendency to exaggerate a practice's functional and formative dimensions. Within discourse on Christian practice, particular rituals are often examined in relative isolation from other religious, political, and social processes. The result is that singular practices—the celebration of the Eucharist, for example—are depicted as accomplishing an astonishing amount of social and political work: reorienting communal imaginations, transcending racial and social divisions, deploying an efficacious counterpolitics to the destructive and atomizing power of the state, and so on.[19] Not only can individual liturgical practices not be relied upon to accomplish the work of social equality, very often they crack under the pressure put upon them to do so. When, for example, it is revealed that the Eucharist does not ameliorate racism or transcend human divisions or contain the seeds of a viable and comprehensive counterpolitical blueprint, we are left feeling that our cherished practices have betrayed us. This sort of analysis abandons us to a choice between two bad options: Either we retreat from history in order to persist in the belief that our practices function in the ways we imagine them to, or we retreat from ecclesial practice, disillusioned by its contradictions and inadequacies and the variegated hypocrisies of its practitioners. I've chosen to foreground non-Eucharistic rituals in order to foreclose the temptation—including my own—to succumb to precisely this rose-colored vision of unilateral liturgical efficacy. Taking an integral view, eschewing both cynicism and theological fantasy-fulfillment, leaves us with a chastened yet more hopeful understanding of ritual's place in the slow work of community.

Communitas or Solidarity?

Navigating schools of thought on the relationship between ritual and solidarity requires that we clarify not only what we mean by ritual, but also (and perhaps more urgently) what we mean by solidarity. Solidarity, not unlike communion, is a term so capacious and pliable that we risk rendering it meaningless through imprecision. By solidarity, are we referring primarily to a feeling of intimacy and connectedness or to a pattern of action? In Catholic social thought and magisterial writing, solidarity indicates both a feeling of profound kinship and the concrete moral work of binding together one's lot with the lot of another for the sake of justice, salvation, and the common good. In ritual studies literature, solidarity is more strongly identified with the former—an almost ineffable feeling of unity and common belonging that arises in the ritual process and helps to undergird, and sometimes transgress, the social order. In *The Elementary Forms of Religious Life*, Émile Durkheim identifies the unique power of communal ritual to generate what he calls collective effervescence, "a sort of electricity" among those gathered that "launches them into an extraordinary height of exaltation."[20] For Durkheim, ritual alleviates the individual from the particularities of her own interests and pursuits, enabling her to see herself as united to the collective.[21] Thus, ritual renders society possible by producing social solidarity. Victor and Edith Turner place even greater emphasis on the social solidarity evoked in ritual. Drawing on French ethnographer Arnold van Gennep's classic studies of rites of passage, the Turners describe *communitas* as the intense feeling of universal kinship, intimacy, and egalitarianism that arises during ritual's liminal state, during which social boundaries are temporarily suspended.[22] Like Durkheim, Victor Turner notes the power of ritual to "convert the obligatory into the desirable,"[23] imbuing the moral order with a compelling aesthetic power. What characterizes effervescence (for Durkheim) or *communitas* (for the Turners) is its separateness from the structures and processes of ordinary life. Durkheim's theory of religious experience, and thus his understanding of ritual effervescence, relies on a firm distinction between sacred and profane.[24] For the Turners, *communitas* is bound up with the condition of "anti-structure"; it is the temporary suspension of social roles during the liminal phase of the ritual process that makes the experience of *communitas* possible.

From a scholarly standpoint, it is admittedly tempting to overplay St. Mary's thoroughly liminal history and identity by suggesting that the parish is a place where social structures are perpetually suspended and transgressed—a space of *communitas*. There are ways in which this is true: To exist on the margins, away from the eyes and authorities of the center, is to exist in a world of unexpected possibility. The friendships and, in their own way, even the conflicts at St. Mary's testified to how profoundly the parish had defied the segregated status quo of Catholic Boston. But liminality in the Turnerian sense is, by definition, temporary. The *communitas* that arises within this liminal state is something like what I experienced in the candlelit darkness at the Easter Vigil Mass. Collective effervescence, *communitas*, or its analogues arise, often spontaneously, during the part of a ritual that is most unlike everyday life—say, the moment you're cocooned in night and the warmth of three hundred pairs of shoulders as a singer with a Spanish guitar and a voice like a cry intones an ancient hymn about the splendor of God destroying the world's darkness. *"Esta es la noche"*—this is the night—the Pregón repeats, bespeaking the Vigil's distinctiveness in much the same way as the question that begins the Ma Nishtana at a Jewish Passover Seder: "Why is this night different from all other nights?" There was a moment during my first St. Mary's Vigil Mass in which I felt nearly overcome by the rush of love I felt for these people, most of whom I didn't even know. The moment was unbidden, irreplicable. This was ritual's magical realism at work, that elusive inbreaking of another world.

But the type of solidarity that this book has examined is not principally that epiphanic, ephemeral sensation of universal sisterhood and brotherhood. Liminality at St. Mary's was not a phase. Indeed, to call St. Mary's a borderland is different than calling it liminal in the Turnerian sense. As in a liminal space, the in-between condition of a borderland can give rise to new and unexpected modes of cultural expression and belonging. But real borderlands do not alleviate the intricate complexities of power relationships. If anything, they magnify them. Romanticizing the borderland as a utopia only gives rise to the sort of ambivalence about difference that we have already identified as the primary problem with communion as a metaphor for the church's mission. (Indeed, there are notable parallels between the Turners' description of *communitas* and theological descriptions of communion). Neither would it be quite accurate to posit that the ecstatic paschal experience of *communitas* is what regulates the parish's social structures during Ordinary Time.[25] The phenomenon at the center of this book is that form of practiced kinship that is quieter and more ordinary—not only a divine gift, but also a human task.

Thus, it is solidarity in the second sense that is our primary focus— the sustained, creative, sometimes costly pattern of morally inflected action and commitment across difference, motivated by love, justice, and concern for the common good. We should be careful not to view solidarity-as-labor in opposition to solidarity-as-feeling. Instead, I am raising a distinction between solidarity as a kind of communal practice—one that invariably involves profound emotional investment—and a more superficial understanding of solidarity as the affective by-product of communal practice. In short, I am suggesting that in order to understand what it takes to sustain a community like St. Mary's, we should view solidarity as a process, not a product. For this task, we need to look both at and beyond worship. Rather than limiting our account of parish ritual to occasional, set-apart forms of action, we should instead, with Bell, attend to the verdant ecology of deeply ordinary ritual practices through which parishioners at St. Mary's perform and maintain these commitments to one another and the place. Ritual theorists could readily offer one hundred different explanations for my rush of emotion during the effervescent Easter Vigil Mass, my realization that I loved all these people. More mysterious, and frankly more enchanting, was Amelia's experience, recounted in chapter 3, of looking around the room at a Tuesday night Parish Council meeting, overhead fluorescent lights blinking, table strewn with agendas and budgets, and thinking, "I love all these people!" To perceive the love that arises within this everyday ritual requires a wider lens.

Ritualizing Solidarity

Ritual as the Language of Community

To understand the intricate relationship between ritual and solidarity at St. Mary's, we, like Bell, must first keep in mind that ritual is not a form of representative action that symbolizes social solidarity in a once-removed sort of way. Rather, ritual is itself a practice of solidarity, action through which relationships form and commitments arise. Rituals of ecclesial solidarity like those we have examined in this book in some sense enact the thing they celebrate: complex relationships between and among God and community. In a community of many languages, nations of origin, and life situations, Catholic ritual serves as a common vernacular. At St. Mary's, ritual is the language of community. There, the highly structured, embodied, movement-oriented character of Catholic ritual becomes its greatest asset. As Alyssa Maldonado-Estrada has suggested, Catholic ritual is a kind of body language.[26] Before Catholics are formed into believers of doctrines and creeds, they are formed into actors, people who know how to move a certain kind of way through a certain kind of space. Such bodily habituation helps even newcomers to intuit, for example, the peripatetic movement of a Via Crucis, or the ebb and flow of a procession, or the impatient rustle of coats and purses when Mass announcements run on too long. Consequential variations in dialect exist, of course, something that becomes obvious every time Massgoers find themselves tripping over one another to receive Communion at a bilingual liturgy. The physical and psychic confusion that result during this part of the Mass attests to the durability of ritual conditioning. It is as though parishioners hear the same song and break into two different dances, crashing into one another as they move yet unable to do otherwise. Yet there is also a surprising theological honesty in the ritual mess. In the Eucharist, Augustine writes, believers "become what they receive"—that is, the Body of Christ.[27] The chaos and confusion of bilingual Communion performs with chastened realism an addendum to Augustine's remark: Becoming the Body of Christ is hard work. Gradually, hybrid vernaculars emerge: the unique sign of peace in the sanctuary aisles, the eclectic musical repertoire of the Easter Vigil, the Palm Sunday passion mime, the mixed-up sidewalk procession and seating arrangement of Palm Sunday. Through ritual's body language, parishioners form and perform themselves into a community.

This use of "perform" should not imply that such action is inauthentic or meaningless.[28] No one would accuse a soccer team of merely "acting" like a team. The performance of teamwork is itself teamwork. Never mind that the team is just a collection of individuals who never would have given one another a second thought, or even met in the first place, if not for the league. But the team is the occasion of their meeting; through the ritual of soccer practice, they become better and better at being a team by conditioning their bodies to move as a team and, through muscle memory, form their intuitions to think as a team.[29] Gradually, through sustained practice, they become known to one another not merely as players but as human beings; they check one another's motives, celebrate one another's victories, and lament one another's injuries—not first and foremost because these things bear on the outcomes of soccer games, but because collective action has, paradoxically, taught them to perceive more acutely the particular reality of another. Similarly, ritual is parishwork—it is practice for being a community of difference.

Embodied Dialogue

In *Gaudium et Spes*, the Pastoral Constitution on the Church in the Modern World, solidarity between church and world arises principally through dialogue. Transposing Vatican II's call to solidarity *ad extra* into a vision of ecclesial solidarity *ad intra* suggests that dialogue also has an important role to play in the local church. In communities of difference, however, asymmetries of power hinder efforts at dialogue. Dialogue in the form of formal verbal exchange rewards linguistic sophistication and access to certain modes of expertise, privileging texts, doctrines, and academic literature rather than the lived concerns and experiences of those on the ground. Dialogue's outcomes ultimately lie in the hands of leaders tasked with implementing them, where the interests of marginalized participants again risk being misrepresented or ignored. On its own, dialogue is an imperfect means of cultivating relationships across difference.[30]

If we understand ritual as body language, however, then we can view ritual practice as a form of embodied dialogue and thus as a companion to solidarity. Over decades of fieldwork among Catholic and Hindu communities in Tamil Nadu, India, the late Indian ethnographer Selva J. Raj observed that local ritual practice often functioned as "dialogue on the ground," a form of "intimate, subtle" exchange that emerged often organically among laity. Raj observed how ordinary people of faith improvised on rituals from their religious traditions to help them navigate everyday religious and cultural divides. In contrast to what he acidly termed "cocktail *communitas*," the self-congratulatory, superficial overtures toward diversity and multiculturalism nurtured in elite spaces, embodied ritual exchange among neighbors at the grassroots level marked a more genuine crossing of boundaries.[31] While Raj's interpretive framework is burdened by its overly airtight distinction between laity and religious elites, people and institution, and religion "from below" and "from above," his fundamental insight is a valuable one. The embodied dialogue of ritualization gives people who would otherwise view one another with indifference, suspicion, or hostility a way of practicing life together. At its best, ritual exchange can be an expression of what Joris Geldhof terms a "peculiar form of love."[32]

Two dimensions of ritual dialogue are worth noting. First, what is most central is not first and foremost the exchange of ideas but rather the exchange of relationships. In Raj's analysis, ritual dialogue on the ground serves the practical end of enabling neighbors to live together in peace. It helps people construct a life with one another, to perceive themselves joined as part of the same community. Each of the rituals of ecclesial solidarity we have examined in this book so far does precisely that. In Egleston Square, ritual mourning gave teenagers space and permission to grieve before seeking revenge and helped neighbors to tell their stories. It did so not in the first place by advancing particularly incisive moral claims (though it did that as well) but by being itself a middle space, an occasion of joining. Reciting the parish mission statement before Parish Council meetings was about articulating a shared vision of church, but it was also about gathering around a table and eating shared food and making decisions communally and bilingually, even when doing so felt painfully inefficient. Ritual makes space for embodied encounters that transform relational imaginations. It is this transformation that renders solidarity across difference conceivable.

Second, the goal of ritual dialogue is not consensus. Far from consolidating group identity or communicating a uniform set of cultural values, the embodied language of ritual practice gives participants space to dwell in ambiguity and difference rather than trying to resolve it. Raj's case studies of Catholic practice in pluralistic Indian contexts underscore the idea that ritual participation does not dissolve people's differences, nor should we want it to. Rather, effective ritual gives participants a way of encountering one another without absolutizing their differences or pretending them away.[33] This capaciousness is especially vital in a community where perspectives, memories, cultural norms, and spiritual commitments vary widely and where parishioners are thus challenged to find ways of practicing togetherness while affirming unique cultural identities.[34] Ritual didn't "solve" the challenges posed by diversity at St. Mary's. Rather than forming participants into a single ecclesial culture that professes to transcend particularity, ritual practice makes space for encounter in and through difference.

To understand this idea more clearly, let us turn to the work of Adam Seligman and Robert Weller, whose three-volume study of ritual and pluralism sheds light on the ritual dynamics of communities like St. Mary's. Seligman and Weller identify three ways that diverse communities navigate their internal boundaries: *notation, ritual,* and *shared experience.*[35] The practice of identifying difference—what they term "notation"—is vital for upholding the recognition of identity groups within a society or institution. In the context of a parish, notation would include, for example, ensuring that Mass is offered in the languages its members speak. While an important first step, however, cultural recognition can only take a community so far.[36] Naming difference does not help people to live with it, nor does it offer them resources for constructing meaningful relationships across their differences. They argue that the two practice-oriented categories—ritual and shared experience—function, by contrast, as both notational (or boundary-defining) and ambiguous (or boundary-transgressing). Following pragmatist philosopher John Dewey, Seligman and Weller argue that "the work of ritual," when understood as a form of shared experience, allows communities defined by difference to take practical action. Their fundamental insight echoes the one raised in the previous chapter: More important than what a ritual says is what it enables participants to do. Ritual "teaches us how to live within and between different boundaries rather than seeking to absolutize them" or, on the other hand, to imagine them gone.[37]

The paradoxical notion that ritual cultivates solidarity by affirming difference lies in stark contrast to the way that studies of multiethnic congregations often frame the role of ritual. In many such congregations, ritual exists primarily to imbue their diverse members with a common, supraethnic religious culture. In a study of large, multiethnic Mosaic Church in Los Angeles, for example, sociologist Gerardo Martí traces how the community used ritual to construct and affirm a shared congregational culture that explicitly sought to transcend ethnicity, race, and nationality. While the church embraced its multiethnic identity, members eschewed the idea that the congregation was multicultural, emphasizing instead that there was only one culture at the church: Christianity.[38] In an opening vignette, Martí narrates a "dirt dance" during a worship service at Mosaic in which four mud-covered male dancers of different races and ethnicities performed a melting pot–style take on unity in Christ. In churches like these, ritual often serves to downplay individual differences while emphasizing a shared "Christian culture."[39]

A West Coast megachurch may appear to have little in common with a small Catholic parish in Boston. Yet there are unexpected similarities in the ways that Mosaic's hip evangelical leaders talked about the cultural function of congregational ritual and the ways that Catholic liturgists sometimes do. As we noted in chapter 1, within ecclesiological discourse, liturgical participation is often portrayed as the momentary inbreaking

of an eschatological future in which human difference is rendered incon-
sequential, even nonexistent, a sign of the equality of all persons in the
eyes of Christ. As I argued, the implication that unity in Christ is bound
up, even implicitly, with the dissolution of difference leads to the prolif-
eration of ecclesial colorblindness, the feigned unseeing of race and ethnicity that norms white, Euro-American practices and bodies.

At St. Mary's, by contrast, constructing a shared ecclesial life across
boundaries is precisely what ritual practice enabled parishioners to do. Far
from consolidating group identity, ritual participation discloses a unique
capacity to encompass difference and make space for encounter.[40] Seligman and Weller put it this way:

> We are constituted on our boundaries, that is to say, constituted on a
> plane we do not totally control, one that is always also open to the other,
> to the stranger, to what is different and unknown and beyond the con-
> trolling power of the center. This is what makes boundaries dangerous.
> Rather than trying to eliminate boundaries or to make them into un-
> breachable walls—the two approaches that so typified the twentieth
> century—ritual continually renegotiates boundaries, living with their
> instability and labile nature. Only by paying closer attention to the play
> of ritual—to its formal elements, even when those formal rhythms may
> overwhelm claims of content—can we find the way to negotiate the
> emergent demands of our contemporary world.[41]

In the final sentence of the introduction to the second edition of *This Bridge
Called My Back*, Gloria Anzaldúa wrote, "Caminante, no hay puentes, se
hace puentes al andar" (*Traveler, there are no bridges, one builds them as one
walks*).[42] The line was Anzaldúa's reimagining of the famous words of
Spanish poet Antonio Machado, "Caminante, no hay camino, se hace
camino al andar"—*Traveler, there is no road, the road is made by walking*.
Ritual is border work. By risking shared practice, people build bridges as
they go. Of course, a bridge is different than a road. To walk where there
is no road requires only sturdy shoes. To walk where there is no bridge,
one risks falling off a cliff. It seemed to me that the people of St. Mary's
took their parish rituals so seriously because they viewed solidarity as a
matter of life or death, the work of physical and spiritual survival. Paradoxically, the result of this seriousness was joy.

Conclusion

The dynamics that have shaped St. Mary's for a century are today transforming the entire landscape of U.S. Catholicism. Among these are new and expanded contexts of migration, sweeping regional shifts in parish growth and decline, an ever-increasing need for lay leadership, limited resources, deep institutional mistrust and betrayal propelled by the clergy sexual abuse crises, and mounting calls for racial and economic justice. In their own way, each of these forces raises complex questions for ecclesial practice, questions that can only be answered by coming to terms with the inevitability of instability and change in the first place. Denying ambiguity leaves institutions grasping nostalgically at the chimera of an imagined past, reforming practices to fortify boundaries rather than to build bridges.

In this age of ambiguity, ritual's durable structure allows participants the paradoxical freedom to dwell in the unknown, in-between present rather than to run from it or react to it by closing ranks. "Tolerance for ambiguity" can easily be dismissed as a postmodern trope, so its practical significance bears emphasizing. The American parish has never not been in transition. Indeed, the unique but in many ways broadly relatable history of St. Mary's offers a hint that idealized visions of the parish worlds of generations past are likely less than accurate. In unstable times, embodied engagement has the capacity to cultivate solidarity without demanding consensus. Participants need not think the same things or believe in exactly the same ways in order to build an ecclesial life with one another. Recalling, for example, the differences between the ways that parishioners Marisol, Ramón, Olivia, Ximena, and Omar interpreted the Way of the Cross in chapter 4, internal differences of belief and experience did not empty the Via Crucis of meaning or render it somehow inauthentic. Instead, ritual's structured but inventive nature imbues it with both durability and flexibility, giving it the capacity to bear generously the phenomenological excess that it invites.

6 Staying Alive

We go as one, or we don't go. I love my church. I'm not going anywhere else.

Janice Chinn, longtime African American parishworker[1]

When I heard the news I was so angry and sad I couldn't even cry. It's like losing a life. There's no reason to close our parish and separate us. Everyone is willing to do whatever it takes to stay here.

Maria Chavez, lay leader from the Dominican Republic[2]

This is a very beautiful community. When I first came to St. Mary's ten years ago, I found friends who were so helpful. It's very important for immigrants to have connections. I don't know what I will do if it closes. I just want to say to the leaders, please, listen to us with your ears and hearts.

Xaivong Termong, parishioner and Cambodian refugee[3]

The racial and cultural integration of this Catholic parish has been the product of decades of work. Few churches in Boston have achieved this goal and been so visibly an anchor of stability in their neighborhoods. Our example of parish needs to be encouraged and used as a model— not abandoned.

Letter from the Parish Pastoral Council to Archbishop Seán O'Malley[4]

At 11:00 a.m. on May 25, 2004, Fr. David Gill, S.J., answered a knock at the parish house door. Gill, a Jesuit priest and professor of classics at Boston College, had been serving as interim pastor of St. Mary's since the previous November.[5] He unlatched the heavy wooden door to find a FedEx deliveryman standing on the front porch with a letter from Archbishop Seán O'Malley. "After careful consideration, and an extensive process and review," the letter read, "I am writing to inform you that I have decided that Saint Mary of the Angels Parish must close." It went on: "The small number of worshipers, and the relatively low sacramental index have led me to conclude that the pastoral and spiritual needs of the People of God of Saint Mary of the Angels can be appropriately served by the remaining parishes in the area."[6]

Gill was stunned. Threats of a shutdown were nothing new to St. Mary's—the specter of closure had loomed over the community since the 1970s. Yet after nearly a century of precarity, the parish was thriving. While Egleston Square continued to struggle with poverty and violence, conditions were nothing like they had been during the 1980s and '90s. The parish's social justice, religious education, and youth ministries were flourishing. A new church roof and other improvements had slowed the building's deterioration. Everyone in Boston knew that closures were coming, but St. Mary's had not been recommended for suppression (the canonical term for closure) in the process leading up to the announcement. An official visit and review by the archdiocese less than two years earlier reportedly elicited praise for the uniquely intercultural and joyfully collaborative nature of the church's liturgical, spiritual, and social life. Parishioners assumed they were safe. They were wrong.

Pastors across the city opened their rectory doors that morning to similar news. Letters had gone out to all 357 parishes in the archdiocese informing them of their fates. Of them, 55 others received the same verdict as St. Mary's: They were to close their doors by that fall. Five more would close and become chapels of surviving parishes. Ten more were to merge. Additional churches in surrounding towns such as Lawrenceville and Lowell were added to the list in separate decisions. In all, 82 parishes were set to be suppressed or merged—nearly a quarter of the parishes in the archdiocese. The morning of the announcement, Archbishop O'Malley held a somber press conference. Expressing sympathy for the roughly twenty-eight thousand Boston Catholics whose parishes had learned of their impending closures that day, he emphasized the inevitability of the shutdowns:

> Changes in population, the movement of people from the cities to the suburbs, [and] the decrease in the number of active Catholics have all contributed to the present predicament. At this time, over one third of

our parishes are operating in the red, the deterioration of our parish buildings and churches (that in the city of Boston alone would cost over 100 million dollars to repair), and the aging clergy (130 pastors are over 70 years of age) have forced us to make the hard decisions that we have announced today.[7]

Like many once-thriving centers of urban Catholic life in the Northeast, twenty-first-century Boston was burdened with a surfeit of aging church buildings, declining Mass attendance, an increasingly dire clergy shortage, and financially unsustainable infrastructure. Closures were inevitable.

But it was a much darker crisis that had truly done in the Archdiocese of Boston. In January 2002, the *Boston Globe* broke its first "Spotlight" investigation detailing the massive cover-up of the sexual abuse of minors by clergy. Church leaders had spent decades shuffling known abusers from parish to parish while working to silence and discredit their victims. St. Mary's was not untouched by the crisis: At least two priests later accused of abuse had been assigned to the parish during the 1960s and 1970s.[8] The "Spotlight" reports unearthed revelations that decimated Boston Catholics' trust in church leaders and the institution. Many left the church for good. Others who stayed reoriented their relationship to the church, withholding financial contributions or joining Boston-based Voice of the Faithful, an organization of laity working for accountability in the wake of the crisis. While O'Malley clarified that no proceeds from the sale of parish properties would be used to pay the archdiocese's $85 million settlement with abuse survivors, many Boston Catholics approached the reconfiguration process with suspicion and resentment. The closures felt like another abuse of power—salt in the wounds of a people already aching from betrayal and sensitized to the destructive force of institutional secrecy.

It soon became clear, too, that the closures affected some communities more than others. Large, wealthy, and well-staffed parishes in the suburbs and more upscale parts of the city were largely spared. By contrast, urban parishes serving poor and working-class communities of color appeared disproportionately targeted.[9] Targeted churches tended to be small, like St. Mary's, with an average Sunday Mass attendance of roughly half that of parishes that survived.[10] They were also disproportionately multilingual and multicultural. More than a quarter of parishes that regularly offered Mass in a language other than English, and almost a third of the city's national and ethnic "personal parishes," were being ordered to close.[11] In East Boston, Our Lady of Mount Carmel, a storied Italian community, faced the heartache of looming closure. In South Boston, parishioners at St. Peter Lithuanian were shocked to find their church on the list.[12] Two Roxbury churches, both products of previous mergers—St. Francis/St. Philip and St. John/St. Hugh—would be combined into a single Black Catholic "mother church" to be named after St. Katharine Drexel. St. Mary's would be the third Roxbury parish closed in less than two years.[13]

For parishioners, confusion fueled indignation. Seventeen years earlier, anticipating precisely the sort of announcement that Archbishop O'Malley made on the morning of May 25, 2004, the Parish Council and Fr. Jack Roussin had made a risky decision: St. Mary's would become financially self-sustaining. The chancery had been supplementing the parish's operational budget, and Fr. Jack wasn't even taking a salary. But protracted financial negotiations with the archdiocese over the cost of a new roof in 1987 had convinced Fr. Jack that the writing was on the wall for St. Mary's: If the parish continued to operate in the red, he forecasted, it wouldn't be long before the archdiocese decided that the cost of keeping the parish open outweighed the benefits. If they wanted to survive, they needed to stop accepting financial subsidies from the archdiocese. Sr. Margaret, then the director of youth ministry and religious education at St. Mary's, recalled the deliberations:

> It was our own Parish Council . . . that said, they're beginning to close churches all around. And they're talking about it. If we continue to be on [archdiocesan] subsidy, we're going to be on that list. We're small, and we're costing them money. Let's go self-supporting. . . . And so the Parish Council for a number of Sundays made this presentation to the community. It was a fearsome thing because, what if it doesn't work? *What if it doesn't work?* The [archdiocese] told us we could not go back.[14]

But the move was a success. Offertory collections, which had barely reached two hundred dollars most weeks, leapt into the thousands.[15] The spring Grand Annual fund-raiser garnered tens of thousands of dollars more to cover—just barely—the cost of keeping St. Mary's afloat. By the time the closure notice was handed down in 2004, St. Mary's hadn't accepted operational subsidies from the archdiocese in almost two decades. To parishioners, the idea that shuttering St. Mary's would help rectify the archdiocese's financial situation rang hollow. The three-quarters of an acre the church occupied was worth relatively little on the real estate market.[16] If sold to a developer, whatever the property would become would likely do little for the poor, working-class, and immigrant families who called St. Mary's home. To parishioners, the decision felt like more betrayal from church leaders who offered lofty rhetoric about the value of cultural diversity while shutting down one of the only parishes in the city to have ever meaningfully achieved it.

The archbishop's letter to the parish struck a nerve—two, actually. First, it seemed that the church was being suppressed because it was small. Parishioners were incredulous. *Of course* St. Mary's was small. It always had been. But it wasn't invisible: By most accounts, the church was serving around four hundred parishioners at the time, a small but hardly insignificant number.[17] Equating its viability with its low sacramental index[18]—a figure bound to be low in a community of its size—ignored almost everything the church actually did. In a list of "Ten Reasons Not to Suppress St. Mary of the Angels," parishioners suggested that the archbishop attend instead to their high "spirituality index." Half of parishioners, including many families and almost all youth, had made a bilingual retreat. They participated in Jesuit-led spiritual direction during Advent and Lent, and groups gathered every Sunday after Mass to reflect on Scripture. The parish buzzed with more than two dozen lay-led parish committees, many of them focused on spiritual formation and social justice outreach. Massgoers worshipped and worked across ethnic, racial, and socioeconomic lines.[19] In an indignant response to the decision printed in the parish bulletin the Sunday after the announcement, Fr. Dave reacted with exasperation that none of this seemed to have been taken into account, citing O'Malley's own words: "As if the 'spiritual needs of the People of God' did not include such things."[20]

Second, and even more infuriating to parishioners, was that O'Malley had proposed breaking up the community along ethnic lines. "The Hispanic community presently worshipping at Saint Mary of the Angels will be invited to join the existing Hispanic community already worshipping at Our Lady of Lourdes, Jamaica Plain," the closure letter stated.[21] In the Sunday bulletin, Gill had choice words for that suggestion:

Not only did [the archbishop] not acknowledge our efforts at being one multi-cultural Catholic community, he effectively insulted it with his—no doubt well-intentioned—welcoming of our Hispanic members to Lourdes, as if they were some kind of separate group that could be simply broken off and sent elsewhere without reference to the rest of us—or to their own wishes. And where, pray tell, would the rest of us be welcome?[22]

Parishioners from across racial and ethnic groups bristled at the insinuation that they only cared about fellow community members who belonged to their own demographic. "We are not a parish that is ethnically-divisible," wrote the incensed cochair of the Parish Council, a longtime African American parishioner and community leader. "Our Latino members cannot just "move" to Our Lady of Lourdes. Please do not assume that our African-American members will automatically go to the new 'Black parish.' Nor can our white and Laotian members just 'find' some other receiving parishes. We are one church, one faith community."[23] In a formal response letter to the chancery, Gill tried to explain that the unique, highly integrated cultural identity at St. Mary's was "hard won," "precious and unusual," and "a real gift to the Church in Boston."[24] Quoted in a *Boston Globe* article on the shutdowns, parish matriarch Janice Chinn put the point more bluntly: "We go as one, or we don't go."[25]

Ritual Solidarity as a Response to Closure

As soon as news of St. Mary's impending closure broke, the Parish Council called an emergency meeting to formulate an action plan, hastily establishing a Committee to Save St. Mary of the Angels (CSSMA) to lead the effort. Throughout the city, outcry over the shutdowns raged. But to a parish of seasoned community organizers, it was already clear that many of the burgeoning resistance efforts were bound to fail. First, much of the protest appeared too sentimental to succeed. *Telling the archbishop that your parish is special because it's where your parents got married isn't going to keep its doors open*, they reasoned. *You need to prove your church has a future, not just a past.* Second, many Catholics focused their outrage, understandably, on the institutional betrayal and hypocrisy the shutdowns represented in the wake of the clergy sexual abuse crisis. Voice of the Faithful had assumed a central role in leading the anti-closure resistance effort.

But the problem of clericalism in the Catholic church wasn't going to be solved in time to save people's parishes from closing, and anyway, if 2002 had proven anything, it was that church leaders weren't about to be shamed into doing the right thing. At some suburban parishes, laity resisted the shutdowns by occupying their sanctuaries, holding around-the-clock vigils, and taking turns sleeping in the pews. Some parishes filed civil lawsuits against the archdiocese contesting its ownership of parish property.[26] Others contacted the State Attorney General's office encouraging the state to open an investigation into whether the shutdowns unjustly targeted parishes serving nonwhite and hearing-impaired communities.[27] In nearby Newton, the Board of Aldermen voted to rezone the land on which St. Bernard's Parish sat in an attempt to lower its property value.[28] In Lowell, the mayor explored having one church declared a historic site to keep it from being sold off.[29] Fifteen parishes went the canonical route, appealing their closures to the Vatican.[30]

The CSSMA knew they had to be strategic. Rather than relying on sentimentality, drilling down on unwieldy grievances with the Catholic hierarchy, or getting mired in litigation they couldn't afford, they would mount a case aimed at proving only one argument: St. Mary's was too important to Egleston Square to close. To make their case, they would need to harness the sources of power to which they had access: vast networks of marrow-deep relationships and a flair for public ritual. At meetings, the committee urged parishioners and neighbors to "stay on message."[31] No amount of heartache would win their cause. They had to prove that saving St. Mary's wasn't only, or even primarily, about them: Closing the church would kill the neighborhood.

After nearly a century in Egleston Square, St. Mary's had become the thread that knit the neighborhood together. The parish house still served as gathering space for peacebuilding efforts in times of crisis and hosted meetings for more than a dozen community organizations. Local residents relied on the Wednesday food pantry run out of the parish basement. Beyond its liturgical, spiritual, and catechetical ministries, parishioners served the homeless, imprisoned, elderly, and people living with HIV/AIDS.[32] They advocated for fair and affordable housing, immigrant justice, youth services, and jobs for formerly incarcerated people. In many ways, the campaign to keep St. Mary's alive would mark the ultimate test of the parish's mission of solidarity. During the darkest days of violence in Egleston Square, St. Mary's had helped to resurrect the neighborhood. Now it was up to the neighborhood to bring St. Mary's back from the brink of death.

"Lifeblood of the Neighborhood"

While Gill fended off phone calls from speculators itching to buy the church's stained-glass windows and appraise its contents,[33] the CSSMA pulled together a massive solidarity effort. They began by mounting a pressure campaign, flooding the chancery with letters and local media with the voices of parishioners and their advocates. To do this, they tapped into the diverse religious and secular ecologies within which St. Mary's existed. At the first committee meeting, someone taped a large piece of sky-blue poster paper to the wall. Attendees listed every community leader, media outlet, local organization, politician, and public figure they could think of: The Boston Globe and the Jamaica Plain Gazette and Spanish-language newspaper El Mundo, National Public Radio and local Spanish-language stations; then mayor Tom Menino and City Counselor Felix Arroyo, State Representative Liz Malia and former representative John McDonough, parish house resident-emeritus Paul Farmer and Egleston YMCA Director Will Morales and local police officer Sixto Merced, a former youth group kid and gang member whose life was transformed by Fr. Jack. They listed longtime neighborhood partners like affordable housing association Urban Edge and bilingual Rafael Hernández School across the street and every Egleston Square neighborhood association in existence. Boston College and Harvard were on the list, the Jesuit Volunteer Corps and Jewish Memorial Hospital. They named every parishioner who had received the archdiocese's prestigious Bishop James Augustine Healy Award, an honor given annually for service to the Black Catholic community in Boston. When they ran out of space on the front of the poster, they turned it over and kept writing.

Next to each individual and organization on the list, they scribbled the name of a parishioner who had a connection, flipping feverishly through the marigold-yellow pages of the parish directory. The parish yellow pages not only collated members' contact information but also organized them by parish activity, neighborhood, country of origin, profession, skills and talents, hobbies, interests, occupation, place of employment, high school or college of graduation, and languages spoken. It was easy to see who had connections where and to whom. Committee members worked their networks to solicit letters of support from everyone on their list, parishioners young and old, and anyone else who might help to convince the archbishop that St. Mary's was integral to the fabric of the neighborhood. Sr. Margaret, who had since left Boston to work as a missionary in Peru, penned a three-page letter of her own. "I ended [it] by saying, 'This is not nostalgia,'" she recalled. "'I'm not like the people on the corner saying, *I got all my sacraments there.* . . . It's more than that. It's more than that.'"[34]

Another letter was from the Rev. Dr. Ray A. Hammond, founder of Boston's Bethel A.M.E. Church and chairman of the ecumenical antiviolence organization Boston Ten Point Coalition. Widely recognized as one of the city's most important community leaders, Hammond provided testimony on behalf of the parish that would prove powerful. In their request for his support, the CSSMA offered Hammond a draft letter to work from. But the pain in their letter was too raw, their accusations of church leaders' absence from the fight for racial justice too acerbic.[35] Perhaps aware of his delicate position as a Catholic outsider, and perhaps because experience had taught him the value of diplomacy, Hammond struck a more measured and compassionate tone. "I can only imagine how difficult these days have been for you," he consoled the archbishop. "I have prayed for you knowing that the gravity of church closings has weighed heavily on your mind and soul." The letter continued:

> In Boston, the churches in the minority community have played a significant role in reducing violence, providing constructive opportunities for youth, addressing affordable housing, and developing communities of hope and opportunity. Without question, in this area, the Catholic Church with the greatest presence in this work has been St. Mary of the Angels. . . . If. St. Mary closes a primary meeting place and resource for this community will be lost and the Catholic Church will have lost one of its greatest witnesses to the spiritual and social mission of the Church.

Hammond corroborated the unique role St. Mary's occupied in church and neighborhood. "I have always seen St. Mary's as a model of the Catholic Church of the 21st century—multi-lingual and multi-racial, with all parishioners knowing and caring about one another and working collaboratively for the sake of all," Hammond wrote. He concluded by suggesting

Unase a nosotros apoyando nuestra

Campaña para Salvar la Comunidad de Santa Maria de los Angeles

La Iglesia Santa Maria de los Angeles en Egleston Square ha recibido notificación de que tiene que cerrar. Les pedimos que se alie a los parroquianos, vecinos, oficiales elegidos, y grupos de la comunidad para apoyar el esfuerzo de mantener a Santa Maria abierta. Unase a nosotros este Domingo para los eventos siguientes:

Este Domingo, 13 de junio

10:00 AM   **Misa mulit-lingüe** (ingles, español, khmer, lenguaje de señas americano), todos están invitados – en Santa Maria de los Angeles

11:30 AM   **Apoyadores de la Comunidad se reunen en el Jardin de Paz en Egleston Square** para caminar juntos a Santa Maria y unirse con los parroquianos después de la misa.

12:00 MD   **Reunión festiva y "Manos alrededor de Santa Maria"** en la iglesia Santa Maria de los Angeles. Se les invita a los parroquianos y otros apoyadores de la comunidad de Egleston Square

Para más información, por favor llame a Santa Maria al 617-445-1524

¡Por favor únase a nosotros y nuestros apoyadores el Domingo! Nuestros apoyadores incluyen:

Concilio Pastoral de Santa Maria de los Angeles, Representante estatal Liz Malia, Representante Jeffrey Sánchez, Representante Marie St. Fleur, Representante Byron Rushing, Representante Gloria Fox, Consejero municipal Chuck Turner, Consejera Maura Hennigan, Consejero Felix Arroyo, Consejero John Tobin, Urban Edge, ESAC City Life/Vida Urbana, Egleston Square Main Streets, Egleston Square Neighborhood Association, Egleston Square Merchants Association, the Grace & Hope Mission, la escuela Rafael Hernandez y el Centro de Salud Brookside.

FIGURE 15. Members of the Committee to Save St. Mary's distributed flyers in English and Spanish throughout Egleston Square notifying neighbors of the Mass, march, and Hands Around St. Mary's campaign to save the church. A long list of campaign supporters, including local politicians and community leaders, follows the announcement, June 13, 2004. Courtesy of Maria Quiroga.

that saving the parish would "be an unmistakable sign of your commitment to communities of color in Boston."[36]

Letters of support for St. Mary's poured into the Lake Street chancery from every corner of the city. Even so, "Simply writing eloquent
letters will not be enough," an internal committee memo warned. "We
need the kind of visibility given to St. Albert the Great, St. Catherine's,
and St. Susanna's," predominantly white parishes outside the city limits whose parishioners had the resources to mount high-profile appeals
and whose plights had thus far occupied most of the media headlines
about the closures. Demographically, the public face of the shutdown
response had begun to look a lot like the lay protests that followed the
"Spotlight" reports on clergy abuse, the memo observed: "The Cathedral is used to seeing the survivor groups and white suburbanites." The
public needed to see them, too—"black and white, Latino, Anglo, and
Asian."[37]

Hands Around St. Mary's

Parishioners concluded that they needed to do something "visible and
dramatic"[38]—something that spoke louder and more clearly than even the
most compelling letter could. Knowing well the power of ritual to unite
the community, they planned a massive multilingual liturgy, procession,
and public demonstration on the parish lawn. The morning of June 13,
2004, the whole parish gathered in the small sanctuary to celebrate Mass
together. It was the Solemnity of the Most Holy Body and Blood of Christ.
The program for the liturgy was emblazoned with the headline, "We are
bread for the community." The liturgy's prayers, readings, and music wove
together all of the community's primary languages and spiritual traditions.
The Gloria rang out in English, Spanish, and Kmhmu.[39] The liturgy program included the English and Spanish refrains and a transliteration of the
text in Kmhmu. This meant that everyone could participate in all three.

Fr. Joe Bruce, a deaf Jesuit priest and longtime friend of the parish,
concelebrated the Mass in American Sign Language (ASL), as he often
did.[40] Hymns in French and Swahili evoked the memory of other cultural
communities that had once called St. Mary's home.

While parishioners prayed inside, reporters assembled on the parish
lawn. Down the street, neighbors, community leaders, local politicians,

and friends from across the city gathered at the Egleston Square Peace Garden, a mural-lined, daffodil-dotted green space that neighbors had cultivated at the once-abandoned lot next to the spot where Hector Morales was killed by police in 1990.[41] As the Mass was about to end, supporters marched from the Peace Garden up Columbus Avenue to the church. Parishioners processed outside to greet their neighbors. Together, everyone encircled the church, singing and dancing as they walked. Standing shoulder to shoulder, it was impossible to tell parishioners from community members, Catholics from non-Catholics, Spanish Massgoers from English Massgoers. In the middle of the circle, on the parish house lawn, a smaller group of parishioners formed another circle: parish elders, newborn babies and recently baptized children in their parents' arms, recent first communicants and newly confirmed teenagers, and representatives of the parish's many nations. The circle on the lawn represented a visual rebuke of the points in the archbishop's letter that had so incensed parishioners: Theirs was a church rich in sacraments, teeming with both history and new life, and united in difference.

At noon, everyone joined hands and sang "We Shall Not Be Moved," an African American spiritual of resistance. Beginning in the 1990s, community leader and parishioner Delphine Walker had helped to organize an annual celebration called Hands Around Egleston Square. Neighbors would flood the streets and join hands in a symbolic demonstration of friendship, solidarity, and care. Intentionally echoing that ritual, parishioners named today's event Manos Alrededor de Santa María de los Ángeles—Hands Around St. Mary's. The protest liturgy united the community against the closure. It also succeeded in its other, more pragmatic objective: St. Mary's was now at the center of the shutdown story. In article after article, the voices and images of St. Mary's parishioners assumed center stage. The day after the event, the *Boston Globe* declared St. Mary's "the lifeblood of the neighborhood."[42]

All Night, All Day

Parishioners had campaigned and strategized and demonstrated. Now, they prayed. Taking inspiration from churches whose members had occupied their sanctuaries indefinitely to protest their shutdowns, St. Mary's parishioners held a twenty-four-hour prayer vigil in the pews. But the vigil wasn't just for them. At the top of every hour, they recited the names of three parishes due to be closed, ringing a bell after each one. After sitting in silent prayer, they concluded each hour with an invocation:

> God of Light, we know you have been with us during this time of vigil. Continue to shine in our hearts as we leave this sanctuary. Let the light of your love be with us and all parishes so that our Spirits will not be extinguished but will continue to shine wherever the people of God may be. Amen.[43]

Invoking the litany of communities on the edge, parishioners made clear that the fight to save their church was about more than their love for a particular place. It was about a larger power structure that pitted poor communities against one another and deprived laity of the authority to determine their future. The future they prayed for was not only one in which the doors of St. Mary's remained open. Their hope was for a new way of being church altogether.

An Ecclesiology of Solidarity

Of the dozens of Boston parishes that contested their closures, only a small fraction achieved success.[44] Among them, incredibly, was St. Mary of the Angels. That fall, in response to overwhelming testimony from parishioners, neighbors, and other supporters, St. Mary's received a two-year reprieve from closure. The following June, O'Malley reversed the decision for good, quietly announcing that St. Mary's would remain open indefinitely. How had a parish that had been on the brink of closure since the day workers broke ground on its foundation managed to evade one of the most sweeping parish shutdowns in U.S. history?

What was distinctive about the campaign St. Mary's mounted was that it was not, ultimately, about resistance alone but about solidarity. The CSSMA assembled a community coalition that intentionally downplayed individual sentimental connections to the parish and instead demonstrated its decisive stabilizing role in the social and cultural ecology of the neighborhood. The coalition's ecumenical, interreligious, and secular composition helped to defuse the temptation to make the campaign a referendum on the credibility and moral authority of the Catholic hierarchy, at least not explicitly. Ritualizing the relationship of mutuality between church and neighborhood, and strategically using media in English and Spanish to open these rituals of solidarity to multiple publics, the community successfully demonstrated that the parish was too vital to the peace and survival of Egleston Square to shutter. In the end, it was solidarity that saved St. Mary's—both the solidarity that bound together the fates of parish and neighborhood and the elusive, hard-won solidarity that united parishioners themselves, propelling their backlash to the idea of being split up along racial, ethnic, and linguistic lines. The mutual garment of destiny had won out.

Parishioners' refusal to be divided was ultimately the refusal of a certain kind of ecclesiology. As Gill intimated in his emergency letter to the parish printed in the bulletin the Sunday after the closure announcement, the archbishop's assumptions were telling. Church leaders assumed that English-speaking and Spanish-speaking parishioners didn't matter enough to one another to desire a shared future. They presumed the Black parishioners would want to leave St. Mary's for the new Black Catholic parish anyway, the Latinos would be just as happy at another Spanish Mass, that the white members could fit in anywhere, and they seemed to forget that the small but still-active Kmhmu community existed at all. All told, the future that the archdiocese suggested for St. Mary's parishioners betrayed a tacit assumption that the only relationships that genuinely mattered to the people were those formed along racial and ethnic lines—that as long as people could continue going to Mass with "their own," they would be content. It did not seem to have occurred to anyone at the chancery that the people of St. Mary's actually meant what they put in their mission statement and wrote in their report to the archdiocese two years prior. Despite relentless archdiocesan rhetoric about celebrating diversity, within its operative ecclesiological vision cultural difference was a problem to be solved. According to a vision like this one, the highest ideals a diverse community can strive for are mutual recognition and tolerance and a concession to the idea of sharing space. At best, groups can become tourists to one another's realities. But this thin understanding of unity precludes the idea of a shared future. If anything, groups become threats to one another's futures, because the existence of these others represents alternative futures for the institution. It wasn't that the archdiocese disapproved of a parish like St. Mary's—it was that it couldn't even imagine one.

The shutdowns betrayed a vision of parish life that equated size with success, privileging larger, wealthier, suburban parishes over small, poor, urban ones. Condensing the purpose of the parish into a sacramental dispensary made the rest of parish life and practice extraneous. Within this metrics-based model, diversity is good when it is useful, when culturally responsive ministry bears fruit in Sunday collections and vocations to the priesthood. If these are the metrics that determine parish survival, churches like St. Mary's will always be the first to go. The solidarity campaign challenged institutional leaders to consider whether there was any room in the church for a parish that was poor and for the poor and at the same time an agent of its own future. The people of St. Mary's didn't want to be a mission of some other, bigger and wealthier church, or a self-selecting alternative community. They wanted to be an ordinary city parish, a place for those who were there for the first time and those who had been away for a while and returned.

Conclusion

The introduction to this book describes the chapters that follow as a winding attempt to understand the mystery of love in a community of difference. My years at St. Mary's taught me that people only fight to save what they love. People loved the youth of Egleston Square, so they marched and prayed and worked to save them. People loved the neighborhood, so they marched and prayed and worked to save it, too. People loved the God they could not see, so they worked side by side with the neighbors they could. People loved the Catholic church, in spite of everything, so they worked to save a place in it. And people loved St. Mary's, so they fought to save it, and they won. To trace the history of St. Mary's is to chronicle more than a century of people willing to risk their lives in order to save the things they loved. In the final case, what they loved was one another; what they risked was love itself.

Love does not erase risk. If anything, it magnifies it, raises its stakes. St. Mary's is still a community on the edge. A month after I moved into the parish house, in October 2011, a Whole Foods opened two miles away in Jamaica Plain's Hyde Square, replacing Hi-Lo Foods, a Latin American grocer that had been in the neighborhood for forty-seven years. A debate over gentrification erupted. But even then, Jamaica Plain's hipster coffee

shops and organic, fair-trade Centre Street boutiques felt like a world away
from the corner of Columbus and Walnut Avenue I occupied. Today, gentrification has started to come for Egleston Square, too, driving up rents
in the buildings around St. Mary's. Roxbury, one of the last affordable
places to live in the city, is slowly becoming inaccessible to the people
St. Mary's serves. In 2020, the COVID-19 pandemic came even closer to
closing the parish than the archdiocese did in 2004. The sort of liturgical
adaptations employed by other congregations during the pandemic lock-
down were inaccessible at St. Mary's. The church building doesn't even
have bathrooms, much less a high-speed Wi-Fi connection, making
livestreaming Mass unsustainable. When churches reopened, parishioners
who had gotten in the habit of attending Mass virtually at other parishes
realized that they had a choice to make—and not all of them chose to return to St. Mary's. Some elderly parishioners were unable to return at all.
Many churches sustained their finances during the shutdown by encouraging members to give online. But it is hard to rely on automatic monthly
deposits in a community where many people live paycheck to paycheck
and others are unbanked. St. Mary's weathered the pandemic, but the crisis revealed new fissures in the community's foundation. Relationships of
solidarity rely on mutual commitment and mutual need. As the neighborhood around St. Mary's changes, the parish's commitment to Egleston
Square remains. But a new generation will have to decide whether its salvation is bound up with St. Mary's.

"People Get Ready," the civil rights anthem–turned–Communion
hymn, prophesied a vision of the kingdom of God toward which St. Mary's
worked to orient people—a place where you don't need money or a ticket
or just about anything else to get on board. *All you need is faith!* Anita would
intone as we swayed our way to Communion—and even if you didn't have
that, there was probably somebody around who would lend you some. To
call St. Mary's a way station is no metaphor: The church was essentially a
subway station, underground and generally in need of repair, either teeming or empty, host to a real here-comes-everybody of the people of God.
To descend the outdoor stairs into the sanctuary was to be overcome with
the sensation that you were standing in the good-enough present of some
engineer's grand vision a century ago. St. Mary's was a place for people
traveling together toward that kingdom—a place, as the song goes, of
"hope for all among those loved the most."[45]

In 2006, having stayed alive, St. Mary's celebrated its centennial anniversary as only it could. There was a trilingual Mass in English, Spanish, and Kmhmu, followed by a potluck feast on the parish lawn. And of course, there was a procession. Parishioners invited Archbishop O'Malley—hard feelings from the closure attempt all water under the bridge—to lead a march to the church from the corner of Washington and School Street: the corner once home to the streetcar barn that housed the first makeshift sanctuary, where shadows from the Egleston Square Orange Line station once stretched, where Hector Morales and the X-Men painted their mural and where Hector was killed by police, where Hector's mother stood on Good Friday to mark the neighborhood's passion, where the long-awaited YMCA finally opened in a building they renamed for Fr. Jack, where neighbors planted a Peace Garden, and where the whole city assembled to process to the church to demand its survival. Side by side, parishioners and neighbors marched through the street, past Egleston Pizza and Skippy White's Record Shop and the hair salon, past the Hernández School and the library, and down the stairs to church.

Appendix: Interviews

Semistructured interviews with parishioners and community members were an invaluable dimension of the research upon which this book is based. Some of my conversation partners provided vivid personal accounts of their migration journeys, faith lives, parish practices, and family stories. Others offered rich oral histories of St. Mary's and Egleston Square. I conducted two primary rounds of interviews, the first during Holy Week in 2013 and the second four years later in 2017. As my project evolved and I became more embedded in the life of the parish, I began to rely more heavily on informal conversations, which I recounted in field note memos, as well as various forms of participant observation, archival research, and photography. Part of me was relieved at this turn: The formality of conducting recorded interviews always activated an anticipatory anxiety within my chest, making me nervous for conversations with people with whom I'd otherwise gladly talk for hours. Nevertheless, these formal interviews laid this book's foundation. Without them, the entire project would have toppled over. As importantly, the disciplined practice of conducting, transcribing, and analyzing formal interviews helped me to ensure that the work included an expansive array of voices. I returned to these stories again and again in the process of research and writing. The following is a list of participants, identified by pseudonyms, whose stories you encountered in the pages of this book.

Pseudonym

Country/region of origin, gender, age at time of interview (if known)
Date, location, and language of interview

Omar

Cuban-born Spanish Mass parishioner, male, 57
March 29, 2013, Parish House office, English

William Morales

New York–born community leader of Puerto Rican heritage, male, 43*
April 2, 2013, YMCA of Greater Boston, Egleston Square, English
A local public figure; this is Morales's real name.

Amelia and Tom

Euro-American married couple, female and male, late 50s
April 3, 2013, their home in Jamaica Plain, English

Sr. Josephine

Boston-born Irish American religious sister, female, 83
April 4, 2013, Parish House chapel, English

Martin

African American lay leader, male, 72
April 4, 2013, Parish House chapel, English

Olivia and Megan

Euro-American married couple, female and female, early 30s
April 7, 2013, their home in Roxbury, English

Marisol

Dominican neighbor and mother of three, female, mid-30s
April 7, 2013, and April 14, 2017, her home in Roxbury, Spanish

Jael

Dominican-born mother and Spanish Mass parishioner, female,
early 40s
April 9, 2013, Parish House office, Spanish

Ximena

Colombian mother of two, female, 52
April 9, 2013, Parish House office, English and Spanish

Florence

African American longtime parishioner and neighbor, female, 83
April 9, 2013, Parish House chapel, English

Pablo, S.J.

Spanish Jesuit in formation at Boston College, male, 32
April 18, 2013, Parish House office, English

Sr. Margaret

Euro-American religious sister, female, early 70s
April 21, 2013, Parish House office, English

Ramón

Ecuadorian parishioner and lay leader, male, 40
April 23, 2013, Parish House chapel, English

Claudia

Dominican American lay leader, female, 60s
December 8, 2015, her place of business, Spanish and English

Gayle

Euro-American lay leader, female, 73
November 14, 2015, my home, and April 15, 2017, Parish House
    office, English

Yamaris

Spanish Mass parishioner from the Dominican Republic, female,
    mid-30s
April 14, 2017, Parish House chapel, Spanish

Gina

Retired English Mass parishioner, female, age unknown
April 14, 2017, Parish House office, English

Eugene

Retired English Mass parishioner, male, 70s
April 14, 2017, Parish House office, English

Michelle

African American English Mass parishioner, female, 70s
April 14, 2017, Parish House chapel, English

Marielena

Dominican-born neighbor, female, early 40s
April 14, 2017, a neighbor's home, Spanish

Victoria

Jamaican-born English Mass choir member, female, age unknown
April 14, 2017, Neighborhood Way of the Cross, English

Alma

English Mass lay leader of South American descent, female, mid-60s
April 15, 2017, Parish House office, English

The shape of these interviews evolved significantly throughout the course of my research. I believe it is helpful, however, to offer a glimpse into the way these early conversations unfolded—or, at the very least, the way I prepared for them ahead of time. Once underway, very few followed the road map I'd laid out precisely; some didn't follow it at all. Nevertheless, I include my initial interview questions here in order to offer some insight into this dimension of the research process. Without fail, the most important question was the one I asked early on: "What brought you here?" This simple inquiry seemed to open up entire worlds, inviting participants to narrate the often-complex cartographies that led them to St. Mary's.

Interview Questions (English)

WELCOME

I. INTRODUCTIONS

    1) Let's begin with some introductions. Could you tell me a little bit about the things you're involved with here at St. Mary's?

II. ENGAGEMENT QUESTIONS

    2) When did you first start coming to St. Mary's of the Angels (SMA)? What brought you here?

    3) In what ways is it similar to/different from other parishes you have attended?

        a. *Probe for connections to parish multicultural identity*

    4) Do you live within the territorial boundary of SMA? Or how did you find your way here?

    5) If you were to describe SMA to a friend who has never been to the parish, what would you say?

        a. *Probe: mission/identity of the parish*

        b. OR, if you could describe St. Mary's in one word, what would it be?

    6) How, if at all, have you seen the parish change during your time here? What has that been like for you?

        a. *Probe: Demographically . . . culturally . . . racially . . . socially . . . spiritually/theologically . . . leadership-wise . . .*

III. EXPLORATION QUESTIONS

    7) The SMA mission statement describes St. Mary's as a "multicultural and multilingual" community. When, if at all, do you tend to interact most with people from the [opposite community—English/Spanish] at SMA?

        a. *Probe for specific examples*

    8) What are those interactions like for you?

    9) What tends to be positive for you about these experiences? What is challenging?

    10) In your experience, what are things that promote multicultural collaboration at SMA?

        a. *Probe/examples: events, practices, liturgies, attitudes, mission statements, etc.*

11) What do you see as barriers to intercultural collaboration at SMA?

    a. *Probe: If you could change or improve one thing with respect to SMA's approach to multicultural community, what would it be?*

12) For you personally, what's your favorite part of Holy Week at SMA? Why?

    a. *Probe for specific examples, memories, and descriptions*

IV. EXIT QUESTION

13) Is there anything else you would like to add?

Interview Questions (Spanish)

BIENVENIDOS

I. INTRODUCCIONES

1) Empezamos con algunas presentaciones. Por favor, cuéntame un poco sobre las principales cosas que está involucrado aquí en St. Mary's.

II. PREGUNTAS DE LA VIDA PARROQUIAL DE STA. MARIA

2) ¿Cuándo comenzó a venir a SMA? ¿Por qué decidiste venir a este parroquia?

    a. De qué manera es similar o diferente a otras parroquias a las que has asistido?

    b. *Probe: Identidad multicultural*

    c. *Probes: ¿Usted vive dentro del límite territorial de SMA? ¿O cómo encontraste tu camino aquí?*

3) Si usted describiera a SMA a un amigo que nunca ha estado en la parroquia, ¿qué diría usted?

    a. Probe: misión / identidad de la parroquia

    b. O, si pudieras describir a St. Mary's en una palabra, ¿cuál sería?

4) ¿En tú opinión, cómo ha cambiado la parroquia a lo largo de su tiempo aquí?

    a. *Probe: Demográficamente . . . culturalmente . . . racialmente . . . socialmente . . . espiritualmente / teológicamente . . . en terminos de liderazgo . . .*

    b. *¿Qué le ha parecido?*

III. PREGUNTAS DE EXPLORACIÓN

5) La declaración de misión de la SMA describe a Santa María como una comunidad "multicultural y multilingüe." ¿Cuándo, en todo caso, suele a interactuar más con personas de la [comunidad opuesta—inglés / español] en SMA?

    a. *Probe: Ejemplos específicos?*

    b. *¿Cómo son esas momentos de interacción para usted?*

    c. *¿Qué son algunas cosas positivas para usted acerca de estas experiencias? ¿Qué es un desafío?*

6) En su experiencia, ¿cuáles son las cosas que promueven la colaboración multicultural en SMA?

    a. *Probe: Ejemplos, e.g., eventos, prácticas, liturgias, las actitudes, las declaraciones de misión, etc.*

7) ¿Qué ve usted como barreras para la colaboración intercultural en SMA?

    a. *Probe: Si pudiera cambiar o mejorar una cosa con respecto al enfoque de la comunidad multicultural de SMA, ¿cuál sería?*

8) Para ustedes, hablando personalmente, ¿Cuál es su parte favorita de la Semana Santa en SMA? ¿Por qué?

    a. *Probe: ejemplos específicos, memorias y descripciones*

IV. PREGUNTA FINAL

9) ¿Hay algo más que quiere usted decir?

Acknowledgments

The first person I met at St. Mary of the Angels was a woman who, in these pages, I've called Florence. I rang the doorbell of the parish house, and she peered out at me through lace curtains. Our eyes met, and I had a fleeting urge to sprint down the front steps and back to the bus stop whence I came. She opened the door and asked who I was. I responded, and she threw one arm around my shoulder. The other she used to hold a cane, which for a brief moment supported the weight of us both. This book is a product of that embrace and the embrace of so many other parishioners and community members who became my primary teachers of theology during the decade over which this project evolved. William Morales, Sr. Katherine McGrath, Maria Chavez, and Alvin Shiggs were indispensable historical guides. I am indebted to Maria Quiroga, whose impeccable record-keeping during Boston's 2004 parish closure era offered me a striking glimpse into a community fighting for survival. My parish house roommate, Catherine Kirwan-Avila—now Sr. Catherine Kirwan-Avila, A.C.J.—guided me through my first year in a new city with patience, kindness, and wisdom. I could fill pages with the names of those whose friendship and insight made this book possible: Juan Pablo Moyano Pérez, S.J., Gregoire Catta, S.J., Ana Lopez, Gloria Celado, Joyce Harvey, Theresa and Melissa Vela, Cynthia Kennedy, Carl Stamm, Marina Pastrana, Kitty Ryan, Joe Vallely, Janice Chinn, Shauna Townsend, John and Kathy Rood, Ann Grady, Wilson Villamar, and so many more.

I am exceedingly grateful to archivist Thomas Lester at the Roman Catholic Archdiocese of Boston archives in Braintree, Massachusetts. Much of the historical research for this book was facilitated by his expertise. Archival research, travel, and editorial assistance for this book were supported by grants from the Brewer Fund for Congregational Research at Candler School of Theology, Emory University's Center for Faculty Development and Excellence, and Boston College School of Theology and

Ministry. I am particularly grateful to Jonathan Strom for his support. A Manuscript Completion Grant from Candler helped to ensure this book's timely completion, as, in a different way, did the generous and humane maternity leave granted to me by Dean Jan Love.

I am indebted to Natalia Imperatori-Lee, Kwok Pui-Lan, Kristy Nabhan-Warren, and Nancy Pineda-Madrid, each of whom read and responded to this project at multiple stages. Their generous feedback shaped this book immeasurably, and I remain deeply grateful for their mentorship and accompaniment. Deborah Kanter read the entire manuscript with a historian's sharp eye and offered detailed feedback. I could not ask for a more magnanimous conversation partner throughout the evolution of this work than Hosffman Ospino. Brett Hoover's early support for my research was a source of deep encouragement, and his own pastorally sensitive parish ethnography served as a model of fieldwork in theology as my project developed. I am grateful, too, to those colleagues and friends who offered feedback on pieces of this manuscript as it took shape. In a particular way, I thank Sarah Bogue, Lucila Crena, Joel Kemp, Kyle Lambelet, Deanna Womack, and Peng Yin, inaugural members of the Candler Junior Faculty Writing Group. Jennifer Ayres and Ellen Ott Marshall provided virtual companionship during early-morning writing sessions throughout the first year of the COVID-19 pandemic. Everyone should be so fortunate to have such colleagues. My brilliant and dedicated research assistant, Lindsey Faust, supported the completion of this book in numerous ways. Several chapters benefitted from the editorial expertise of Ulrike Guthrie. I thank John Garza for his unwavering enthusiasm for this project and everyone at Fordham University Press who helped to bring this book to fruition.

Several pieces of this book first saw the light of day as conference papers shared in the Fieldwork in Theology Interest Group of the Catholic Theological Society of America, the Ecclesiology section of the College Theology Society, and at gatherings of the American Academy of Religion and the Association of Practical Theology. A much earlier version of a portion of chapter 1 was published as "Beyond Unity and Diversity: Race, Culture, and Communion Ecclesiology in U.S. Catholicism," *American Catholic Studies* 130, no. 4 (Winter 2019): 31–57. A previous iteration of part of chapter 2 was published as "Fieldwork in Ecclesial Borderlands: Culture, Community, and Belonging in a Multiethnic Boston Parish," *Exchange* 48, no. 3 (2019): 225–35.

I owe my deepest gratitude to my family. My sister, Abby Bigelow, traveled across the country on more than one occasion to provide childcare at crucial moments, and my heart was buoyed by the support of many family members and relatives. Above all, this work was animated by the love and unyielding encouragement of my husband, Drew, and our three daughters, Nora, Lucy, and Julia. Drew made this work possible through generous family caretaking and unyielding encouragement and, in a deeper sense, through a commitment to justice and community that continues to orient our lives. Nora and Lucy were born while I was a doctoral student. In the womb, they accompanied me to classes and conferences, quietly inaugurating me into the mystery of the incarnation. Later, they slept in carriers and played on blankets as I conducted interviews, strolled through city streets on the Way of the Cross, toddled up and down church aisles during Mass, and took crayons to the pages of manuscript drafts. Julia entered the world a year after I joined the faculty at Candler, just in time to become a wellspring of delight to our family during the strange and dark days of the pandemic. You four are the joy of my life and the surest sign I know of God's love.

Notes

Introduction: Unstable Communities of the Faithful

1. The Impressions, "People Get Ready," lyrics and music by Curtis Mayfield, recorded October 26, 1964, ABC-Paramount, track 1 on *People Get Ready*, 1965, vinyl single.

2. Cf. The Impressions, "People Get Ready."

3. Cf. Noel Ignatiev, *How the Irish Became White* (New York: Routledge, 1995).

4. "A Statement of the Black Catholic Clergy Caucus, 1968," in *Black Theology: A Documentary History, Volume 1: 1966–1979*, 2nd ed., ed. James Cone and Gayraud S. Wilmore (Maryknoll, N.Y.: Orbis, 1993), 230.

5. Peter DeMarco, "Church Faithful Protest Closings," *Boston Globe*, June 14, 2004, B4.

6. Tracy Kidder, *Mountains Beyond Mountains: The Quest of Dr. Paul Farmer, a Man Who Would Cure the World* (New York: Random House, 2003), 129–34.

7. See John C. Seitz, *No Closure: Catholic Practice and Boston's Parish Shutdowns* (Cambridge, Mass.: Harvard University Press, 2011).

8. In Massachusetts, I learned, CORI—or Criminal Offender Record Information—includes records related to an individual's interactions with the criminal justice system. CORI records posed employment challenges for those with criminal backgrounds, especially prior to a 2010 reform of the system. On an information table in the back of the sanctuary, St. Mary's maintained a list of "CORI-friendly" employers.

9. For a sample, see Joseph H. Fichter, S.J., *Southern Parish: The Dynamics of a City Church*, vol. 1 (Chicago, Ill.: University of Chicago Press, 1951) and *Social Relations in the Urban Parish* (Chicago, Ill.: University of Chicago Press, 1956); Charles W. Dahm, O.P., *Parish Ministry in a Hispanic Community* (Mahwah, N.J.: Paulist Press, 2004); William A. Clark, *A Voice of Their Own: The Authority of the Local Parish* (Collegeville, Minn.: Liturgical Press, 2005); Mark R. Francis, CSV, *Local Worship, Global Church: Popular Religion and the Liturgy* (Collegeville, Minn.: Liturgical Press, 2014); Ricky Manalo, *The Liturgy of Life: The Interrelationship of*

Sunday Eucharist and Everyday Worship Practices (Collegeville, Minn.: Liturgical Press, 2014); and Brett C. Hoover, *The Shared Parish: Latinos, Anglos, and the Future of U.S. Catholicism* (New York: NYU Press, 2014) [Hoover notes that he was a priest at the time of his research]. A recent counterexample to the trend is Alyssa Maldonado-Estrada, *Lifeblood of the Parish: Men and Catholic Devotion in Williamsburg, Brooklyn* (New York: NYU Press, 2020).

10. Gloria Anzaldúa, *Borderlands/La Frontera* (San Francisco, Calif.: Aunt Lute, 1987), Preface to the first edition (no pagination).

11. See Charles E. Zech, Mary L. Gautier, Mark M. Gray, Jonathan L. Wiggins, and Thomas P. Gaunt, S.J., *Catholic Parishes of the 21st Century* (New York: Oxford University Press, 2017), 108–9; and Hoover, *The Shared Parish*. According to the Center for Applied Research in the Apostolate (CARA), using data primarily from 2010 and 2011, roughly 35.9% of U.S. parishes serve multiple racial, ethnic, cultural, and/or linguistic communities. Of the 6,332 multicultural parishes identified by CARA, the vast majority—almost 70 percent—serve Spanish-speaking communities. CARA's figure significantly exceeds the 25 percent of parishes identified as *multiracial* in the 2012 phase of the National Congregations Study. CARA data likely include parishes that serve cultural or racial communities that do not necessarily meet or exceed 20 percent of the parish's membership, the threshold used by the NCS and other studies to identify a congregation as multiracial. Additionally, 14 percent of the multicultural parishes identified by CARA serve European and other linguistic and cultural communities that would be considered racially white (e.g., Polish, Ukrainian, French Canadian) and thus would not have been identified by the NCS as multiracial. I privilege the CARA figures because they account for nuances particular to the parish context. See Mark Gray, "Cultural Diversity in the Catholic Church in the United States" (Washington, D.C.: Center for Applied Research in the Apostolate, 2016), 7.

12. See Hoover, *The Shared Parish*.

13. See, for example, Nicholas M. Healy, "Ecclesiology and Communion," *Perspectives in Religious Studies* 31 (2004): 274; and Nicholas M. Healy, *Church, World and the Christian Life: Practical–Prophetic Ecclesiology* (Cambridge: Cambridge University Press, 2000).

14. Gustavo Gutierrez, "Conversion to the Neighbor," in *Gustavo Gutiérrez: Essential Writings*, ed. James B. Nickoloff (Minneapolis, Minn.: Fortress Press, 1996), 149–55. Gutiérrez references Yves Congar's notion of "the sacrament of our Neighbor" (154–55).

15. The phrase *locus ecclesiologicus* appears in John O'Brien, "Ecclesiology as Narrative," *Ecclesiology* 4 (2008): 153.

16. Natalia Imperatori-Lee, *Cuéntame: Narrative in the Ecclesial Present* (Maryknoll, N.Y.: Orbis, 2018), 84; citing Ada Maria Isasi-Díaz, "La Habana:

The City That Inhabits Me. A Multi-Site Understanding of Location," in *La Lucha Continues: Mujerista Theology* (Maryknoll, N.Y.: Orbis, 2004).

17. Robert A. Orsi, "Crossing the City Line," in *Gods of the City: Religion and the American Urban Landscape*, ed. Orsi (Bloomington: Indiana University Press, 1999), 41–42; cf. Mircea Eliade, *The Sacred and the Profane: The Nature of Religion*, trans. Willard R. Trask (New York: Harcourt, Brace & Co., 1959).

18. See Imperatori-Lee, *Cuéntame*, 24ff; María Pilar Aquino, "Theological Method in U.S. Latino/a Theology," in *From the Heart of Our People* (Maryknoll, N.Y.: Orbis, 1999): 39; Carmen M. Nanko-Fernández, "Lo Cotidiano as Locus Theologicus," in *The Wiley-Blackwell Companion to Latino/a Theology*, ed. Orlando O. Espín (Malden, Mass.: John Wiley & Sons, 2015), 15–16; Ada María Isasi-Díaz, *En La Lucha/In the Struggle: Elaborating a Mujerista Theology* (Minneapolis, Minn.: Fortress Press, 1983); Michelle A. González, "Who We Are: A Latina/o Constructive Anthropology," in *In Our Own Voices: Latino/a Renditions of Theology*, ed. Benjamin Valentin (Maryknoll, N.Y.: Orbis, 2011), 64.

19. On this point, see Imperatori-Lee, *Cuéntame*. The quoted text is from Clare Watkins with Deborah Bhatti, Helen Cameron, Catherine Duce, and James Sweeney, "Practical Ecclesiology: What Counts as Theology in Studying the Church?" in *Perspectives on Ecclesiology and Ethnography*, ed. Pete Ward (Grand Rapids, Mich.: Eerdmans, 2012), 169.

20. Imperatori-Lee, *Cuéntame*, 5, 76. See also Orlando O. Espín, *The Faith of the People: Theological Reflections on Popular Catholicism*, especially chapter 3, "Tradition and Popular Religion" (Maryknoll, N.Y.: Orbis, 1997), 63–90.

21. See Timothy Matovina, *Latino Catholicism: Transformation in America's Largest Church* (Princeton, N.J.: Princeton University Press, 2012), 24–25.

22. Anita Talsma Gaul, "'Living in Perfect Harmony:' A Multiethnic Catholic Parish on the Minnesota Prairie, 1881–1910," *Journal of American Ethnic History* 30, no. 1 (Fall 2010): 49. See also James Hennessey, *American Catholics: A History of the Roman Catholic Community in the United States* (New York: Oxford University Press, 1981), 75. Hennessy notes that as of 1785, the first parish in New York City served English, Irish, French, Spanish, Dutch, and Portuguese Catholics.

23. Paula M. Kane, *Separatism and Subculture: Boston Catholicism, 1900–1920* (Chapel Hill, N.C.: UNC Press, 2017), 5.

24. See Leslie Woodcock Tentler, *Seasons of Grace: A History of the Catholic Archdiocese of Detroit* (Detroit, Mich.: Wayne State University Press, 1990).

25. Brett Hoover, "A Place for Communion: Reflections on an Ecclesiology of Parish Life," *Theological Studies* 78, no. 4 (2017): 825–49.

26. Karl Rahner, S.J., "Theology of the Parish," in *The Parish: From Theology to Practice*, ed. Hugo Rahner (Westminster, Md.: Newman Press, 1958), 34.

27. A small sample of ethnographic accounts of diverse Protestant congregations includes Rebecca F. Spurrier, *The Disabled Church: Human Difference and the Art of Communal Worship* (New York: Fordham University Press, 2019); Mary McClintock Fulkerson, *Places of Redemption: Theology for a Worldly Church* (New York: Oxford University Press, 2010); Gerardo Martí, *Worship Across the Racial Divide: Religious Music and the Multiracial Congregation* (New York: Oxford University Press, 2012); Kathleen Garces-Foley, *Crossing the Ethnic Divide: The Multiethnic Church on a Mission* (New York: Oxford University Press, 2007); Gerardo Martí, *A Mosaic of Believers: Diversity and Innovation in a Multiethnic Church* (Bloomington: Indiana University Press, 2005).

28. Michael O. Emerson with Rodney M. Woo, *People of the Dream: Multiracial Congregations in the United States* (Princeton, N.J.: Princeton University Press, 2008). The Multiracial Congregations Study found that Catholic parishes were nearly three times more likely to be multiracial than were Protestant congregations, but more recent data suggest a narrowing gap.

29. Kathleen Garces-Foley, "Comparing Catholic and Evangelical Integration Efforts," *Journal for the Scientific Study of Religion* 47, no. 1 (2008): 17–22.

30. See, for example, *Lived Theology: New Perspectives on Method, Style, and Pedagogy*, edited by Charles Marsh, Peter Slade, and Sarah Azaransky (New York: Oxford University Press, 2016); and Natalie Wigg-Stevenson, *Ethnographic Theology: An Inquiry into the Production of Knowledge* (New York: Springer, 2014).

31. See Robert A. Orsi, *History and Presence* (Cambridge, Mass.: Harvard University Press, 2016); Orsi, "Abundant History: Marian Apparitions as Alternative Modernity," *Historically Speaking* 9, no. 7 (2008): 12–16; Orsi, ed., *Gods of the City*; Orsi, *Thank You, St. Jude: Women's Devotion to the Patron Saint of Hopeless Causes* (New Haven, Conn.: Yale University Press, 1996); and Orsi, *The Madonna of 115th Street: Faith and Community in Italian Harlem, 1880–1950* (New Haven, Conn.: Yale University Press, 1985).

32. Maldonado-Estrada, *Lifeblood of the Parish*.

33. For refractions of and engagements with this question, see Sara A. Williams, "From Disciplinary Transactions to Political Practice: Moving Past Theology and Anthropology 'in General,'" *Political Theology Network* (May 12, 2022), https://politicaltheology.com/from-disciplinary-transactions-to-political -practice-moving-past-theology-and-anthropology-in-general/; Todd D. Whitmore, "Bringing the Mess That is Life into Theology: The Representational Task of Ethnography, *Ecclesial Practices* 8 (2021): 142–64; Whitmore, *Imitating Christ in Magwi: An Anthropological Theology* (London: T&T Clark, 2019); J. Derrick Lemons, ed., *Theologically Engaged Anthropology* (New York: Oxford University Press, 2018); Christian Scharen and Aana Marie Vigen, eds.,

Ethnography as Christian Theology and Ethics (New York: Continuum, 2011); and Joel Robbins, "Anthropology and Theology: An Awkward Relationship?" *Anthropological Quarterly* 79, no. 2 (Spring 2006): 285–94. Religious studies scholars negotiate the question in a somewhat analogous way, interrogating the relationship between research and embodied and affective entanglements. See, for example, Robert A. Orsi, "The Study of Religion on the Other Side of Disgust," *Harvard Divinity Bulletin* (Spring/Summer 2019), https://bulletin.hds .harvard.edu/the-study-of-religion-on-the-other-side-of-disgust/; Kristin Norget, Valentina Napolitano, and Maya Mayblin, eds., *The Anthropology of Catholicism: A Reader* (Berkeley: University of California Press, 2017); Elizabeth Pérez, *Religion in the Kitchen: Cooking, Talking, and the Making of Black Atlantic Traditions* (New York: New York University Press, 2016); Orsi, "Roundtable on Ethnography and Religion: Doing Religious Studies with Your Whole Body," *Practical Matters* no. 2 (Spring 2013): 1–6; Pérez, "Cooking for the Gods: Sensuous Ethnography, Sensory Knowledge, and the Kitchen in Lucumí Tradition," *Religion* 41, no. 4 (December 2011): 665–83; Kristy Nabhan-Warren, "Embodied Research and Writing: A Case for Phenomenologically Oriented Religious Studies Ethnographies," *Journal of the American Academy of Religion* 79, no. 2 (June 2011): 378–407; and Katherine P. Ewing, "Dreams from a Saint: Anthropological Atheism and the Temptation to Believe," *American Anthropologist* 96, no. 3 (September 1994): 571–83.

34. Maldonado-Estrada, *Lifeblood of the Parish*, 81–82, citing Erving Goffman, *The Presentation of Self in Everyday Life* (New York: Anchor Books, 1959), 24, 106, 112. On "devotional labor," see Elaine A. Peña, *Performing Piety: Making Space Sacred with the Virgin of Guadalupe* (Berkeley: University of California Press, 2011).

35. Karen Mary Davalos, "The Real Way of Praying: The Via Crucis, *Mexicano* Sacred Space, and the Architecture of Domination," in *Horizons of the Sacred: Mexican Traditions in U.S. Catholicism*, ed. Timothy Matovina and Gary Riebe-Estella (Ithaca, N.Y.: Cornell University Press, 2002), 41–68; Alyshia Gálvez, *Guadalupe in New York: Devotion and the Struggle for Citizenship Rights Among Mexican Immigrants* (New York: NYU Press, 2010); Roberto S. Goizueta, *Caminemos Con Jesús: Toward a Hispanic/Latino Theology of Accompaniment* (Maryknoll, N.Y.: Orbis, 1995); Virgilio P. Elizondo, *Galilean Journey: The Mexican-American Promise*, 2nd ed. (Maryknoll, N.Y.: Orbis, 2005); Elizondo and Timothy Matovina, *San Fernando Cathedral: Soul of the City* (Maryknoll, N.Y.: Orbis, 1998); Elizondo and Matovina, *Mestizo Worship: A Pastoral Approach to Liturgical Ministry* (Collegeville, Minn.: Liturgical Press, 1998); and Christopher Tirres, *The Aesthetics and Ethics of Faith: A Dialogue Between Liberationist and Pragmatic Thought* (New York: Oxford University Press, 2013).

36. Amelia and Tom, interview, April 3, 2013.

37. Following Anfara, Brown, and Mangione, I engaged in surface content analysis through initial open coding. After this initial coding, I then engaged in axial coding. During this phase, I applied concepts from research questions to emerging themes in an iterative manner. I then utilized these themes as heuristic devices to interpret and analyze interview data. I ensured factual rigor by triangulating multiple data sources, including parishioner interviews, historical and social scientific studies of the archdiocese and local neighborhood, census data, city and archdiocesan newspaper articles, and my own participant-observations. See Vincent A. Anfara, Kathleen M. Brown, and Terri L. Mangione, "Qualitative Analysis on Stage: Making the Research Process More Public," *Educational Researcher* (October 2002), 28–38; and Amanda Coffey and Paul Atkinson, "Concepts and Coding," in *Making Sense of Qualitative Data: Complementary Research Strategies* (Thousand Oaks, Calif.: Sage, 1996), 26–53.

38. Claudia, interview, December 8, 2015; and Marisol, interview, April 14, 2017.

39. In 2020, *The Chicago Manual of Style* updated their recommendations to preference the capitalization of Black. See "Black and White: A Matter of Capitalization," *CMOS Shop Talk*, June 22, 2020, http://cmosshoptalk.com /2020/06/22/black-and-white-a-matter-of-capitalization/; *Chicago Manual of Style*, 17th ed. (Chicago, Ill.: University of Chicago Press, 2017), section 8.38.

1. Beyond Unity in Diversity

1. George E. Ryan, "Re: Boston Priests and 'March on Washington,'" Archdiocesan News Bureau Release, August 28, 1963, *The Pilot* News Release Archive, Roman Catholic Archdiocese of Boston; National Association for the Advancement of Colored People, Boston Branch, "The New Boston NAACP (Activities Since June)," October 1963, Northeastern University Library, Archives and Special Collections, Freedom House, Inc. records (M16), https://repository.library.northeastern.edu/downloads/neu:rx914022d ?datastream_id=content.

2. "March on Roxbury; March on Roxbury," September 22, 1963, GBH Archives, 11:20–11:25, https://openvault.wgbh.org/catalog/A_47A310B09A58411 89161E4B8389B4072; Robert L. Levey, "6,000 March for Rights in Boston," *Boston Globe*, September 23, 1963, 1, 4, 5; Freedom House, "Flier for March on Roxbury for better schools on September 22, 1963 with map showing the route of the march," September 1963, Northeastern University Library, Archives and Special Collections (M16) Box 31, Folder 1058; Melvin King, *Chain of Change: Struggles for Black Community Development* (Boston, Mass.: South End Press,

1999), 32–36; Leroy Ryan (photographer), "Boston Artist Dana Chandler," *Boston Globe* via Getty Images, September 14, 1963.

3. "March on Roxbury; March on Roxbury," GBH Archives, 0:01–0:22. The day after the march, Sherwin School burned to the ground.

4. Press release, "Cardinal Departs Thursday for Re-Opening of Council," Archdiocesan News Bureau, Boston, Mass., September 20, 1963.

5. "Flier for March on Roxbury for better schools on September 22, 1963 with map showing the route of the march," 2.

6. Press release, "Cardinal Issues Statement on 'Inter-racial Justice,'" Archdiocesan News Bureau, Boston, Mass., August 22, 1963.

7. Two days after the March on Roxbury, Hicks won the 1963 school committee primary election by a wide margin. King, *Chain of Change*, 36. See also, for example, Robert Coles, "The White Northerner: Pride and Prejudice," *Atlantic Monthly* 217 (June 1966): 53–57; and John T. McGreevy, "Racial Justice and the People of God: The Second Vatican Council, the Civil Rights Movement, and American Catholics," *Religion and American Culture* 4, no. 2 (Summer 1994): 231–32.

8. "Solemn Opening of the Second Session of the Second Vatican Ecumenical Council, Address by His Holiness Paul VI," September 29, 1963, https://www.vatican.va/content/paul-vi/es/speeches/1963/documents/hf_p-vi _spe_19630929_concilio-vaticano-ii.html. Translation from Latin and Spanish versions of the text my own.

9. On the relationship between the civil rights movement and Vatican II, see Joseph P. Chinnici, *American Catholicism Transformed: From the Cold War Through the Council* (New York: Oxford University Press, 2021), 84–104; and McGreevy, "Racial Justice and the People of God," 221–54.

10. Quoted by Ormond Rush, *The Vision of Vatican II* (Collegeville, Minn.: Liturgical Press, 2019), 221.

11. On the impact of preconciliar social, political, liturgical, and ecclesial movements on Catholics' changing relationship with society, including church renewal efforts such as the Liturgical Movement, Catholic Action, and the International Congress of the Laity, see Chinnici, *American Catholicism Transformed*, 3–52. Theologically, the *nouvelle théologie* movement of Yves Congar, Marie-Dominic Chenu, Jean Daniélou, Henri de Lubac, and others should be considered. The influence of modernism on Catholic architecture, art, and aesthetics was also a vanguard of the new Catholic relationship with the modern world. See Catherine R. Osborne, *American Catholics and the Church of Tomorrow: Building Churches for the Future (1925–1975)* (Chicago: University of Chicago Press, 2018).

12. The language of "transaction" follows Massimo Faggioli, "Vatican II and the Church of the Margins," *Theological Studies* 74, no. 4 (2013): 816.

13. Faggioli similarly notes the tendency among scholars to appeal to the ecclesiology of Vatican II without consideration of *Gaudium et Spes*: "One of the forgotten lessons of Vatican II is the necessity of a synergy between ecclesiology and moral theology, because each discipline contributes to the formation of a *habitus* toward the particular and the universal. It is the particular, concrete, real situations that most challenge us as moral individuals. It is the universal that is typical of the Catholic understanding of the church." Faggioli, "Vatican II and the Church of the Margins," 815.

14. The Sanctuary Movement of the 1980s and the anticlosure protests in Boston in 2004 are two such examples of parish-based activism animated, in different ways, by the spirit of Vatican II. See, for example, Mario T. García, *Father Luis Olivares: A Biography. Faith Politics and the Origins of the Sanctuary Movement in Los Angeles* (Chapel Hill: UNC Press, 2018), 112, 171; and Seitz, *No Closure*, 23–32ff.

15. Meghan J. Clark argues that solidarity should be understood as a social virtue: "Anatomy of a Social Virtue: Solidarity and Corresponding Vices," *Political Theology* 15, no. 1 (2014): 26–39. I have drawn the phrase "ecclesial virtue" from three sources: Gerard Mannion, who proposes "virtue ecclesiology" to support the work of ecumenism and the cultivation of a compelling pastoral vision; and Paul Lakeland and Richard R. Gaillardetz, both of whom propose humility as an ecclesial virtue. See Gerard Mannion, *Ecclesiology and Postmodernity: Questions for the Church in Our Time* (Collegeville, Minn.: Liturgical Press, 2007), 198, 230; Paul Lakeland, "'I Want to be in That Number:' Desire, Inclusivity, and the Church," *CTSA Proceedings* 66 (2011): 16–28; and Richard R. Gaillardetz, *An Unfinished Council: Vatican II, Pope Francis, and the Renewal of Catholicism* (Collegeville, Minn.: Liturgical Press, 2015), 73–158.

16. Rush, *The Vision of Vatican II*, 225.

17. Throughout this book, I primarily rely on Austin Flannery, O.P.'s translations of *Gaudium et Spes* and *Lumen Gentium*. Austin Flannery, ed. *Vatican Council II: Constitutions, Decrees, and Declarations: The Basic Sixteen Documents* (Collegeville, Minn.: Liturgical Press, 1996), 1–96, 163–282. The Vatican translation of GS 1 uses the phrase "the deepest of bonds" rather than solidarity, which I believe conveys a similar sentiment. See "Pastoral Constitution on the Church in the Modern World: *Gaudium et Spes*," December 7, 1965, 1, https://www.vatican.va/archive/hist_councils/ii_vatican_council/documents/vat-ii_const_19651207_gaudium-et-spes_en.html.

18. Reacting to socialism and Marxism, *Rerum Novarum* rejects the idea that the poor should take political action to change their situation by force, encouraging instead union among the classes in friendship and brotherly love (RN 25). See Steinar Stjernø, *Solidarity in Europe: The History of An Idea* (Cambridge: Cambridge University Press, 2009), 65.

19. See Gerald J. Beyer, "The Meaning of Solidarity in Catholic Social Teaching," *Political Theology* 15, no. 1 (2014): 13.

20. For a probing examination of the still-unfinished development of the notion of solidarity in Catholic social thought, see Anna Rowlands, *Towards a Politics of Communion: Catholic Social Teaching in Dark Times* (London: T&T Clark, 2021), 329–67. Rowlands emphasizes that the political language of solidarity "is itself a migration and secularization of a previously Christian set of ideas" (240); the political notion of solidarity migrated back into the ecclesial lexicon, as it were, as Catholic social doctrine developed.

21. World Synod of Catholic Bishops, *Justicia in Mundo* (Justice in the World), 1971, §6.

22. James McEvoy, *Leaving Christendom for Good: Church-World Dialogue in a Secular Age* (Lanham, Md.: Lexington Books, 2014), 74, quoted in Rush 255: Dialogue is the council's "fundamental metaphor in interpreting the church-world relationship." Similarly, Bradford Hinze argues, "Vatican II laid the groundwork for a dialogical approach to the church's internal and external relations." See Hinze, *Practices of Dialogue in the Roman Catholic Church* (New York: Continuum, 2006), 4.

23. Marie-Dominic Chenu, quoted in Guiseppe Alberigo, "Transition to a New Age," 589n37; quoted in Rush, *The Vision of Vatican II*, 254.

24. Hinze, *Practices of Dialogue in the Roman Catholic Church*, 4.

25. Sandra Schneiders, "The Word in the World," *Pacifica* 23, no. 3 (2010): 251.

26. Schneiders, "The Word in the World," 251.

27. Kristin M. Colberg, *Vatican I and Vatican II: Councils in the Living Tradition* (Collegeville, Minn.: Liturgical Press, 2016), 40.

28. Ulrich Horst, *Unfehlbarkeit und Schachter: Studien zur Unfehlbarkeitsdiskussion von Melchoir Cano bis zum I. Vaticakanischen Konzil* (Mainz: Matthias-Grunewald-Verlag, 1982), cited by Colberg, *Vatican I and Vatican II*, 26.

29. Patrick Granfield, "The Church as *Societas Perfecta* in the Schemata of Vatican I," *Church History* 48, no. 4 (1979): 437.

30. In contrast to the *societas perfecta* notion, *Gaudium et Spes* acknowledges the church's dependence on the world: "Whoever contributes to the development of the human community on the level of family, culture, economic and social life, and national and international politics, according to the plan of God, is also contributing in no small way to the community of the church insofar as it depends on things outside itself" (GS 44). An aim of the council, according to Yves Congar, "is a full recognition of the historicity of the world and of the Church itself which, though distinct from the world, is nonetheless bound up with it. Movements in the world must have their echo

in the Church, at least to the extent that they raise problems." Quoted by Rush, *The Vision of Vatican II*, 176, fn 50.

31. Rush 165ff; John O'Malley, S.J., "Reform, Historical Consciousness, and Vatican II's Aggiornamento," *Theological Studies* 32, no. 4 (1971): 573–601. O'Malley identifies several different, sometimes competing modes of historical thinking at play throughout the council (590–95). On the council's acknowledgment of the influence of evolutionary theory on its conception of nature and time, see GS 5 and Leo J. Donovan, "Was Vatican II Evolutionary? A Note on Conciliar Language," *Theological Studies* 36, no. 3 (1975): 493–502.

32. Ormond Rush, *Still Interpreting Vatican II: Some Hermeneutical Principles* (Mahwah, N.J.: Paulist Press, 2004), 9, referencing Giuseppe Ruggieri, "Towards a Hermeneutic of Vatican II," *Concilium* 1 (1999): 3. The phrase "sign of the times" (*signa temporum*) has roots in Mt 16:4. The subcommission charged with drafting a chapter on the human condition utilized the following "working definition" of the term: "The phenomena which occur so frequently and so pervasively that they characterize a given epoch and seem to express the needs and aspirations of contemporary humanity." See Rush, *The Vision of Vatican II*, 176, fn 49.

33. Rush, *The Vision of Vatican II*, 179, emphasis in the original; referencing *Dei Verbum* 8.

34. Council of Trent, Session 13, "Decree Concerning the Most Holy Sacrament of the Eucharist," October 11, 1551; Session 25, "Decree on Reformation," December 4, 1563; Session 25, "On Receiving and Observing the Decrees of the Council," December 4, 1563. I owe this observation to O'Malley, "Reform, Historical Consciousness, and Vatican II's Aggiornamento," 581.

35. Vatican I, Session 3, "Canon 4.3. On Faith and Reason," April 24, 1870.

36. The bracketed text is my own disambiguation; the original translation of Austin Flannery, O.P., reads: ". . . no more eloquent expression of *this people's* solidarity."

37. Writes Rahner, "In *Gaudium et spes*, in an action of the entire Church as such, the Church as a totality becomes conscious of its responsibility for the dawning history of humanity." See Rahner, "Towards a Fundamental Theological Interpretation of Vatican II," trans. Leo J. Donovan, *Theological Studies* 40, no. 4 (1979): 719.

38. See, for example, Robert A. Orsi's account of the Italian East Harlem *festa* of the Madonna of Mount Carmel in *Madonna of 115th Street* (New Haven, Conn.: Yale University Press, 1985). Roberto Goizueta makes a similar argument about Latinx popular ritual in *Caminemos con Jesús* (Maryknoll, N.Y.: Orbis, 1995) and "The Symbolic Realism of U.S. Latino/a Popular Catholicism," *Theological Studies* 65, no. 2 (2004): 225–74.

39. On the effect of Vatican II on the relationship between the Eucharist and popular practice, see Ricky Manalo, CSP, *The Liturgy of Life: The Interrelationship of Sunday Eucharist and Everyday Worship Practices* (Collegeville, Minn.: Liturgical Press, 2014), 47–78.

40. O'Malley interprets the image of the church as the people of God as a reversal of previous councils. For example, Vatican I distinguished between the church and its people, preserving the image of a sinless and unchanging church despite the sinfulness of its members. See O'Malley, "Reform, Historical Consciousness, and Vatican II's Aggiornamento," 588.

41. Francis A. Sullivan, *The Church We Believe In: One, Holy, Catholic, and Apostolic* (Mahwah, N.J.: Paulist Press, 1988), 132–51.

42. Michael J. Hornsby-Smith, *The Changing Parish: A Study of Parishes and Parishioners After Vatican II* (London: Routledge, 1989); and Desmond Fisher, *The Church in Transition* (London: Geoffrey Chapman, 1967), 80. See also Avery Dulles, *Models of the Church* (New York: Image Classics, 2002 [1978]), 491; and William J. Clark, S.J., *A Voice of Their Own: The Authority of the Local Parish* (Collegeville, Minn.: Liturgical Press, 2005).

43. Dulles, *Models of the Church*, 39–40, citing Ferdinand Tönnies, *Gemeinschaft und Gesellschaft* (trans. *Community and Society* [New York: Harper Torchbooks, 1963]).

44. Dulles, *Models of the Church*, 51.

45. Bradford E. Hinze, "Ecclesial Impasse: What Can We Learn from Our Laments?" *Theological Studies* 72, no. 3 (2011): 474–75.

46. Hornsby-Smith, *The Changing Parish*, 30.

47. Hornsby-Smith, *The Changing Parish*, 30.

48. Jim Castelli and Joseph Gremillion, *The Changing Parish: The Notre Dame Study of Catholic Life Since Vatican II* (San Francisco, Calif.: Harper & Row, 1987), 3. Notably, the Notre Dame Study of Parish Life did not include non-English-speaking parishes among those surveyed. In such parishes, unpaid lay leadership was likely even higher than the figures indicated here.

49. Hornsby-Smith, *The Changing Parish*, 30–31.

50. Francesco Coccopalmerio, "De Paroecia ut Comminitate Christifidelium," *Periodica* 80 (1991): 22; cited by Clark, *A Voice of Their Own*, 36–37.

51. Dulles, *Models of the Church*, 52. See also Gregory Baum's critique of the image of church as community in "The Church of Tomorrow," *New Horizons: Theological Essays* (New York: Paulist Press, 1972). Hornsby-Smith similarly emphasizes the ambiguity of community as a root metaphor for church; see *The Changing Parish*, 92–93.

52. Karl Rahner, "Towards a Fundamental Theological Interpretation of Vatican II," 717.

53. Rahner, "Towards a Fundamental Theological Interpretation of Vatican II," 717.

54. Rahner, "Towards a Fundamental Theological Interpretation of Vatican II," 719.

55. See, for example, Gerald Arbuckle, *Culture, Inculturation, and Theologians: A Postmodern Critique* (Collegeville, Minn.: Liturgical Press, 2010); Anscar Chupungco, *Liturgical Inculturation: Sacramentals, Religiosity, and Catechesis* (Collegeville, Minn.: Liturgical Press, 1992); Laurenti Magesa, *Anatomy of Inculturation: Transforming the Church in Africa* (Maryknoll, N.Y.: Orbis, 2014); Peter C. Phan, *In Our Own Tongues: Perspectives from Asia on Mission and Inculturation* (Maryknoll, N.Y.: Orbis, 2003); and Aylward Shorter, *Toward a Theology of Inculturation* (Eugene, Ore.: Wipf and Stock, 2006).

56. Rush, *The Vision of Vatican II*, 231.

57. Rahner, "Towards a Fundamental Theological Interpretation of Vatican II," 719. Integrating such leaps into the church's sense of itself was complicated by what John O'Malley identifies as a theological and historical overemphasis on continuity in the church. Without a well-developed theology of transition, there is a Catholic tendency to deny the reality of historical discontinuity and, in turn, the magnitude of the shift this "qualitative leap" represented. The equation of discontinuity with rupture is one reason that the church could not anticipate many of the questions that would arise in the wake of the council. See O'Malley, "Reform, Historical Consciousness, and Vatican II's Aggiornamento," 590, 598–601.

58. 1985 Synod Final Report, I, section 3. 39.

59. 1985 Synod Final Report, I, section 4, 41.

60. 1985 Synod Final Report, II, section C, 53, 54.

61. See Walter Kasper, *The Catholic Church: Nature, Reality, and Mission*, trans. Thomas Hoebel (London: Bloomsbury T&T Clark, 2015), 21.

62. Cited by Nicholas M. Healy, "Ecclesiology and Communion," *Perspectives in Religious Studies* 31, no. 3 (2004): 273.

63. Clare Watkins, "Objecting to *Koinonia*: The Question of Christian Discipleship Today—And Why Communion is Not the Answer," *Louvain Studies* 28, no. 4 (2003): 327.

64. For a review of the ways *communio* has functioned ecclesiologically throughout the history of Roman Catholicism, see Joseph A. Komonchak, "Conceptions of Communion, Past and Present," *Cristianesimo nella storia* 16 (1995): 321–40. For other helpful, positive presentations of communion ecclesiology from a Roman Catholic perspective, see Dennis M. Doyle, *Communion Ecclesiology: Visions and Versions* (Maryknoll, N.Y.: Orbis, 2000); Kasper, *The Catholic Church: Nature, Reality, and Mission*; Richard Lennan, "Communion Ecclesiology: Foundations, Critiques, and Affirmations," *Pacifica*

20, no. 1 (2007): 24–39; Jamie Phelps, O.P., "Communion Ecclesiology and Black Liberation Theology," *Theological Studies* 61, no. 4 (2000): 672–700; J. M. R. Tillard, *Church of Churches: The Ecclesiology of Communion* (Collegeville, Minn.: Liturgical Press, 1980); and Susan K. Wood, "The Church as Communion," in *The Gift of the Church: A Textbook on Ecclesiology in Honor of Patrick Granfield, O.S.B.*, ed. Peter Phan (Collegeville, Minn.: Liturgical Press, 2000). From an Orthodox perspective, see John D. Zizioulas, *Being as Communion: Studies in Personhood and the Church* (Crestwood, N.Y.: St. Vladimir's Seminary Press, 1985); and Zizioulas, *Communion and Otherness: Further Studies in Personhood and the Church* (London: T&T Clark, 2006). For uses of communion ecclesiology in ethnographic studies, see Paul S. Fiddes, "Ecclesiology and Ethnography: Two Disciplines, Two Worlds?" in *Perspectives on Ecclesiology and Ethnography*, ed. Pete Ward (Grand Rapids, Mich.: Eerdmans, 2012), 29–30; and Brett Hoover, *The Shared Parish: Latinos, Anglos, and the Future of U.S. Catholicism* (New York: NYU Press, 2014), 198–216. For critical perspectives, see Nicholas M. Healy, *Church, World, and the Christian Life: Practical-Prophetic Ecclesiology* (Cambridge: Cambridge University Press, 2000); and Gerard Mannion, *Ecclesiology and Postmodernity: Questions for the Church in Our Time* (Collegeville, Minn.: Liturgical Press, 2007), ch. 3.

65. Congregation for the Doctrine of the Faith, Letter to the Bishops of the Catholic Church on Some Aspects of the Church Understood as Communion (*Communionis notio*) (Libreria Editrice Vaticana, 1992), § 3.

66. Dennis Doyle, *Communion Ecclesiology*, 13.

67. The work of John Zizioulas exemplifies this perspective. See Zizioulas, *Communion and Otherness*, 50.

68. See Rush, *The Vision of Vatican II*, 206; Lennan, "Communion Ecclesiology: Foundations, Critiques, and Affirmations," 34ff; and Paul Lakeland, *The Liberation of the Laity: In Search of an Accountable Church* (New York: Continuum, 2003), 226.

69. Kasper, *The Catholic Church*, 21. See also Tillard, *Church of Churches*, 195.

70. Zizioulas, *Being as Communion*, 145.

71. Zizioulas, *Being as Communion*, 150–51.

72. Zizioulas, *Being as Communion*, 153–54.

73. Zizioulas, *Being as Communion*, 162.

74. Zizioulas, *Being as Communion*, 147.

75. Communion ecclesiology is not a paradigm for diversity in the church prior to the mid-1980s. Note, for example, the title of the 1980 bishops' document on diversity in the church, which indicates an active search for new paradigms: *Beyond the Melting Pot: Cultural Pluralism in the United States* (Washington, D.C.: United States Catholic Conference, 1980).

76. Note, again, that communion is not a focus of the document on the proceedings of the 1985 III Encuentro, out of which the National Pastoral Plan developed. The III Encuentro document is more oriented around themes of social justice and prophetic commitment. See Secretariat for Hispanic Affairs, National Conference of Catholic Bishops (NCCB), *Prophetic Voices: The Document on the Process of the III Encuentro Nacional Hispano de Pastoral* (Washington, D.C.: United States Catholic Conference, 1986); NCCB, *National Pastoral Plan for Hispanic Ministry* (Washington, D.C.: United States Catholic Conference, 1987), 28; USCCB, *Encuentro and Mission: A Renewed Pastoral Framework for Hispanic Ministry* (Washington, D.C.: United States Conference of Catholic Bishops, 2002); USCCB, Committee on Cultural Diversity in the Church, *Building Intercultural Competence for Ministers* (Washington, D.C.: United States Conference of Catholic Bishops, 2014), 4; and USCCB, Committee on Cultural Diversity in the Church, *Best Practices for Shared Parishes: So That They May All Be One* (Washington, D.C.: United States Conference of Catholic Bishops, 2013), 32–33. See also NCCB, Bishops' Committee for Hispanic Affairs, *Leaven for the Kingdom* (Washington, D.C.: United States Catholic Conference, 1990), 5–6; and NCCB, U.S. Bishops' Committee on Hispanic Affairs, *Communion and Mission: A Guide for Bishops and Pastoral Leaders on Small Church Communities* (Washington, D.C.: United States Catholic Conference, 1995).

77. USCCB, *Encountering Christ in Harmony* (Washington, D.C.: United States Conference of Catholic Bishops, 2018), 12.

78. USCCB, *Welcoming the Stranger Among Us: Unity in Diversity* (Washington, D.C.: United States Conference of Catholic Bishops, 2000); John Paul II, *Ecclesia in America*, January 22, 1999.

79. USCCB, *Welcoming the Stranger Among Us*, citing John Paul II, *Ecclesia in America*, §34.

80. Again, this is a contrast with its 1979 pastoral on racism, *Brothers and Sisters to Us*, in which the communion framework is not employed.

81. USCCB, *Open Wide Our Hearts* (Washington, D.C.: United States Conference of Catholic Bishops, 2018), 20–21, 30–31; cf. NCCB, *Brothers and Sisters to Us* (Washington, D.C.: United States Catholic Conference, 1979).

82. USCCB, *Open Wide Our Hearts*, 21.

83. The term "folk paradigm," developed by political theorist Nancy Fraser, distinguishes between formal, theoretical understandings and the "folk" understandings that emerge from popular appropriations of them; folk paradigms frame action and condition popular perceptions of social reality. See Hoover, *The Shared Parish*, 185, citing Nancy Fraser and Axel Honneth, *Redistribution or Recognition? A Political-Philosophical Exchange*, trans. Joe Golb, James Ingram, and Christiane Wilke (New York: Verso, 2003), 11.

84. Hoover, *The Shared Parish*, 106ff.

85. Hoover, *The Shared Parish*, 199–200.

86. Vincent A. Miller, "Where is the Church? Globalization and Catholicity," *Theological Studies* 69, no. 2 (2008): 421.

87. Healy, *Church, World, and the Christian Life*, 37.

88. Watkins, "Objecting to *Koinonia*," 328.

89. Watkins, "Objecting to *Koinonia*," 341.

90. Neil Ormerod, "The Structure of a Systematic Ecclesiology," *Theological Studies* 63, no. 1 (2002): 5.

91. Ormerod, "The Structure of a Systematic Ecclesiology," 5, 27. Ormerod argues that communion's "starting point is not the concrete data of history but an idealized version whose contact with that data will always remain problematic" (27).

92. Ormerod, "The Structure of a Systematic Ecclesiology," 28. See also Brian Flanagan, "Communion Ecclesiologies as Contextual Theologies," *Horizons* 40, no. 1 (2013): 53–70.

93. Cf. Ormerod, "The Structure of a Systematic Ecclesiology," 29, emphasis added; Healy, *Church, World, and the Christian Life*, 35.

94. Ormerod, "The Structure of a Systematic Ecclesiology," 27–28.

95. José Comblin, *People of God*, trans. Phillip Berryman (Maryknoll, N.Y.: Orbis, 2004), 59.

96. J. M. R. Tillard, *Flesh of the Church, Flesh of Christ: At the Source of the Ecclesiology of Communion* (Collegeville, Minn.: Liturgical Press, 2001), 68.

97. José Vasconcelos, *The Cosmic Race: Bilingual Edition*, trans. Didier T. Jaén (Baltimore: The Johns Hopkins Press, 1997 [1925]). See also Virgilio Elizondo, *The Future is Mestizo: Life Where Cultures Meet*, rev. ed. (Boulder : University Press of Colorado, 2000). For a critique of the notion of mestizaje-as-theological-paradigm that resonates with the argument of this chapter, see Nestor Medina, *Mestizaje: (Re)Mapping Race, Culture, and Faith in Latino/a Catholicism* (Maryknoll, N.Y.: Orbis, 2009).

98. Zizioulas, *Being as Communion*, 151.

99. See, for example, Demetrius K. Williams, "'Upon All Flesh:' Acts 2, African Americans, and Intersectional Realities," in *They Were All Together in One Place? Toward Minority Biblical Criticism*, ed. Randall C. Bailey, Tat-song Benny Liew, and Fernando Segovia (Atlanta: Society of Biblical Literature, 2009), 289–312.

100. Homi Bhabha, *The Location of Culture*, 2nd ed. (London: Routledge, 2004), 31.

101. Thomas Hylland Eriksen, "Diversity versus Difference: Neo-Liberalism in the Minority Debate," in *The Making and Unmaking of Differences: Anthropological, Sociological, and Philosophical Perspectives*, ed. Richard Rottenburg,

Burkhard Schnepel, and Shingo Shimada (New Brunswick, N.J.: Transaction Publishers, 2006), 14.

102. Bhabha, *The Location of Culture*, 50.

103. Eriksen, "Diversity versus Difference," 14.

104. M. Shawn Copeland, "Toward a Critical Christian Feminist Theology of Solidarity," in *Women and Theology*, ed. Mary Ann Hinsdale and Phyllis H. Kaminski (Maryknoll, N.Y.: Orbis, 1995), 16.

105. Cited by Copeland, "Toward a Critical Christian Feminist Theology of Solidarity," 16.

106. See, for example, Victoria C. Plaut et al., "'What About Me?' Perceptions of Exclusion and Whites' Reactions to Multiculturalism," *Journal of Personality and Social Psychology* 101, no. 2 (2011): 337–53.

107. Zech et al., *Catholic Parishes of the 21st Century*, 112, tables 8.2 and 8.3, summarizing findings from the Center for Applied Research in the Apostolate.

108. Elochukwu E. Uzukwu, *A Listening Church: Autonomy and Communion in African Churches* (Eugene, Ore.: Wipf and Stock, 2006).

109. Bryan Massingale, *Racial Justice and the Catholic Church* (Maryknoll, N.Y.: Orbis, 2010). See also Willie James Jennings, *The Christian Imagination: Theology and the Origins of Race* (New Haven, Conn.: Yale University Press, 2011).

110. Hoover, *The Shared Parish*, 187.

111. Bryan Massingale, "The Challenge of Idolatry and Ecclesial Identity," in *Ecclesiology and Exclusion: Boundaries of Being and Belonging in Postmodern Times*, ed. Dennis M. Doyle, Timothy J. Furry, and Pascal D. Bazzell (Maryknoll, N.Y.: Orbis, 2012): 130–36. Massingale cites the example of EWTN's coverage of a liturgy during Pope Benedict XVI's 2008 visit to Washington, D.C. Following a gospel choir performance, an EWTN commentator remarked: "We have just been subjected to an over-preening display of multicultural chatter. And now, the Holy Father will begin the sacred part of the Mass" (132).

112. Tillard, *Flesh of the Church, Flesh of Christ*, 68.

113. See Lauren F. Winner, *The Dangers of Christian Practice: On Wayward Gifts, Characteristic Damage, and Sin* (New Haven, Conn.: Yale University Press, 2018); and Katie M. Grimes, "Breaking the Body of Christ: Sacraments of Initiation in a Habitat of White Supremacy," *Political Theology* 18, no. 1 (2017): 22–43.

114. Fernando A. Ortiz, "Becoming Who We Are: Beyond Racism and Prejudice in Formation and Ministry," in *To Be One in Christ: Intercultural Formation and Ministry*, ed. Fernando A. Ortiz and Gerard J. McGlone, S.J. (Collegeville, Minn.: Liturgical Press, 2015), 103–20.

115. Grimes, "Breaking the Body of Christ," 23ff.

116. John R. Logan and Brian J. Stults, "The Persistence of Segregation in the Metropolis: New Findings from the 2020 Census," Diversity and Disparities Project, Brown University, https://s4.ad.brown.edu/Projects/Diversity. See also Leah Boustan, "Racial Residential Segregation in American Cities," in *The Oxford Handbook of Urban Economics and Planning*, ed. Nancy Brooks, Kieran Donaghy, and Gerrit-Jan Knaap (New York: Oxford University Press, 2011).

117. John T. McGreevy, *Parish Boundaries: The Catholic Encounter with Race in the Twentieth Century Urban North* (Chicago: University of Chicago Press, 1998), 4–5.

118. McGreevy, *Parish Boundaries*, 5.

119. McGreevy, *Parish Boundaries*, 18.

120. McGreevy, *Parish Boundaries*, 4, 103. See also Matthew J. Cressler, "'Real Good and Sincere Catholics': White Catholicism and Massive Resistance to Desegregation in Chicago, 1965–1968," *Religion and American Culture* 30, no. 2 (Summer 2020): 273–306; and Gerald Gamm, *Urban Exodus: Why the Jews Left Boston and the Catholics Stayed* (Cambridge, Mass.: Harvard University Press, 2001).

121. Miller, "Where is the Church?" 421.

122. Willie James Jennings makes this point powerfully in the conclusion of *The Christian Imagination: Theology and the Origins of Race* (New Haven, Conn.: Yale University Press, 2010), 287.

123. See Eduardo Bonilla-Silva, *Racism Without Racists*, 4th ed. (Lanham, Md.: Rowman & Littlefield, 2014); and Leslie G. Carr, *"Color-Blind" Racism* (Thousand Oaks, Calif.: Sage, 1997). On the implications of colorblindness for ecclesial practice, see Leslie H. Picca, "Race and Social Context: Language, 'Colorblindness,' and Intergroup Contact," in *Ecclesiology and Exclusion*, 119–24.

124. Phelps, "Communion Ecclesiology and Black Liberation Theology," 674.

2. Urban Borderlands

1. Michelle, interview, April 14, 2017.

2. Yamaris, interview, April 14, 2017, translated from Spanish.

3. "Welcome, welcome | To those who come in the name of the Lord!"

4. Brett C. Hoover, *The Shared Parish: Latinos, Anglos, and the Future of U.S. Catholicism* (New York: NYU Press, 2014), 2.

5. Joseph Tondorf File 5.27, 1893, John J. Williams Papers, Roman Catholic Archdiocese of Boston (RCAB).

6. According to Richard Heath of the Jamaica Plain Historical Society, "Egleston Square is a classic example of housing development following public transit lines. It also shows how the expanded capacity of the transit lines made possible public acceptance of increased density with the development of

multi-family housing between 1910 and 1930." See Heath, "History Time: The Origin of Egleston Square's Name," *Boston.com*, November 15, 2011, http://archive.boston.com/yourtown/news/jamaica_plain/2011/11/history_time_the _origin_of_egl.html. See also Gil Propp, "Egleston Square," *Boston Streetcars*, http://www.bostonstreetcars.com/egleston-square.html; "Egleston Square, Roxbury/Jamaica Plain," *Commercial Casebook: Egleston Square, Historic Boston Incorporated, 2009–2011*, http://historicboston.org/wp-content/uploads /Casebook-Egleston-Square.pdf; and "St. Mary's Timeline," St. Mary of the Angels Centennial Liturgy program, September 10, 2006, St. Mary of the Angels Parish File, *The Pilot* Archive, RCAB.

7. Quitclaim Deed, signed and sealed by Samuel Shuman and Julia Shuman to "Our Lady of the Angels, Roxbury" and the Roman Catholic Archbishop of Boston and his successors, July 11, 1906, St. Mary of the Angels (Roxbury) Parish File, RCAB. See also Patrick E. O'Connor, "St. Mary of the Angels, Roxbury Celebrates Centennial Year," *Boston Pilot*, September 15, 2006, https://www.thebostonpilot.com/articleprint.asp?id=3262.

8. Richard Heath, "The Architectural History of Egleston Square," Jamaica Plain Historical Society, accessed August 14, 2017, http://www.jphs .org/locales/2005/9/30/egleston-square-by-richard-heath.html.

9. Gerald Gamm, *Urban Exodus, Why the Jews Left Boston and the Catholics Stayed* (Cambridge, Mass.: Harvard University Press, 1999), 72–73.

10. As Gamm notes, "In the summer of 1908, Archbishop O'Connell appointed a special commission to recommend changes in the parish boundaries in the Dorchester-Roxbury." Such recommendations even included the closure of St. Paul's Parish, which had just opened that year. The suggestion was not implemented. See Gamm, *Urban Exodus*, 72–74.

11. Henry A. Barry to parishioners, September 7, 1906, in St. Mary of the Angels Centennial Liturgy program (copy), September 10, 2006, St. Mary of the Angels (Roxbury) Parish File, *The Pilot* Archive, RCAB.

12. This method of gradually completing church construction as funds were raised was not uncommon in the archdiocese at the time. According to James W. Sanders, the policy in Boston was "one of first designing a monumental church, then building the basement with available funds and roofing it for church services, and then building the upper church as money came in, a process that took ten to twenty years." St. Mary of the Angels is the only remaining "basement church" from this period. See Sanders, "Boston Catholics and the School Question, 1825–1907," in *From Common School to Magnet School: Selected Essays in the History of Boston's Schools*, ed. James W. Fraser, Henry L. Allen, and Sam Barnes (Boston, Mass.: Trustees of the Public Library of the City of Boston, 1979), cited in Gamm, *Urban Exodus*, 155.

13. Gamm, *Urban Exodus*, 1.

14. Gerald Gamm, "In Search of Suburbs: Boston's Jewish Districts, 1843–1994," in *The Jews of Boston*, ed. Jonathan D. Sarna, Ellen Smith, and Scott-Martin Kosofsky (New Haven, Conn.: Yale University Press, 2005), 153.

15. Rev. Finnegan to Archbishop O'Connell, November 12, 1919, St. Mary of the Angels Chancery Correspondence File, RCAB.

16. Gamm, *Urban Exodus*, 69. The iconic building that originally housed Congregation Mishkan Tefila still stands at its original site on Seaver Street, though the congregation relocated to Newton in the 1950s. After the temple was sold, it went through a number of transitions and is currently the home of United House of Prayer For All People.

17. Rev. Charles A. Finnegan to William Cardinal O'Connell, Sept. 1, 1928, St. Mary of the Angels, Parish Boundary Files, RCAB; cited by Gamm, *Urban Exodus*, 81.

18. Theodore H. White, *In Search of History: A Personal Adventure* (New York: Harper and Row, 1978), 22, cited in Gamm, *Urban Exodus*, 78–79.

19. Gamm, *Urban Exodus*, Map 15, 80.

20. Gamm, *Urban Exodus*, 93.

21. Rev. Finnegan to Archbishop O'Connell, October 11, 1935, St. Mary of the Angels Chancery Correspondence File, RCAB.

22. Gamm, *Urban Exodus*, 63.

23. St. Mark Congregational Church was originally established in 1895 as William Lloyd Garrison Memorial Congregational Church, the first Black church in Boston. After a series of transitions, the congregation moved to 200 Townsend Street in Roxbury. The Social Center was the first social service agency for children of its kind in the city. In 1934, St. Mark's sponsored Black Cub Scout pack in the United States and the first Black Boy Scout troop in Boston, among other distinctions. By the 1950s, the Social Center had become a major center of Black life in Boston and played a key role in civil rights organizing in the city. See Robert C. Hayden, *Faith, Culture, and Leadership: A History of the Black Church in Boston* (Boston, Mass.: Boston Branch NAACP, 1983); and Gamm, *Urban Exodus*, 61.

24. Gamm, *Urban Exodus*, 60.

25. Neighborhood transformation in the Egleston Square area was accelerated by the suburbanization of the area's Jewish residents, an "urban exodus" that Gamm traces not to the blockbusting, redlining, and white flight of midcentury, but earlier, to patterns of religious institutional belonging and urban Jewish out-migration set in motion in the 1920s. The Great Depression had a deleterious effect on the finances of Roxbury's Jewish community, which, like Roxbury's Catholics, had building plans that outpaced resources (150–51). At the same time, Jews outpaced Catholics in their ascent from working class to middle class, fueling their exodus from the city to suburbs like Newton and

Brookline. Because Jewish congregations were moveable, communities like Mishkan Tefila were able to abandon their buildings in pursuit of suburban real estate. Catholics, meanwhile, were more likely to remain at their territorially fixed parishes and, in turn, in their urban neighborhoods. Gamm refutes the notion that Mattapan's Jewish community was displaced by the Boston Banks Urban Renewal Group (BBURG), established in 1968 to reverse decades of redlining by providing mortgage loans to low-income and Black families. BBURG had been viewed as fueling the area's "rapid and tense racial transition" (42). In reality, Gamm demonstrates, Boston's urban Jewish communities began to suburbanize decades before the BBURG.

26. Regine O. Jackson, "After the Exodus: The New Catholics in Boston's Old Ethnic Neighborhoods," *Religion and American Culture* 17, no. 2 (Summer 2007): 194.

27. Gamm, *Urban Exodus*, 88.

28. Rev. John J. Roussin to Rev. John F. Mulloy, June 18, 1986, St. Mary of the Angels Parish File, RCAB.

29. Gamm, *Urban Exodus,* 83–88. See also John McGreevy, *Parish Boundaries: The Catholic Encounter with Race in the Twentieth-Century Urban North,* 4–5, 18, 103.

30. Gamm, *Urban Exodus,* 60. The term "defended neighborhoods" is from Gerald D. Suttles, *The Social Construction of Communities* (Chicago: University of Chicago Press, 1972).

31. Gamm, *Urban Exodus,* 60.

32. James L. Franklin, "St. Mary's is a Happier Place Now," *Boston Globe,* February 7, 1977, 1, 6.

33. Thomas Tweed, *Crossing and Dwelling: A Theory of Religion* (Cambridge, Mass.: Harvard University Press, 2009), 54, 73.

34. Yamaris, interview.

35. Ximena, interview, April 9, 2013.

36. See, among others, Allan Figueroa Deck, "A Latino Practical Theology: Mapping the Road Ahead," *Theological Studies* 65, no. 2 (June 2004): 296; and Hosffman Ospino, "Evangelizing US Latinos in the Twenty-First Century: Realities and Possibilities," in *To All The World: Preaching and the New Evangelization,* ed. Michael E. Connors, C.S.C. (Collegeville, Minn.: Liturgical Press, 2016), 95.

37. Amelia and Tom, interview, April 3, 2013.

38. Gayle, interview, November 14, 2015.

39. Victoria, informal conversation during Neighborhood Way of the Cross, April 14, 2017.

40. Michelle, interview.

41. Florence, interview, April 9, 2013.

42. Martin, interview, April 4, 2013.

43. Claudia, interview, December 8, 2015.

44. Marisol, second interview, April 14, 2017, translated from Spanish.

45. See, for example, Gerardo Martí, *Worship Across the Racial Divide: Religious Music and the Multiracial Congregation* (New York: Oxford University Press, 2012).

46. Gina, interview, April 14, 2017.

47. Heidegger's notion of bridges, place, and space illustrates the point. A bridge does not simply unite two preexisting locations. Building a bridge also helps to create the locations it unites. Transposing Heidegger into a practical theological key, one could argue that building bridges between cultural communities does not threaten group identities but has the capacity to strengthen them, even as a shared space is established between them. See Martin Heidegger, "Building Dwelling Thinking," in *Poetry, Language, Thought*, trans. Albert Hofstadter (New York: Harper Colophon, 1971), II.

48. Gloria Anzaldúa, *Borderlands/La Frontera* (San Francisco, Calif.: Aunt Lute, 1987), no pagination. Daisy L. Machado echoes the point with attention to the Latinx context: "The twenty-first-century Latino borderlands are understood as those places where culture, race, identity, politics, and religion intersect in complicated and even violent ways whether in El Paso, in the South Texas Valley, in the mushroom farms of southern New Jersey, in the desert of Arizona, or in the meat packing plants in Iowa, East Los Angeles, the Bronx, and New York." See Machado, "Borderlife in the Religious Imagination," in *Religion and Politics in America's Borderlands*, ed. Sarah Azaransky (Lanham, Md.: Lexington Books, 2013), 81.

49. Sophia Park, S.N.J.M., "The Galilean Jesus: Creating a Borderland at the Foot of the Cross (Jn 19:23–30)," *Theological Studies* 70, no. 2 (2009): 421.

50. See Homi Bhabha, *The Location of Culture*, 2nd ed. (London: Routledge, 2004), 7, referencing Heidegger, "Building Dwelling Thinking," I.

51. Michael Nausner, "Homeland as Borderland: Territories of Christian Subjectivity," in *Postcolonial Theologies: Divinity and Empire*, ed. Catherine Keller, Michael Nausner, and Mayra Rivera (Des Peres, Mo.: Chalice Press, 2004), 129; emphasis in the original.

52. Gregory Fernando Pappas, "Dewey and Latina Lesbians on the Quest for Purity," in *Pragmatism in the Americas*, ed. Pappas (New York: Fordham University Press, 2011), 269.

53. Pappas, "Dewey and Latina Lesbians on the Quest for Purity," 268–70.

54. Roberto Goizueta, *Christ Our Companion: Toward a Theological Aesthetics of Liberation* (Maryknoll, N.Y.: Orbis, 2009), 129.

55. Goizueta, *Christ Our Companion*, 156.

56. Goizueta, *Christ Our Companion*, 129.

57. Goizueta, *Christ Our Companion*, 129. Goizueta's analysis draws on Virgil Elizondo's portrayal of Galilee as the organizing principle for understanding the historical particularity of Jesus Christ. Scholars including Néstor Medina and Jean-Pierre Ruiz have contested Elizondo's symbolic interpretation of Galilee as too great a departure from the historical Galilee. Goizueta responds by citing Michael Lee, who argues that Elizondo's purpose is primarily pastoral. See Elizondo, *Galilean Journey: The Mexican-American Promise*, 2nd ed. (Maryknoll, N.Y.: Orbis, 2005); Goizueta, *Christ Our Companion*, 140; and Michael E. Lee, "*Galilean Journey* Revisited: Mestizaje, Anti-Judaism, and the Dynamics of Exclusion, *Theological Studies* 70, no. 2 (2009): 377–400.

58. Goizueta, *Christ Our Companion*, 129.

59. Sr. Margaret, interview, April 21, 2013.

60. Goizueta, *Christ Our Companion*, 137.

61. My thinking here is influenced by Willie James Jennings, who argues that communion must defy the forces of residential segregation: "The identities being formed in the space of communion may become a direct challenge to the geographic patterns forced upon peoples by the capitalistic logic of real estate. We who live in the new space of joining may need to transgress the boundaries of real estate, by buying where we should not and living where we must not, by living together where we supposedly cannot, and by being identified with those whom we should not." Willie James Jennings, *The Christian Imagination: Theology and the Origins of Race* (New Haven, Conn.: Yale University Press, 2011), 287.

62. See, for example, Miller, "Globalization and Catholicity," 421.

63. Carmen M. Nanko-Fernández, "Alternately Documented Theologies: Mapping Border, Exile, and Diaspora," in *Religion and Politics in America's Borderlands*, 39.

3. Receiving Vatican II in Roxbury

1. 1983 Code of Canon Law, Can. 536 §2.

2. "Parish Visitation: Outline of Written Report and Cardinal's Schedule," November 19, 1990, St. Mary of the Angels internal record. I am grateful to parishioners who shared records from this period with me.

3. According to a parishioner who helped to lead the mission statement discernment process, the goal of creating the statement was both to codify what the parish was already doing and to articulate a future agenda for its ministry.

4. Massimo Faggioli, "Vatican II and the Church of the Margins," *Theological Studies* 74, no. 4 (2013): 816.

5. Joseph E. Hurley to Chancery, June 23, 1933, St. Mary of the Angels Correspondence File, RCAB.

6. John E. Moran to Rt. Rev. T. J. Burke, November 14, 1933, St. Mary of the Angels Correspondence File, RCAB.

7. Daniel L. Shea to Chancery, July 22, 1942, St. Mary of the Angels Correspondence File, RCAB.

8. Timothy Howard to Chancery, February 18, 1935, St. Mary of the Angels Correspondence File, RCAB.

9. Matthew J. Coughlin to Msgr. Jeremiah F. Minihan, August 4, 1942, St. Mary of the Angels Correspondence File, RCAB.

10. Rev. Earl T. Lyons to Bishop John J. Wright, December 1949, St. Mary of the Angels Correspondence File, RCAB.

11. Charles A. O'Connor to Chancery, May 18, 1928, St. Mary of the Angels Correspondence File, RCAB.

12. J. C. McCuller to Arch. O'Connell, undated but followed by internal response dated August 26, 1929, St. Mary of the Angels Correspondence File, RCAB.

13. "Disgusted Parishioner" to Chancellor, February 10, 1937, St. Mary of the Angels Correspondence File, RCAB.

14. Helen L. Mullen to Chancery, October 6, 1942, St. Mary of the Angels Correspondence File, RCAB.

15. Helen L. Mullen to Chancery, October 6, 1942, St. Mary of the Angels Correspondence File, RCAB.

16. J. C. McCuller to Arch. O'Connell; undated but followed by internal chancery response dated August 26, 1929; St. Mary of the Angels Correspondence File, RCAB.

17. Rev. Finnegan to Arch. O'Connell, October 11, 1935, St. Mary of the Angels Correspondence File, RCAB.

18. Michel De Certeau, *The Practice of Everyday Life,* vol. 1, trans. Steven Rendell (Berkeley: University of California Press, 1984), 37. De Certeau writes, "The space of a tactic is the space of the other. Thus it must play on and with a terrain imposed on it and organized by the law of a foreign power. . . . In short, a tactic is an art of the weak."

19. See James M. O'Toole, *Militant and Triumphant: William Henry O'Connell and the Catholic Church in Boston, 1859–1944* (South Bend, Ind.: University of Notre Dame Press, 1992).

20. Helen L. Mullen to Chancery, October 6, 1942, St. Mary of the Angels Correspondence File, RCAB.

21. For example, in 1937 alone, Rev. Edward S. Galvin lasted three months at St. Mary's; Rev. Arthur D. Morley lasted five months. Timothy M. Howard to Rt. Rev. Francis L. Phelan, January 22, 1937; Chancery Secretary to

Rev. Charles A. Finnegan, April 1, 1937; Secretary to Finnegan, May 25, 1937; Secretary to Finnegan, July 16, 1937; Secretary to Finnegan, October 14, 1937; all St. Mary of the Angels Correspondence File, RCAB.

22. James B. Donovan to Rt. Rev. Walter J. Furlong, April 28, 1953, St. Mary of the Angels Correspondence File, RCAB.

23. "The Roxbury Report: A critical analysis prepared by the members of a four-week pastoral program in the inner-city in the summer of 1964—for private distribution among themselves and interested parties," St. John's Seminary, Brighton, Mass., November 8, 1964, 4, Folder M-3038 (Roxbury Apostolate Volunteers), Chancellor's Miscellaneous Files, RCAB.

24. In 1938, the Home Owner's Loan Corporation (HOLC) Residential Security map of Boston graded Roxbury a "D" zone, the category of highest "risk." Comments on the map note an "infiltration" of "foreign[ers] and Negro[es]," "Jews," and "relief families." Designating Roxbury "hazardous" for investment, HOLC encouraged lenders to deny loans to the area in the practice known as redlining. See "Mapping Inequality: Redlining in New Deal America," *American Panorama*, ed. Robert K. Nelson and Edward L. Ayers, accessed July 7, 2020, https://dsl.richmond.edu/panorama/redlining, Boston area D9.

25. Mel King, *Chain of Change: Struggles for Black Community Development* (Boston, Mass.: South End Press, 1981), 26, cited by Peter Medoff and Holly Sklar, *Street of Hope: The Fall and Rise of an Urban Neighborhood* (Boston, Mass.: South End Press, 1994), 13.

26. I use these words because they are the terms employed throughout archdiocesan records during this period to identify Roxbury and the surrounding areas.

27. Medoff and Sklar, *Street of Hope*, 18–20.

28. Martin, interview, April 4, 2013.

29. Boston Redevelopment Authority Housing Market Report, cited by Medoff and Sklar, *Street of Hope*, 16.

30. "The following special statement was issued for the guidance of the faithful of the Archdiocese by Richard Cardinal Cushing on Pentecost Sunday, May 17, 1964," May 17, 1964, 3–4. *The Pilot*/Archdiocesan News Bureau archive, RCAB.

31. "Cardinal Cushing Summons Community to Racial Justice," July 31, 1964, *The Pilot*/Archdiocesan News Bureau archive, RCAB.

32. "Address of Most Reverend Richard J. Cushing, Archbishop of Boston, Saturday, March 8, 1958 at Noon Luncheon, Paulist Information Center, Park Street, Boston, Mass., inaugurating *The Catholic Interracial Council*," March 8, 1958, *The Pilot*/Archdiocesan News Bureau archive, RCAB.

33. Quoted by William Leonard, "The Failure of Catholic Interracialism in Boston Before Bussing," in *Boston's Histories: Essays in Honor of Thomas H.*

O'Connor, ed. Thomas O'Connor, James O'Toole, and David Quigley (Boston, Mass.: Northeastern University Press, 2004), 231.

34. Leonard attributes the difficulty that the Boston CIC and other organizations had in moving the needle on race relations in the city to the fact that their work primarily aimed to change church structures rather than lay attitudes. Their membership was mostly or fully priests and religious, with few laypeople participating. Moreover, before the mid-1970s, there was only one African American priest in the archdiocese. See Leonard, "The Failure of Catholic Interracialism in Boston Before Bussing," 242–43.

35. "The Roxbury Report."

36. "The Roxbury Report," 4.

37. Rush, *The Vision of Vatican II*, 225.

38. The Roxbury Report," 5.

39. Card. Cushing to Rev. John J. Connolly, James J. McCarthy, and William P. Conley, August 28, 1964, Folder M-3038, Chancellor's Miscellaneous Files, RCAB.

40. "Report of the Committee Appointed by Monsignor Stapleton on the Motion of the Group Meeting to Discuss the Inner-City Program," December 4, 1964, 1, Folder M-3038, Chancellor's Miscellaneous Files, RCAB.

41. Rev. Lawrence Perry to Card. Cushing, August 15, 1964; and Rev. James H. Coffey to Cushing, August 8, 1964, Folder M-3038, Chancellor's Miscellaneous Files, RCAB. Both letters, replies to Cushing's call for volunteers, quote text from the original letter.

42. "The Church and the City: A Select Bibliography," November 18, 1964, Folder M-3038, Chancellor's Miscellaneous Files, RCAB.

43. Fourth General Meeting Minutes, December 9, 1964, 2, Folder M-3038, Chancellor's Miscellaneous Files, RCAB.

44. Urban Pastoral Program: General Introductory Meeting, November 4, 1964, Folder M-3038, Chancellor's Miscellaneous Files, RCAB.

45. Urban Pastoral Program: General Introductory Meeting, November 4, 1964, Folder M-3038, Chancellor's Miscellaneous Files, RCAB.

46. "Report of the Committee Appointed by Monsignor Stapleton on the Motion of the Group Meeting to Discuss the Inner-City Program," December 4, 1964, 1, Folder M-3038, Chancellor's Miscellaneous Files, RCAB.

47. Second General Meeting Minutes, November 18, 1964, 1; Fourth General Meeting Minutes, December 9, 1964, 2, Folder M-3038, Chancellor's Miscellaneous Files, RCAB.

48. Fourth General Meeting Minutes, December 9, 1964, 1, Folder M-3038, Chancellor's Miscellaneous Files, RCAB.

49. Third General Meeting Minutes, December 2, 1964, 2, Folder M-3038, Chancellor's Miscellaneous Files, RCAB.

50. Sixth General Meeting Minutes, January 20, 1965, Folder M-3038, Chancellor's Miscellaneous Files, RCAB.

51. Sixth General Meeting Minutes, January 20, 1965; and Third General Meeting Minutes, December 2, 1964, 3; both Folder M-3038, Chancellor's Miscellaneous Files, RCAB.

52. Florence, interview, April 9, 2013.

53. Henry F. Barry to Rt. Rev. Francis J. Sexton, Nov. 13, 1965, Correspondence Files, RG III, C. 3, Boston (Roxbury), St. Mary of the Angels, 1965, 225:5, RCAB.

54. Henry F. Barry to Rt. Rev. Francis J. Sexton, March 10, 1965, Correspondence Files, RG III, C. 3, Boston (Roxbury), St. Mary of the Angels, 1966–1968, 225:6, RCAB.

55. Rt. Rev. Francis J. Sexton to Most Rev. Jeremiah F. Minihan, August 25, 1967, Correspondence Files, RG III, C. 3, Boston (Roxbury), St. Mary of the Angels, 1966–1968, 225:6, RCAB.

56. Fr. Vin Daily to Card. Humberto Medeiros Souza, January 22, 1973, Chancellor's Miscellaneous Files, St. Mary of the Angels (Roxbury), RCAB.

57. John J. White, For the Roxbury Clergy, to Card. Humberto Medeiros, August 8, 1976, Chancellor's Miscellaneous Files, Roxbury Pastoral Development, RCAB.

58. "Meeting: Roxbury Parishes—Pastoral [Illegible]," notes, June 22, 1976, Chancellor's Miscellaneous Files, Roxbury Pastoral Development, RCAB. According to the notes, the priest who made this comment was Rev. Dozia J. Wilson. Ironically, Wilson had firsthand knowledge of bishops' propensity to send "displaced" clergy to inner-city parishes, as Wilson was ordained in the Diocese of Albany, New York. In 1976, Wilson was accused of raping two boys from Sacred Heart School, where he was assigned. Instead of prosecuting Wilson, Bishop Edwin Broderick and District Attorney Sol Greenberg agreed to let him leave the area. Wilson moved to Boston, where he became parish administrator at St. Joseph's, Roxbury, in May 1976, under the auspices of Cardinal Medeiros. In 2003, Wilson was accused of sexually abusing a fifteen-year-old boy at St. Joseph's beginning in 1976. According to reports, Wilson had brought the boy and his younger brother with him from Albany to live with him in the Roxbury rectory. Wilson was sent to the House of Affirmation in Worcester for treatment in November 1978 and left St. Joseph's on April 30, 1979. This is just one of many examples of the ways that bishops used poor, inner-city parishes in Roxbury and beyond as "dumping grounds" for abusive, ineffective, and otherwise problematic priests. Clergy abuse experts have referred to this as the "geographic solution" to the problem of predatory priests. See Kathleen Holscher, "The Catholic Anatomy of a Dumping Ground: Thinking Across the Catholic-ness and the Coloniality of Sexual Abuse in

Indian Country," presentation, Gonzaga University, April 1, 2022; and Patrick J. Wall, "Geographic Solution," personal blog (November 7, 2019), https://patrickjwall.wordpress.com/2019/11/07/geographic-solution/.

59. John J. Roussin to John Mulloy, June 18, 1986, Chancellor's Miscellaneous Files, St. Mary of the Angels Rectory, RCAB.

60. Leonard, "The Failure of Catholic Interracialism in Boston Before Bussing," 242.

61. The idea of diocesan pastoral councils was first raised in *Christus Dominus* (CD), the Decree Concerning the Pastoral Office of Bishops in the Church, promulgated a month before AA. The purpose of these diocesan committees is "to investigate and weigh pastoral undertakings and to formulate practical conclusions regarding them" (CD 27). Some critics, leaning heavily on CD to interpret AA, argued that AA 26 was not calling for standing parish councils but rather for more ad hoc councils to coordinate specific pastoral activities. Critics contended that many fledgling parish councils established in the spirit of Vatican II mistook AA's permission to participate in the coordination of apostolic work with the coordination of the parish overall and expected pastors to cede too much authority to them. For a sample of such critics, see John Keating, "Consultation in the Parish," *Origins* 14, no. 17 (1984): 257–59; William Dalton, "Parish Councils or Parish Pastoral Councils?" *Studia Canonica* 22, no. 1 (1988): 169; Orville Greise, "The New Code of Canon Law and Parish Councils," *Homiletic and Pastoral Review* 85, no. 4 (January 1985): 47–53; Peter Kim Se-Mang, *Parish Councils on Mission: Co-Responsibility and Authority among Pastoral and Parishioners* (Kuala Lumpur: Benih Publisher, 1991); and John A. Renken, "Pastoral Councils: Pastoral Planning and Dialogue Among the People of God," *The Jurist* 53, no. 1 (1993): 132–54. See also Mark F. Fischer, "What Was Vatican II's Intent Regarding Parish Councils?" *Studia Canonica* 33 (1999): 5–25.

62. Guidelines for the Parish Council, Archdiocese of Boston, 3, Folder M-3017 ("Councils"), Chancellor's Miscellaneous Files, RCAB.

63. Sacred Congregation for the Clergy, "Private Letter on 'Pastoral Councils'" (*Omnes Cristifidelis*) January 1, 1973; 1983 Code of Canon Law, Can. 536.

64. St. Mary of the Angels Parish Council to Fr. William Calter, March 16, 1969, RG III C 3, St. Mary of the Angels Parish File (1969–1970), 255:7, RCAB.

65. Rt. Rev. Thomas J. Finnegan, Jr. to Rev. William F. Calter, April 24, 1969, RG III C 3, St. Mary of the Angels Parish File (1969–1970), 255:7, RCAB

66. Darrell G. Simpson to Card. Cushing, May 20, 1969, RG III C 3, St. Mary of the Angels Parish File (1969–1970), 255:7, RCAB.

67. Lawrence Perry to Card. Cushing, June 10, 1969, RG III C 3, St. Mary of the Angels Parish File (1969–1970) 255:7, RCAB.

68. Card. Cushing to Father Perry, June 12, 1969, RG III C 3, St. Mary of the Angels Parish File (1969–1970) 255:7, RCAB.

69. "Your faithful people at St. Marys Parish" to Card. Cushing, May 2, 1969, RG III C 3, St. Mary of the Angels Parish File (1969–1970), 255:7, RCAB.

70. Thomas M. Simmons to Darrell Simpson, June 13, 1969, RG III C 3, St. Mary of the Angels Parish File (1969–1970), 255:7, RCAB.

71. Audre Lorde, "The Master's Tools Will Never Dismantle the Master's House," in *Sister Outsider: Essays and Speeches* (Berkeley, Calif.: Crossing Press, 1984), 110–14.

72. Amelia and Tom, interview, April 3, 2013.

73. Claudia, interview, December 8, 2015.

4. Passion of the Neighborhood

1. Quoted in Tom Coakley, "Procession Mixes Politics, Prayer," *Boston Globe*, March 30, 1991, 24.

2. Sr. Josephine, interview, April 4, 2013.

3. Cesáreo Gabaráin, "Madre, Óyeme" ("Mother, Hear Me"), 1973. Text:

"Mother, hear me, my prayer is a cry in the night.
Mother, look at me, in the night of my youth."

4. Dan Adams and Gal Tziperman Lotan, "Church Prays for Roxbury Youth Hit by Gunfire," *Boston Globe*, January 12, 2013, https://www.bostonglobe.com/metro/2013/01/12/roxbury-shooting-victim-critical-but-stable-condition-today/jZBblvD3tf487D7RbeWkDL/story.html.

5. "We adore you, O Christ, and we bless you. Because by your holy cross, you have redeemed the world."

6. This text was printed in the Neighborhood Way of the Cross program booklet distributed to participants.

7. Neighborhood Way of the Cross program. Ricardo Cantalapiedra, "Pueblo mío, ¿Qué te he hecho?" *Salmos de Muerte y De Gloria* (Pax, 1972). Translation: *"Oh my people, what have I done to you? How have I hurt you? Answer me."*

8. Neighborhood Way of the Cross program. Jesse Manibusan and Rufino Zaragoza, OFM, "Open My Eyes/Abre Mis Ojos," *Spirit & Song* (Portland, Ore.: Oregon Catholic Press, 1998 [1988]).

9. Neighborhood Way of the Cross program. Bernardo Velado, "Perdona a Tu Pueblo" (Portland, Ore.: Oregon Catholic Press, 1992). Translation: *"Forgive your people, Lord. Forgive your people, forgive them, Lord."*

10. Neighborhood Way of the Cross program. "Were You There (When They Crucified My Lord)," Nineteenth-century Spiritual. First printing: William Eleazar Barton, *Old Plantation Hymns* (1899).

11. While the development of the Via Crucis has often been traced to the fourteenth-century Franciscan takeover of the holy sites in Jerusalem after the Crusades, contemporary scholarship suggests a different set of origins, as discussed below. Sarah Lenzi concludes that, contrary to popular belief, the Stations of the Cross were "not enacted on the landscape of Jerusalem until well into the early modern period, the Stations have nothing apparent to do with the Crusades, do not owe their earliest incarnations to the Franciscans specifically, and, in some sense, have little to do with the geographical city of Jerusalem" (49). See Sarah E. Lenzi, *The Stations of the Cross: The Placelessness of Medieval Christian Piety* (Turnhout, Belgium: Brepols, Studia Traditionis Theologiae, 2016).

12. Egeria, *Itinerarium Egeriae*, chapter 36, 79–80; translated in Wilkinson (1999), chapter 36, 154, cited by Lenzi, *The Stations of the Cross*, 28.

13. See John F. Baldovin, S.J., *The Urban Character of Christian Worship: The Origins, Development, and Meaning of Stational Liturgy* (Rome: Pont. Institutum Studiorum Orientalium, 1987); and Baldovin, *Worship: City, Church, and Renewal*, especially "The City as Church, The Church as City" (Washington, D.C.: The Pastoral Press, 1991), 3–11.

14. See Roberto Goizueta, *Caminemos Con Jesus* (Maryknoll, N.Y.: Orbis, 1995).

15. According to Lenzi, the Via Crucis has roots in the devotional and theological turn to the passion of Jesus Christ that occurred around the year 1000, a turn that gave rise to an emphasis on the salvific dimension of Jesus' suffering, as in the work of Anselm of Canterbury and, later, in the affective piety of St. Francis of Assisi. See Lenzi, *The Stations of the Cross*, 10, 14.

16. Lenzi, *The Stations of the Cross*, 32–33, 46–49.

17. See, for example, Alyshia Gálvez's account of the *Viacrucis del Inmigrante* [Way of the Cross of the Immigrant] through Manhattan's financial district in *Guadalupe in New York: Devotion and the Struggle for Citizenship Rights Among Mexican Immigrants* (New York: NYU Press, 2010), 107–39; Gioacchino Campese, *The Way of the Cross of the Migrant Jesus/El Via Crucis De Jesus Migrante*, bilingual ed. (Liguori, Mo.: Liguori, 2006); Virgil Elizondo, ed., *Way of the Cross: The Passion of Christ in the Americas* (Maryknoll, N.Y.: Orbis, 1992); Francisco Pelaez-Diaz, "Central American Migration as the Way of the Cross: Ignacio Ellacuria's Notion of the 'Crucified Peoples' for Theological Reframing of the Migrant Experience," in *Migration and Public Discourse in World Christianity*, ed. Afe Adogame, Raimundo C. Barreto, and Wanderley Pereira da Rosa (Minneapolis, Minn.: Fortress Press, 2019), 229–46; and Stephen Bevans, "Mission *among* Migrants, Mission *of* Migrants: Mission of the Church," in *A Promised Land, A Perilous Journey*, ed. Daniel Groody and Gioacchino Campese (Notre Dame, Ind.: University of Notre Dame Press,

246 NOTES TO PAGES 128–32

2008), 90, 95, 98. See also Felipe de Jesús Vargas Carrasco, "El Vía Crucis del Migrante: Demandas y Membresía," *Trace* 73 (2018): 117–33; and Yuri Arón Inocente Escamilla, "Usos Politicos del Sufrimiento en el Vía Crucis del Migrante, Ixtepec, Oaxaca," *Relaciones: Estudios de Historia y Sociedad* 40, no. 157 (2019), https://doi.org/10.24901/rehs.v40i57.339.

18. "St. Mary's Timeline," St. Mary of the Angels Centennial Liturgy program, September 10, 2006, St. Mary of the Angels Parish File, *The Pilot* Archive, RCAB. For an examination of the category of liturgical protest, see Kyle B. T. Lambelet, *¡Presente! Nonviolent Politics and the Resurrection of the Dead*, especially chapter 2, "Crossing the Line: Liturgical Protest and the Tasks of Practical Reason" (Washington, D.C.: Georgetown University Press, 2019), 24–56.

19. See Johann Baptist Metz, "Communicating a Dangerous Memory," in *Love's Strategy: The Political Theology of Johann Baptist Metz*, ed. John K. Downey (Harrisburg, Pa.: Trinity Press International, 1999), 135–49.

20. Matthew J. Cressler, *Authentically Black and Truly Catholic: The Rise of Black Catholicism in the Great Migration* (New York: NYU Press, 2017), 88.

21. Rev. John J. Roussin to Rev. James J. McCarthy, April 3, 1986, John J. Roussin Personnel File, RCAB. See also comments by Rev. Michael F. Groden, Vicar for Urban Ministry and Director for Social Development, Archdiocese of Boston, in James L. Franklin, "He Must Find Church's Place in Changing City," *Boston Globe*, February 8, 1977, 6.

22. "Guidelines for Interviews," John J. Roussin deaconate exit interview questionnaire, John J. Roussin Personnel File, undated (circa 1971–72), RCAB.

23. Fr. Ryan to Bishop Daley, "Re: St. Mary of the Angels," October 20, 1976, St. Mary of the Angels Parish File, RCAB.

24. James L. Franklin, "St. Mary's is a Happier Place Now," *Boston Globe*, February 7, 1977, 1, 6.

25. Irene Sage, "Father Jack Roussin: A Priest of the Streets," *Boston Globe*, November 5, 1992, 80.

26. Sr. Margaret, interview, April 21, 2013.

27. Patrick E. O'Connor, "St. Mary of the Angels, Roxbury Celebrates Centennial Year," *Boston Pilot*, September 15, 2006), https://www .thebostonpilot.com/article.asp?ID=3262.

28. Sr. Margaret, interview.

29. Rev. John J. Roussin to Rev. John Mulloy, June 18, 1986, St. Mary of the Angels Parish File, RCAB.

30. Irene Sage, "Father Jack Roussin: A Priest of the Streets," 77, 80–81.

31. Sr. Margaret, interview. See also Edgar J. Driscoll, "Pastor Sheds a Positive Light on Egleston Square Youths," *Boston Globe*, December 20, 1990, 33, 42.

32. William Morales, interview, April 2, 2013.

33. John E. McDonough, *Experiencing Politics: A Legislator's Stories of Government and Health Care* (Berkeley University of California Press, 2000), 58–80; David Boeri, "Jamaica Plain's X-Men," WCVB Ten O'clock News, *Boston TV News Digital Library: 1960–2000*, November 27, 1990, http://bostonlocaltv.org/catalog/V_BAON6HSYLLRWC8F.

34. Sr. Margaret, interview.

35. Martin, interview, April 4, 2013.

36. Tom Coakley, "Procession Mixes Politics, Prayer," 21.

37. Sr. Margaret, interview.

38. Sr. Margaret, interview.

39. Sr. Margaret, interview.

40. Sr. Margaret, interview.

41. William Morales, interview.

42. Here I am thinking of Baldovin, "The City as Church, The Church as City," 3–4.

43. Daniel Golden, "Mixed Signals," *Boston Globe Magazine*, February 17, 1991, 59.

44. Onaje X. O. Woodbine argues that in gang-era Roxbury, street basketball possessed strong symbolic power, representing a "pass" from involvement in the gang world. See Woodbine, *Black Gods of the Asphalt: Religion, Hip-Hop, and Street Basketball* (New York: Columbia University Press, 2016); and *Take Back What the Devil Stole* (New York: Columbia University Press, 2021), 8.

45. "An Egleston Square Comeback," *Boston Globe,* July 24, 1990, 10.

46. Mary B. W. Tabor, "In Boston, A Slaying Reawakens Gang Fears," *New York Times,* November 29, 1990, A22; Anthony De Jesus, *Implicit Protest on Urban Battlegrounds: The X-Men, The Greater Egleston Coalition and the Establishment of the Greater Egleston Community High School*, paper presented on COMM-ORG: The On-Line Conference on Community Organizing and Development, 1998, http://comm-org.wisc.edu/papers98/de_jesus.htm.

47. McDonough, *Experiencing Politics,* 75.

48. Sr. Margaret, interview.

49. McDonough, *Experiencing Politics,* 75.

50. Maureen H. O'Connell, *If These Walls Could Talk: Community Muralism and the Beauty of Justice* (Collegeville, Minn.: Liturgical Press, 2012), 188.

51. Walter Brueggemann, *The Prophetic Imagination*, 2nd ed. (Minneapolis, Minn.: Fortress Press, 2001), 45, cited in O'Connell, *If These Walls Could Talk,* 192. See also Brueggemann, "The Costly Loss of Lament," *Journal for the Study of the Old Testament* 11, no. 36 (1986): 57–71.

52. On this point, I am influenced by Don Seeman, "Otherwise than Meaning: On the Generosity of Ritual," *Social Analysis* 48, no. 2 (Summer 2004): 55–71.

53. Justine Schiavo, "Friends of Hector Morales Jr. place a cross last night at the corner of School and Washington streets where the 19-year-old was shot" (photo). Accompanying story by Doreen E. Iudica and Efrain Hernandez, Jr., "Mayor Pledges Inquiry in Death of 19-Year-Old," *Boston Globe*, November 27, 1990, 26. See also McDonough, *Experiencing Politics*, 60.

54. Efrain Hernandez, Jr., and Adrian Walker, "Call for Peace Accompanies Funeral For Young Gunman," *Boston Globe*, November 28, 1990, 8.

55. William Morales, interview.

56. Hernandez and Walker, "Call for Peace Accompanies Funeral," 1, 8.

57. William Morales, interview. See also George Rizer, "A funeral procession in Jamaica Plain for Hector Morales, killed in a shootout with Boston police officers" (photo). Accompanying story by Thomas Palmer, "Truth Elusive When Mood is Explosive," *Boston Globe*, December 2, 1990, A24.

58. Boeri, "Jamaica Plain's X-Men."

59. William Morales, interview.

60. Ashley G. Lanfer, "The Heart of the City" (Working Paper 9, Rappaport Institute for Greater Boston, Kennedy School of Government, Harvard University, Cambridge, Mass., November 22, 2003), 90, https://www.hks.harvard.edu/sites/default/files/centers/rappaport/files/hotc_finalreport.pdf.

61. Coakley, "Procession Mixes Politics, Prayer," 21.

62. Christopher D. Tirres, *The Aesthetics and Ethics of Faith: A Dialogue Between Liberationist and Pragmatic Thought* (New York: Oxford University Press, 2014), 36. See, for example, Davalos, "The Real Way of Praying," 58.

63. Goizueta, *Caminemos con Jesús*; see also Tirres, *The Aesthetics and Ethics of Faith*; Virgil Elizondo and Timothy Matovina, *San Fernando Cathedral: Soul of the City*, (Eugene, Ore.: Wipf and Stock, 2012 [1998]); Timothy Matovina, "Sacred Place and Collective Memory: San Fernando Cathedral, San Antonio, Texas," *US Catholic Historian* 15, no. 1 (1997): 33–50; Timothy Matovina, "San Fernando Cathedral and the Alamo: Sacred Place, Public Ritual, and Construction of Meaning," *Journal of Ritual Studies* 12 (Winter 1998): 1–13; Ellen McCracken, "Reterritorialized Spirituality: Material Religious Culture in the Border Space of San Fernando Cathedral," *Arizona Journal of Hispanic Cultural Studies* 4, no. 1 (2000): 193–210; and Stacy Connelly, "Performance Review: The *Via Crucis*: San Fernando Cathedral's Passion Play and Procession, Dir. Mario Mandujano," *Baylor Journal of Theatre and Performance* 3, no. 2 (2006): 139–46.

64. Davalos, "The Real Way of Praying," 46–47. On Catholic parish practice in Chicago, see also Deborah Kanter, *Chicago Católico: Making Catholic*

Parishes Mexican (Champaign: University of Illinois Press, 2020); and Timothy B. Neary, *Crossing Parish Boundaries: Race, Sports, and Catholic Youth in Chicago, 1914–1954* (Chicago: The University of Chicago Press, 2016).

65. Davalos, "The Real Way of Praying," 56.

66. Davalos, "The Real Way of Praying," 46.

67. Davalos, "The Real Way of Praying," 67.

68. Matthew J. Cressler, "The Living Stations of the Cross: Black Catholic Difference in the Black Metropolis," in *Authentically Black and Truly Catholic*, 83–115.

69. Most of the aforementioned accounts of the Via Crucis include ardent disavowals of the idea that the ritual in question is a "mere" passion play but insist it is instead something more authentic and sincere. Here, I make the same claim, but without the insinuations of superficiality that the passion-play genre evidently carries in the instances. For example, see Davalos, "The Real Way of Praying," 41; and Cressler, *Authentically Black and Truly Catholic*, 91.

70. Davalos, "The Real Way of Praying," 67.

71. Cressler, *Authentically Black and Truly Catholic*, 99.

72. Wayne Ashley, "The Stations of the Cross: Christ, Politics, and Processions on New York City's Lower East Side," in *Gods of the City: Religion and the American Urban Landscape*, edited by Robert A. Orsi (Bloomington: Indiana University Press, 1999): 341–64.

73. Martin, interview.

74. Martin, interview.

75. Gayle, interview, November 14, 2015.

76. Marisol, first interview, April 7, 2013, translated from Spanish.

77. Ramón, interview, April 23, 2013.

78. See Nancy Pineda-Madrid, "Traditioning: The Formation of Community, the Transmission of Faith," in *Futuring Our Past: Explorations in the Theology of Tradition*, ed. Orlando Espín and Gary Macy (Maryknoll, N.Y.: Orbis, 2006).

79. Olivia, interview, April 7, 2013.

80. Omar, interview, March 29, 2013.

81. Ximena, interview, April 9, 2013.

82. Ximena, interview.

83. Catherine Bell, *Ritual Theory, Ritual Practice* (New York: Oxford University Press, 1992), 208.

84. Although this conception of ritual is outdated in the field of ritual studies, it remains a common popular understanding of the function of liturgy, sacrament, and other forms of ritual practice in ecclesial communities. It is typified by approaches in classical cultural anthropology that regard ritual's primary function as creating social concord. The ritual theory of Clifford

Geertz similarly takes for granted the general coherence of belief, viewing ritual as meaning-bearing action and cultural symbols as disclosing commonly held meanings. See Geertz, *The Interpretation of Cultures* (New York: Basic Books, 1973) and *Local Knowledge* (New York: Basic Books, 1983). See also Talal Asad's critique of Geertz in Asad, "Anthropological Conceptions of Religion: Reflections on Geertz," *Man* 18, no. 2 (1983): 237–59.

85. See Don Seeman's critique of this position in "Otherwise than Meaning," 61.

86. I am thinking of Jon Sobrino's notion of crucified people as the unnamed victims of history, living and dead. See Sobrino, *The Principle of Mercy: Taking the Crucified People from the Cross* (Maryknoll, N.Y.: Orbis 1994).

87. David Kertzer, *Ritual, Politics, and Power* (New Haven, Conn.: Yale University Press, 1988), 76.

88. Seeman, "Otherwise than Meaning," 55–72.

89. Seeman, "Otherwise than Meaning," 55, 59.

90. Adam B. Seligman, Robert Weller, Michael J. Puett, and Bennett Simon, *Ritual and Its Consequences: An Essay on the Limits of Sincerity* (New York: Oxford University Press, 2008), 4.

91. See Lenzi, *The Stations of the Cross*, 10, 14.

92. The understanding of redemption I summarize in this paragraph characterizes a broad trajectory of interpretation that followed Anselm of Canterbury's theology of atonement in *Cur Deus Homo* (1094–98).

93. For this reason, Pineda-Madrid cautions that the practice of the Via Crucis "can be interpreted as an affirmation of Anselmian atonement, an occasion in which Catholics lift up the death of Jesus as redemptive, leaving all else in a secondary position." See Pineda-Madrid, *Suffering and Salvation in Ciudad Juarez* (Minneapolis, Minn.: Fortress Press, 2011), 92. As noted above, Lenzi traces the origins of the genre of devotion to which the Via Crucis belongs to the eleventh-century rise of pietistic practices centered on Jesus's bodily suffering, a turn often associated with Anselm. See Lenzi, *The Stations of the Cross*, 10, 14.

94. Nancy Pineda-Madrid, *Suffering and Salvation in Ciudad Juarez*, 69–95.

95. I am grateful to Ernesto Valiente for this insight.

96. Martin Luther King, Jr., "Letter from a Birmingham Jail," April 16, 1963.

97. Joanna Watson, "Lilla Watson," *Queensland Review* 14, no. 1 (2007): 47.

98. This is a play on the Roman Catholic maxim, *extra ecclesiam nulla salus*, "Outside the Church, there is no salvation." Jon Sobrino turns the phrase on its head, declaring "*extra pauperes nulla salus*"—"There is no salvation outside the poor." See Sobrino, "*Extra Pauperes Nulla Salus*: A Short Utopian-

Prophetic Essay," in *No Salvation Outside the Poor: Prophetic-Utopian Essays* (Maryknoll, N.Y.: Orbis, 2008).

99. See M. Shawn Copeland, *Enfleshing Freedom: Body, Race, and Being* (Minneapolis, Minn.: Fortress Press, 2009).

100. I am grateful to my colleague Joel Kemp for insight on this point, noting resonances between the Roxbury Way of the Cross and the ways in which ritually remembering the Exodus journey becomes the "price of admission" into the community of memory in ancient Israel.

5. Ritualizing Solidarity

1. Yamaris, interview, April 14, 2017, translated from Spanish.

2. Michelle, interview, April 14, 2017.

3. The understanding of practice that grounds this work is influenced from several different directions, by turns contrasting and complementary. Alasdair MacIntyre, building on Aristotle, positions practice as a form of habit that cultivates virtue. While practice helps one develop skills toward particular ends (say, mastering a concerto), the habit of practice itself is also a good in its own right, and perhaps an even deeper one. If, for MacIntyre, practice is a teacher of virtue and community is its school, then through a MacIntyrian lens, we can view the ecclesial community as a school of solidarity—as a community formed in the virtue of solidarity through sustained intercultural practice. As at St. Mary's, practice is guided by tradition, sustained through the institution of the church, but it is also itself the work of tradition. Such practice thus speaks back to and pushes the boundaries of the institutional church. Yet MacIntyre leaves relatively open the question of power, necessitating a more critical conversation partner. Pierre Bourdieu's notion of practice as collective strategization emphasizes the role of the *habitus*, the embodied conditioning that manifests in the taken-for-granted norms and unwritten rules of the social world. Bourdieu draws our attention to the ways that ecclesial practices are shaped by—and often become complicit in naturalizing—power structures. Yet if MacIntyre's understanding of practice neglects the question of power, Bourdieu complicates the possibility of transformative actions that run counter to the dominant social structure, a critique developed by Michel de Certeau. See Alasdair MacIntyre, *After Virtue: A Study in Moral Theory*, 3rd ed. (Notre Dame, Ind.: University of Notre Dame Press, 2007), 187–203; Pierre Bourdieu, *The Logic of Practice* (Stanford, Calif.: Stanford University Press, 1980); and Michel de Certeau, *The Practice of Everyday Life*, 3rd ed. (Berkeley, Calif.: University of California Press, 2011 [1984]).

4. Michelle, interview.

5. Amelia, with Tom, interview, April 3, 2013.

6. Yamaris, interview.

7. Jael, interview, March 2017.

8. Jael, interview, translated from Spanish.

9. Bourdieu, *The Logic of Practice*, 53ff.

10. Karl Rahner, S.J., "Theology of the Parish," in *The Parish: From Theology to Practice*, ed. Hugo Rahner (Westminster, Md.: Newman Press, 1958), 28–29.

11. For further exploration of this point, see Alyssa Maldonado-Estrada, *Lifeblood of the Parish* (New York: NYU Press, 2020).

12. Cf. Andrew Greeley, *The Catholic Imagination* (Berkeley: University of California Press, 2001).

13. Nancy Ammerman and collaborators foregrounded the relationship between urban ecology and congregational culture and practice in *Congregation and Community* (New Brunswick, N.J.: Rutgers University Press, 1997). My understanding of ritual ecology also transposes insights from human development studies. See Urie Bronfenbrenner, *The Ecology of Human Development* (Cambridge, Mass.: Harvard University Press, 1979).

14. Catherine Bell, *Ritual Theory, Ritual Practice* (New York: Oxford University Press, 1992), especially chapter 4, "Action and Practice," 69–93, chapter 8, "Ritual, Belief, and Ideology," 182–96, and chapter 9, "The Power of Ritualization," 197–223.

15. Bell, *Ritual Theory, Ritual Practice*, 81ff. See also Pierre Bourdieu, *Outline of a Theory of Practice* (Cambridge: Cambridge University Press, 1972), chapter 5.

16. Translation: "Everything is a gift of God . . ."

17. The liturgy for the Easter Vigil includes seven readings from Hebrew Scripture, of which many parishes read only a selection. While the reading from Exodus is the third reading in the full liturgy, it is the second at St. Mary's.

18. When used as a strategy for increasing congregational diversity, Gerardo Martí calls this pluralist approach a "musical buffet." See Marti, *Worship Across the Racial Divide: Religious Music and the Multiracial Congregation* (Oxford: Oxford University Press, 2012), 132.

19. I have in mind the trajectory of Eucharistic political theology influenced by radical orthodoxy, as in the work of William T. Cavanaugh, especially *Torture and Eucharist* (Oxford: Blackwell Publishing, 1998), *Theopolitical Imagination* (London: T&T Clark, 2003), and *Migrations of the Holy: God, State, and the Political Meaning of the Church* (Grand Rapids, Mich.: Eerdmans, 2011). See also Kyle B. T. Lambelet's critique of Cavanaugh's unidirectional understanding of liturgical formation in *¡Presente!, Nonviolent Politics and the Resurrection of the Dead* (Washington, D.C.: Georgetown University Press, 2019), 24–56.

20. Emile Durkheim, *The Elementary Forms of the Religious Life*, trans. Joseph Ward Swain (New York: Free Press, 1965 [1912]), 218.

21. See Robert N. Bellah, "Durkheim on Ritual," 194, here also referencing Durkheimian Roy Rappaport, *Ritual and Religion in the Making of Humanity* (Cambridge: Cambridge University Press: 1999).

22. For example, Victor Turner, "Passages, Margins, and Poverty: Religious Symbols of *Communitas*," in *Dramas, Fields, and Metaphors* (Ithaca, N.Y.: Cornell University Press, 1974), 232; Victor and Edith Turner, *Image and Pilgrimage in Christian Culture*, rev. ed. (New York: Columbia University Press, 2011 [1978]); and Edith Turner, *Communitas: The Anthropology of Collective Joy* (New York: Palgrave MacMillan, 2012).

23. Victor Turner, *The Forest of Symbols*, (Ithaca, N.Y.: Cornell University Press, 1967), 30. See also Tim Olaveson, "Collective Effervescence and *Communitas*: Processual Models of Ritual and Society in Emile Durkheim and Victor Turner," *Dialectical Anthropology* 26, no. 2 (2001): 98.

24. Durkheim, *The Elementary Forms of the Religious Life*, 52–56. See also Mircea Éliade, *The Sacred and the Profane: The Nature of Religion* (New York: Houghton Mifflin Harcourt, 1959).

25. Here I am referring to what the Turners call "normative *communitas*," which is the organization of spontaneous *communitas* into a permanent system for the purpose of social control. In other words, I do not perceive spontaneous *communitas* as giving rise to the parish's structures.

26. Alyssa Maldonado-Estrada, "Masculinity and the Body Languages of Catholicism, *The Religious Studies Project*, May 24, 2021, https://www .religiousstudiesproject.com/podcast/masculinity-and-the-body-languages-of -catholicism/. On the idea of ritual as a form of language, see for example, Aurora Donzelli, "Material Words: The Aesthetic Grammar of Toraja Textiles, Carvings, and Ritual Language," *Journal of Material Culture* 25, no. 2 (2020): 167–95; and Bellah, "Durkheim on Ritual," 186–89.

27. Augustine of Hippo, Sermon 227, in *The Works of Saint Augustine: A Translation for the 21st Century*, Part III—Sermons, vol. 4, trans. Edmund Hill, O.P. (Hyde Park, N.Y.: New City Press, 1991); Augustine of Hippo, Sermon 272B, in *The Works of Saint Augustine: A Translation for the 21st Century*, Part III— Sermons, vol. 7, trans. Edmund Hill, O.P. (Hyde Park, N.Y.: New City Press, 1993), 300–1.

28. On the question of authenticity, sincerity, and ritual action, see Adam Seligman, Robert P. Weller, Michael J. Puett, and Bennett Simon, *Ritual and Its Consequences: An Essay on the Limits of Sincerity* (New York: Oxford University Press, 2008).

29. Bourdieu, *The Logic of Practice*, 57.

30. See Selva J. Raj, "Dialogue 'On the Ground,'" in *Vernacular Catholicism, Vernacular Saints: Selva J. Raj on "Being Catholic the Tamil Way*," ed. Reid J. Locklin (New York: SUNY Press, 2017), 177. Raj died unexpectedly in 2008, leaving his already pathbreaking work unfinished. Some of his most important writing was compiled posthumously into this volume.

31. Raj, "Transgressing Boundaries, Transcending Turner," in *Vernacular Catholicism*, 109.

32. Joris Geldhof, "Epilogue: Inter-riting as a Peculiar Form of Love," in Marianne Moyaert and Joris Geldhof, ed., *Ritual Participation and Interreligious Dialogue: Boundaries, Transgressions and Innovations* (London: Bloomsbury, 2015), 218–23.

33. Seligman et al., *Ritual and Its Consequences: An Essay on the Limits of Sincerity* (New York: Oxford University Press, 2008), 7.

34. See Bell, *Ritual Theory, Ritual Practice*, 221–22.

35. Adam B. Seligman and Robert P. Weller, *Rethinking Pluralism: Ritual, Experience, and Ambiguity* (New York: Oxford University Press, 2012), 8.

36. Cf. Charles Taylor, *The Politics of Recognition* (Princeton, N.J.: Princeton University Press, 1994), 25–74.

37. Seligman et al., *Ritual and Its Consequences*, 7. The authors contrast ritual with deritualized, "sincere" frames of action, which they contend are more concerned with boundary maintenance than boundary negotiation.

38. Gerardo Martí, *A Mosaic of Believers: Diversity and Innovation in a Multiethnic Church* (Bloomington, Ind.: Indiana University Press, 2005).

39. See also Kathleen Garces-Foley, "Comparing Catholic and Evangelical Integration Efforts," *Journal for the Scientific Study of Religion* 47, no. 1 (2008): 21–22.

40. As noted in the previous chapter, this should be understood in contrast to the notion in anthropology that ritual functions mainly to create social cohesion or concord (the work of Alfred Reginald Radcliffe-Brown is often cited as illustrative of this view) or to resolve social ambiguity. A difference-centric understanding of ritual should also be understood as a critique of the idea that ritual, as "meaning-bearing action," expresses a coherent set of beliefs or functions according to its place in a cultural system of meaning, as in the ritual theory of Clifford Geertz. See Geertz, *The Interpretation of Cultures* (New York: Basic Books, 1973) and *Local Knowledge* (New York: Basic Books, 1983).

41. Seligman et al., *Ritual and Its Consequences*, 11.

42. Gloria E. Anzaldúa, *This Bridge Called My Back: Writings by Radical Women of Color*, 2nd ed., ed. Gloria Anzaldúa and Cherrie Moraga (Berkeley, Calif.: Third Woman Press, 1983). The English translation is part of the original text; emphasis in original. Cf. Antonio Machado, "Proverbs and Songs,

29" in *Border of a Dream: Selected Poems of Antonio Machado*, translated by Willis Barnstone (Port Townsend, Wash.: Copper Canyon Press, 2014), 281.

6. Staying Alive

1. Quoted by Paysha Stockton, "Parishioners Praying to Save St. Mary's," *Boston Globe*, June 28, 2004, B2. Unless otherwise noted, all documents, records, letters, and media articles cited in this chapter related to the closure of St. Mary's were generously provided to me by parishioners who had helped to lead the Committee to Save St. Mary's.

2. Quoted by John Swan, "Church Rallies Against Closing," *Jamaica Plain Gazette*, June 11, 2004, 1, 23

3. Quoted by Swan, "Church Rallies Against Closing," 23.

4. Parish Pastoral Council Co-Chair to Arch. O'Malley, June 9, 2004.

5. "St. Mary's Timeline," St. Mary of the Angels Centennial Liturgy program, September 10, 2006. The timeline was compiled through parishioner research for the occasion of the parish's one-hundredth anniversary celebration.

6. Arch. O'Malley to Rev. David Gill, S.J., May 24, 2004.

7. "Remarks of Boston Archbishop O'Malley on Parish Reconfiguration," May 25, 2004, https://www.bostoncatholic.org/sites/g/files/zjfyce871/files /financial-statements/Parish_Reconfiguration_statement040525.pdf.

8. At least one claim of abuse was settled against Rev. Michael D. Sullivan, who was assigned to St. Mary of the Angels from 1960 to 1964. Rev. Anthony J. Vasaturo, assigned to St. Mary's from 1975 to 1976, admitted to sexual activity with a sixteen-year-old girl at a previous assignment, a case the Archdiocesan Review Board ruled as unsubstantiated. See "Assignment Record—Rev. Michael D. Sullivan," https://www.bishop-accountability.org /assign/Sullivan_Rev_Michael_D.htm, and "Assignment Record—Rev. Anthony J. Vasaturo," https://www.bishop-accountability.org/assign/Vasaturo _Anthony_J.htm, accessed May 17, 2021.

9. Twenty-seven percent of urban parishes were ordered closed on May 25, 2004, versus 18 percent of parishes in the suburbs and 10 percent in small and rural towns. See Bill Dedman, "The breakdown," *Boston Globe*, May 26, 2004, 1A. See also Bill Dedman, "Closings at a Glance," *Boston Globe*, http://archive.boston.com/news/specials/parishes/. Figures do not include parishes closed separately from the May 25, 2004, announcement.

10. Parishes to be closed had an average Sunday Mass attendance of 559; parishes that remained open had an average attendance of 1,068. Dedman, "Closings at a Glance."

11. Among personal parishes, 31.7 percent (13 of 41) were initially slated to be closed, as were 27 percent of parishes with Masses in languages other than

English. By contrast, roughly 19 percent of English-only parishes were closed. Monica Rhor, "For Lithuanians, Identity Threatened," *Boston Globe*, May 31, 2004.

12. Rhor, "For Lithuanians, Identity Threatened." St. Peter ultimately remained open.

13. Ray Hammond to Arch. O'Malley, July 20, 2004.

14. Sr. Margaret, interview, April 21, 2013.

15. Sr. Margaret, interview.

16. Estimate by Mossik Hacobian, Director of Urban Edge, in *Jamaica Plain Gazette*, June 11, 2004, 23. For an analysis of the broader community impacts of Boston's church closures and the sale of church property, see Claire Sadar and Alyssa Maldonado-Estrada, "Greater Boston's Church to Condo Pipeline," *DigBoston*, October 1, 2021. https://binjonline.com/2021/10/01/special-feature -greater-bostons-church-to-condo-pipeline/.

17. "St. Mary of the Angels Parish, Roxbury, Massachusetts, Visitation Report," March 2–3, 2002, 4.

18. St. Mary's sacramental index ranked 336th out of the archdiocese's 357 parishes. Boston's sacramental index is calculated by adding the number of baptisms and funerals and twice the number of marriages performed in a parish during a given year. Closure decisions in 2004 were based in part on sacramental index figures from July 1, 2002, to June 30, 2003. See Anne E. Kornblut, "Parishes Calculate Their Future: 'Sacrament Index' Part of Decision on Closings," *Boston Globe*, March 9, 1998, B1.

19. Parishioners of St. Mary of the Angels to Arch. O'Malley, "Ten Reasons Not to Suppress St. Mary of the Angels," undated (Spring–Summer 2004).

20. Rev. Gill to Members of Saint Mary of the Angels Parish, Parish Bulletin, May 30, 2004.

21. Arch. O'Malley to Rev. Gill, May 24, 2004.

22. Rev. Gill to Members, Parish Bulletin.

23. Parish Pastoral Council Co-Chair to O'Malley, June 9, 2004.

24. Rev. Gill to Arch. O'Malley, June 3, 2004.

25. Janice Chinn, quoted in *Boston Globe*, B2, June 28, 2004.

26. Seitz, *No Closure*, 12.

27. Meeting notes, "Partnerships Work Group" (multiparish organizing meeting), July 14, 2004.

28. "Church Property is Rezoned," *Boston Globe*, July 13, 2004. Article text circulated via community e-mail, July 13, 2004.

29. "Partnerships Work Group," July 14, 2004.

30. Seitz, *No Closure*, 12.

31. Committee to Save St. Mary's (CSSMA) Meeting Minutes, July 7, 2004.

32. Raymond Chretien to Alvin Shiggs, e-mail (printed), June 2, 2004.

33. CSSMA Meeting Minutes, July 7, 2004.

34. Sr. Margaret, interview.

35. CSSMA cochairs to Rev. Dr. Hammond, undated letter draft.

36. Rev. Dr. Hammond to Arch. O'Malley, July 20, 2004.

37. CSSMA, undated internal memo.

38. CSSMA, undated internal memo.

39. Hands Around St. Mary's liturgy program, June 13, 2004.

40. Rev. Joe Bruce, S.J., who was also fluent in Spanish and Guatemalan Sign Language, worked with the parish's deaf immigrants, celebrated trilingual (English, Spanish, ASL) weddings for deaf couples, offered daily Mass in ASL, and interpreted Parish Council meetings and other gatherings.

41. The Peace Garden was created in 2002 after the shooting death of neighborhood teen Pedro Sajous, through the advocacy of community groups, headed by the Ecumenical Social Action Committee (ESAC). The lot, which included a fifteen-foot-tall billboard left over from the days when elevated Orange Line tracks ran above the street, was owned by Clear Channel Entertainment, which agreed to lease the lot to the community. Students from Greater Egleston Community High School, an alternative school established after Hector Morales's killing to support gang-involved youth, painted a six-panel mural there entitled *Peace Throughout History*. At the time of this book's writing, the future of the Peace Garden is in jeopardy. Clear Channel sold the lot to a developer in January 2022, signaling the impact of neighborhood change on the local community. Andrew Brinker, "Memorial in Egleston Square May Disappear," *Boston Globe*, January 23, 2022, B1, B3. See also "Our History," *ESAC Boston*, https://www.esacboston.org/our-history.

42. Peter DeMarco, "Church Faithful Protest Closings," *Boston Globe*, June 14, 2004, B4.

43. "St. Mary of the Angels Prayer Vigil Hourly Meditation Schedule," June 26–27, 2004.

44. Mark Pratt, "Two More Churches Remain Open; Closing Dates Rescinded for Others," Associated Press/ *Boston Globe*, June 17, 2005.

45. The Impressions, "People Get Ready," lyrics and music by Curtis Mayfield, recorded October 26, 1964, ABC-Paramount, track 1 on *People Get Ready*, 1965, vinyl single.

Index

ambiguity, 12, 40, 54–55, 84–85, 96, 184–85, 187

American Sign Language (ASL), 198

announcements, 9, 12, 22, 27, 63–64, 165

Anzaldúa, Gloria, 7, 84, 186

Archdiocese of Boston, 108; and neglect of inner city, 27, 70–72, 92, 99–100, 104, 130; and parish closures, 29, 188–204; and race, 31, 97–98; and Roxbury Apostolate, 27, 98–107, 129, 158; and sexual abuse, 5–6, 187, 190, 193, 198; and St. Mary's, 65–68, 89–90, 95, 108–111, 130–31, 176

arson, 103, 133, 135

assimilation, 50, 144, 169

authority: of the archdiocese, 106; conflicts of, 52, 61, 110–12, 170; of laity, 26, 43, 95, 114, 165, 174, 200; moral, 176. *See also* power

baptism, 10, 33, 41–43, 47–48, 54, 58, 112, 146, 174

Barry, Fr. Henry A., 2, 68, 103

Barry, Fr. Henry F., 103–4

basement church, 2, 18, 69, 78, 103, 134, 203

Bell, Catherine, 28, 153, 166, 175, 181

belonging: and choice, 78, 86; across difference, 25, 84, 166, 168; local, 34, 51, 59–60, 136, 146; transnational, 73–74

Bhabha, Homi K., 56, 84

bilingual liturgies. *See* multilingual liturgies

bilingual meetings, 89–90

Black Catholics: clergy, 106; in Chicago, 145; and the parish, 15, 56–57, 70, 191; and segregation, 13, 77, 98; at St. Mary's, 8, 65, 76, 78, 108, 131, 193, 201; theology, 61

Borderland, 7, 84–87, 186; neighborhood as, 9, 12–13, 66, 128; St. Mary's as, 7–8, 28, 65–66, 72, 83–87, 160, 165, 179–80

Borders: within Boston, 33–34, 44, 65, 70–71, 114, 133, 136; within the church, 27, 43; between church and world, 26, 32, 34, 45. *See also* boundaries; parish

Boston Redevelopment Authority, 97

boundaries, parish, 15–16, 59, 70–71, 74; crossing, 28, 72, 74, 86–87, 94–95, 128, 165; of St. Mary's, 7, 65, 67–69, 71, 78, 91

bus, 9, 83, 136–37, 160. *See also* MBTA

bussing, 98, 129

Calter, Fr. William A., 108–10

Caribbean, 3, 8, 21, 25, 73, 127–76

Catholic Interracial Council (CIC), 98–99

Catholic social thought, 35–36, 178

change, 56; in the church, 29, 33, 39, 52–53, 84, 86–87, 95, 103, 112, 161, 187; in the community, 13, 63, 68, 189, 203

Chao, Roberto, 134

Chenu, Marie-Dominique, OP, 36–37

Christ: belief in, 89, 157; presence of, 42, 48, 85, 101, 126, 134, 144, 146, 159, 163, 172; redemption through, 38, 99, 155–56, 177; suffering of, 147–48; unity in, 10, 16, 41, 47–48, 54–55, 61, 174, 185–86; way of, 32, 85, 151, 154, 157. *See also* Eucharist; incarnation; Jesus

civil rights movement, 1, 29–32, 46, 203

class: divisions between, 8, 34, 44, 62, 65, 101, 174; solidarity between, 7, 33, 35–36, 62, 83–84, 91, 99; theological reflection and, 10. *See also* middle-class Catholics; poor, the; poor Catholics; poverty; upper-class Catholics; working-class Catholics

SUSAN BIGELOW REYNOLDS is assistant professor of Catholic Studies at Candler School of Theology at Emory University, where her research focuses on public ritual, culture, and questions of marginality and suffering in ecclesial communities.

CATHOLIC PRACTICE IN THE AMERICAS

Gerald J. Beyer, *Just Universities: Catholic Social Teaching Confronts Corporatized Higher Education*

Brandon Bayne, *Missions Begin with Blood: Suffering and Salvation in the Borderlands of New Spain*

Susan Bigelow Reynolds, *People Get Ready: Ritual, Solidarity, and Lived Ecclesiology in Catholic Roxbury*